Innovation and the State

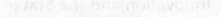

Innovation and the State

Political Choice and Strategies for

Growth in Israel, Taiwan,

and Ireland

Dan Breznitz

Yale University Press

New Haven and London

Set in Adobe Garamond by Binghamton Valley Composition

Printed in the United States of America.

Library of Congress Cataloging-in-Publication Data
Breznitz, Dan.
Innovations and the state : political choice and strategies for growth in Israel, Tai-
wan, and Ireland / Dan Breznitz.
   p.   cm.
Includes bibliographical references and index.
ISBN 978-0-300-12018-9 (cloth : alk. paper)   1. Information technology—
Israel.   2. Information technology—Taiwan.   3. Information technology—
Ireland.   4. Israel—Economic policy.   5. Taiwan—Economic policy.
6. Ireland—Economic policy.   I. Title.
HC415.25.Z9I553   2007
338.9—dc22

                        2006038733

A catalogue record for this book is available from the British Library.

10 9 8 7 6 5 4 3 2 1

To my loving mother Tamar and my beloved wife Shiri, the two women who make my life a joy

Contents

Illustrations

TABLES

Acknowledgments

Writing a book is a long but, thankfully, not a lonely journey. An embarrassingly large number of people have helped me when I, quite often, stumbled. I would like to thank my friends for this journey at MIT and afar: David Art, Sean Safford, Amos Zehavi, Carlos Martínez-Vela, Douglas Fuller, Edward Cunningham, Guy Hachlili, Yoav Ezer, Dirk Zorn, Fabio Fonti, and Carsten Zimmermann. Many other wise friends and mentors have assisted me along the way; standing high among them are Andrew Schrank, Gary Herrigel, Ashish Arora, Alfonso Gambardella, Douglas Guthrie, Niel Fligstein, Mark Granovetter, Walter Powell, Manuel Trajtenberg, Dan Peled, Ehud Harari, Arnon Bentur, Nadav Liron, Martin Kenney, Benjamin Coriat, Giovanni Dosi, Suma Athreye, Mary O'Sullivan, William Lazonick, Stephen Klepper, Morris Teubal, Arnaldo Camuffo, Gil Avnimelech, Richard Locke, Jonah Levy, Edward Roberts, Thomas Allen, Mauro Guillen, and John Zysman. John also proved instrumental in moving me in the right direction during the last set of revisions, when my ability to think straight was questionable.

In every one of my host countries, there have been many institutions and people to thank. In Israel, I especially thank the Neaman Institute for Advanced Studies and its program in Science, Technology, and the Economy for giving me an intellectual home away from home, as well as the Institute's administrative staff, in particular Rebecca Best, for protecting me from myself for the past four years. In the field, Orna Berry, Jon Medved, Ed Malvaski, and Avner Halperin contributed over and above the call of duty. Glorianna Davenport stands as a guardian angel of my forays into Ireland; without her I would probably not have been able to conduct the extensive field research I did. The dismantled Media Lab Europe (MLE) should also be thanked for giving me institutional support and a warm house in its first two very optimistic years. I am happy that my memories of MLE are of that period. Breffni Tomlin and the National Institute of Technology Management in University College Dublin have also provided a home away from home. The Coughlans—Sean, Michelle, and Anna—gave a real home for Shiri and me. Sean also proved that Irish men know not only how to be true friends and climb rocks, but also how to cook. Cathal Friel took me under his wing and introduced me to a different Dublin many a time, giving me his wise counsel and deep friendship. In the "sunny" Southeast, the Griffins—Michael, Jasmine, and Myla-Ling—have shown us what Irish hospitality is all about, and in Kerry, Peter Bellew proved that this art is not unique to the East. Throughout my long endeavor, Brendan Touhy, Brian Caulfield, Helen Keelan, and Sean O'Sullivan have always been there to save a lonely Danny Boy from getting lost. In Taiwan, special thanks is owed to the managers and staff of the Department of Industrial Technology at the Ministry of Economic Affairs; at both NTU and MIT, Ji-Ren Lee was invaluable, Wen-Yueh (James) Wang and Yu-Chen (Jesse) Lan supplied superb research assistantship; and Alan Chen and Hsin Hsin Lin gave superb logistic support.

The many interviewees in Israel, Ireland, Taiwan, and the United States who gave me, a complete stranger, so much of their time stand in a category of their own. Back at MIT, Helen Ray consistently nurtured me back to mental health in the Department of Political Science. The people of the Writing Center have seen me struggling, probably more times than I care to admit, with writing all my bubbling ideas into a coherent essay; in particular, Thalia, Marilyn, and Susan have faced this daunting task with a smile and wry sense of humor. During the summer of 2004, this task was delegated in England to Hatuly, who took it in brave stride, each and every afternoon. At the IPC, Anita Kafka has always been my Seraph, and my colleagues in the globalization project—in particular, Akintunde Akinwande, Charles Sodini, Timothy Sturgeon, Sara Jane McCaffrey, and Edward Steinfeld—gave me constant advice and counsel.

Starting in August 2005 the Sam Nunn School of International Affairs and the School of Public Policy of Georgia Institute of Technology gave me a friendly home and more support, friendship, and time than an assistant professor can ever hope for. I am especially in debt for all of the above to William Long. In addition, Kirk Bowman, Michael Best, Hans Klein, Seymour Goodman, and Richard Doner made our transit to Atlanta a much more intellectually thriving one. During spring 2006, the Stanford Project on Region of Innovation and Entrepreneurship at Stanford's Institute of International Studies gave me a home and needed solitude to finish the last revisions of this book as a visiting scholar. I especially thank Henry Rowen, William Miller, Marguerite Hancock, and Rafiq Dossani for making the experience a productive one. Lesa Mitchell, Robert Litan, and Robert Strom at the Kauffman Foundation were there to give me, and this book, the final needed push.

In addition, two sets of annual scholarly meetings were important to keep me going. The first has been DRUID in Copenhagen, where special thanks are owed to Mark Lorenzen, Peter Maskell, Henrik Sornn-Friese, and Bent Dalum. The second has been EGOS, where special thanks are owed to the members of the Standing Working Group One, especially Richard Whitley, Glenn Morgan, Arndt Sorge, and Peer Hull Kristiansen. Lastly, at Yale University Press, my editor, Michael O'Malley, his editorial assistants Steve Colca and Alex Larson, and my manuscript editor Dan Heaton proved both invaluable and utterly encouraging.

However, none of this research would have come together as one coherent body of work without four people. Suzanne Berger, has been both a true friend and a harsh master, knowing when to push me forward and when to save me from despair. Richard Samuels has always been more than just the superb mentor he is, and, together with Debbie, they gave us an extended family in Massachusetts. Michael Piore always knew how to keep me going, and to whom and where to send me before I fell. Richard Lester helped me find a home and stability in this hectic period within the rich community he nurtures at the IPC.

Financial support made this research possible: from a Sloan Foundation graduate fellowship; the STE program of the Neaman Institute in the Technion in Israel; the SSRC program on the Corporation as a Social Institution through a grant given by the Sloan Foundation; the MacArthur Foundation, through two grants given by the Center for International Studies at MIT; MIT Industrial Performance Center; MediaLabEurope; MIT's Department of Political Science; and the Kauffman Foundation.

Last but not least, without the enduring support of my family in all of its branches, blood and law, I would have never survived this journey. My mother, Tamar, prevented me from losing my balance and hope. Dafna showed what sisters are all about, heroically reminding me what life is in Dublin and Tel Aviv. Finally, Shiri, my companion and wife, has repeatedly proved that she is a saint reborn; she is truly my song. The existence of this book has at least as much to do with her as it has with me; only she and god know why she puts up with me.

Abbreviations

ASIC	application-specific integrated circuit
BES	business expansion scheme (Ireland)
BIOS	basic input-output system
BIRD	Bi-national (Israel-U.S.) Research
BOI	Bank of Israel
CBS	Central Bureau of Statistics (Israel)
CCL	Computer and Communication Lab (Taiwan)
CMOS	complementary metal oxide semiconductor
CORBA	common object request broker architecture
CPU	central processing unit
CRM	customer-relationship management
CSIA	Information Service Industry Association (Taiwan)
CSIST	Chungshan Institute of Science and Technology (Taiwan)
DOIT	Department of Industrial Technology (Taiwan)
DRAM	dynamic random access memory
DSP	digital signal processing
EDIP	Electronic Industry Development Program (Taiwan)
EDP	Enterprise Development Program (Ireland)

EI	Enterprise Ireland
ERSO	Electronic Research and Service Organization (Taiwan)
EU	European Union
FDI	foreign direct investment
FRP	fantasy role playing
FT	*Financial Times*
GDP	gross domestic product
HEA	Higher Education Authority (Ireland)
IAEI	Israel Association of Electronic and Information Industries
IASH	Israeli Association of Software Houses
IC	integrated circuit
IDA	Industrial Development Agency (Ireland); renamed in 1993 as IDA Ireland
IDB	Industrial Development Bureau (Taiwan)
IDM	integrated device manufacturer
IEP	Irish punt
III	Institute for Information Industry (Taiwan)
IP	Internet protocol
IPO	initial public offering
IPR	intellectual property rights
IRDA	Israeli R&D Associates
ISA	Irish Software Association (formerly known as ICSA)
ISP	International Services Program (Ireland)
IT	information technology
ITRI	Industrial Technology Research Institute (Taiwan)
ITV	Israeli Technology Ventures
IVA	Israel Venture Association
KMT	Kuomintang
LAN	local area network
LCD	liquid crystal display
LDLP	Leading Product Development Program (Taiwan)
MAGNET	generic noncompetitive R&D (Hebrew acronym)
M&A	merger and acquisition
MBO	management buyout
MCP	Multi-Client Project (Taiwan)
MIC	Market Intelligence Center (Taiwan)
MNC	multinational corporation
MoEA	Ministry of Economic Affairs (Taiwan)

MOTI	Ministry of Trade and Industry (Israel)
NESC	National Economic and Social Council (Ireland)
NIC	newly industrialized countries
NID	National Informatics Directorate (Ireland)
NSC	National Science Council (Taiwan); National Software Center (Ireland)
NSD	National Software Directorate (Ireland)
NT$	new Taiwanese dollars
NTBF	new technology–based firm
OBM	own-brand manufacturing
OCR	optical character recognition
OCS	Office of the Chief Scientist (Israel)
ODM	original-design manufacturing
OECD	Organization for Economic Co-operation and Development
OEM	original-equipment manufacturing
OMG	object-management group
PBX	private-branch exchange
PKI	public key infrastructure
PRTLI	Programme for Research in Third-Level Institutions (Ireland)
RAD	rapid application development; not to be confused with the Israeli RAD group of telecommunications companies
R&D	research and development
RIB	rapid innovation–based
RIT	Regional Institute of Technology (Ireland)
RTC	Regional Technical College (Ireland)
S&T	science and technology
SBIR	small-business innovation research
SCS	Seed Capital Scheme (Ireland)
SFI	Science Foundation Ireland
SI	systems of innovation
SME	small and medium-sized enterprises
SO	Stationary Office (Ireland)
SoC	system on chip
STAG	Science and Technology Advisory Group (Taiwan)
TCP	transmission control protocol
TDP	Technology Development Program (Taiwan)
TVCA	Taiwan Venture Capital Association
UCD	University College Dublin

USAID	United States Agency for International Development
USD	United State dollar
VC	venture capital, venture capitalists
VLSI	very large–scale integration
VoIP	voice over Internet protocol
WB	World Bank
WLAN	wireless local area network

Innovation and the State

Chapter 1 Plurality, Choice, and the Politics of Industrial Innovation

> Action, the only activity that goes on directly between men without the intermediary of things or matter, corresponds to the human condition of plurality, to the fact that men, not Man, live on the earth and inhabit the World. While all aspects of the human condition are somehow related to politics, this plurality is specifically *the* condition—not only the *conditio sine qua non,* but the *conditio per quam*—of all political life.
>
> —*Hannah Arendt,* The Human Condition

This book is about choice. Its main argument is that, contrary to what we are led to believe, the current processes of intensified globalization give emerging economies a larger number of economic-development alternatives than they have had since World War II. This is especially true, I argue, in the case of rapid innovation–based (RIB) industries. A general truism today is that both the onslaught of international economic forces and the fragmentation of production limit the power of states to set unique courses of successful economic growth. And yet in this book I argue that these same conditions have given states more choices of action than ever before, for the increasing complexity and openness of the world allow developing states that wish to engage with the international economic system a far larger number of entry points than in any other period.

This does not mean that emerging economies have an easier task of development, or that success, even if and when it is achieved, is without cost. The options facing states today are real, and each has its own negative as well as positive consequences. It is true that old methods of industrialization no longer work. However, I contend that this means only that the role of the state in economic development has changed, not that its power has diminished. The world has evolved, and with it we need to transform our understanding of industrial development.

One of the most unexpected developments of the 1990s is that firms in a number of emerging states not known for their high-technology industries in the past moved to the forefront in new information technologies (IT). Even more surprising from the point of view of comparative political economy theories, the IT industries of these countries seem to embody different business models and to carve out different positions in the global production network of the U.S.-dominated IT industry. Of these emerging economies, the Taiwanese, Israeli, and Irish indigenous IT industries, riding what seems to be one of the greatest waves of industrial innovation ever, have become hotbeds of new technology–based firms (NTBF). Some of these firms have become global players over the past ten years.

That very different IT industries working in the same sectors and markets have grown in emerging economies challenges two central ideas in the comparative political economy literature. First, it suggests that there is a way for less-developed countries to become successful players in rapid innovation–based industries, something that was not considered plausible in the past. Second, it suggests that there are multiple choices for industrial development. The cases of Ireland, Israel, and Taiwan demonstrate that states and societies, even under conditions of intense globalization in one of the most globalized industries, can pursue different strategies of economic growth.

Contemporary political economy literature cannot satisfactorily explain many of the changes in industrial systems in the past few decades. This is especially true in the case of rapid innovation–based industries in emerging economies. Contemporary political economists take a dismal view of the prospects for RIB industrial leapfrogging by backward societies—that is, transformation of such societies to front-rank competitors in technological innovation in the span of one generation. While each of the standard theories has a particular approach, each unites in pessimism about the possibility of using government policies to leapfrog in rapid innovation–based industries.[1] Furthermore, none of the theories can accommodate a situation in which a few emerging countries, each employing very different industrial policies, planned and implemented by very different bureaucracies, with very different labor market regulations, financial institutions, and educational and training systems, achieve success at the same time in the same research and development (R&D)–intensive sectors.

Against these bleak predictions, the stories of Israel, Ireland, and Taiwan offer cases of successful rapid innovation–based industrial growth in the time span of one generation in countries with very different political and institutional systems. These stories offer us multiple puzzles, the answers to which are intimately linked to important debates in comparative political economy. First, comparing these three stories provides us with insights into a highly contested issue of economic growth—the role of the state in the development of high-technology industries in less-developed economies. Second, comparing the three very different paths of science-and-technology industrial policy regimes and development bears upon the question of whether states and societies have choices in their economic development strategies. Finally, comparing the three different positions and relationships of the local IT industry with the global IT production networks offers us an understanding of how globalization, and especially the radical transformation of production, influences development opportunities of peripheral economies.

Politics is about crafting and picking alternatives. Politics matters, therefore, only if choices can be made and if making them has real consequences. In the past three decades students of politics have done their best to convince us that choosing between alternatives, even if choices exist, no longer truly matters. Nowhere is this more evident than in comparative political economy, particularly in the study of industrial development, where the plurality of positive actions has been diminished to one. Both the neoclassical economists, in their belief that the only choice is to let the market rule, and the developmental statists, who argue that only specific structures of states bring forth industrial success, have marginalized the importance of picking between true alternatives. Furthermore, even the varieties of capitalism and the development-path literatures, by focusing on how different established institutions grant different comparative and competitive advantages, offer path-dependent explanations that maintain diversity only by limiting choice.

Yet I believe that choices still exist, that states and societies, through the political process of crafting and picking alternative modes of action, can follow diverse paths and still achieve industrial success. Furthermore, this book demonstrates that the outcome of each path is a different socioindustrial system with different strengths, different weaknesses, and a different distribution of the fruits of success. With this book I set out to confirm that emerging economies have a plurality of options with regard to their industrial development. Moreover, I advance a framework of thinking about how different choices lead to long-term consequences and the development of successful *and* radically different industrial systems. I strive in short to give politics—the art and profession of creating alternatives and the social struggles of choosing between, and acting upon, them—the importance that it seems to have lost in the social sciences.

To this end, one goal of this book is to expand our understanding of the role of the state in the development of the rapid innovation–based industries—not only to clarify what options less-developed states have to spur and sustain IT industrial growth but also to analyze and map the limits of state actions and the dynamics of state-industry interactions. To do so, I focus my analysis on the ways in which the three states have influenced the skills and capabilities acquired and developed by the private IT industry. Another goal is to explain how the different approaches of the three states shaped the IT industries and influenced the particular development path of, and the particular capabilities developed by, each industry. In doing so, I seek to move beyond the question of whether the state has a role in industrial development. I propose a theory concerning the influence of particular policies on the development of rapid innovation–based industries in emerging economies. While much of the literature in comparative political economy sees the existence of different industrial and capitalistic systems as givens, and explains their influence on the behavior of firms and economies under the same global conditions, in this book I seek to understand how different industrial systems are created in the first place.[2] I argue that state actions give rise to different high-technology industries, and that these industries not only utilize different business models, position themselves differently in the global production network, and acquire different skills and capabilities, but also have very different strengths and weaknesses with regard to their sustainability and profitability. In addition, I demonstrate that these industries allocate the economic benefits of success very differently within their host societies, and thus choices are made, actions are taken, and these choices and actions have consequences.

Thus the story is both simple and complex. I argue that in the case of rapid innovation–based industries two major facts not accounted for in the literature—that new technologies in themselves have become the final product, and that production is increasingly fragmented internationally—have altered the way in which industrial production is taking place. Accordingly, these changes transform the ways in which emerging economies can take part in the international economy.

With the fragmentation of production and the rise of global production networks, no longer do whole industries locate in one specific geographical location. Instead, a particular set of activities takes place in one country, while others take place in different ones (Arndt and Kierzkowski 2001a, Gereffi 1994, Gourevitch 2000, Henderson et al. 2002, Sturgeon 2000, 2002, 2003). Consequently, states now excel in a definite set of activities rather than in specific industries. For example, Taiwan, China, Israel, and the United States all have large and successful semiconductor industries; however, each of these countries specializes in a particular set of activities and has continued to develop a significantly different set of capabilities.

If in the past, late-developing countries were expected to utilize a strategy of imitation, technology transfer, and competition on the basis of scope and scale, aiming to build whole industries that can compete in global markets, this strategy has become suspect because production in all those industries had become fragmented (Amsden 1989, 2001, Gerschenkron 1962, Johnson 1982, Wade 1990). Moreover, if in the past one could claim that states need to develop capabilities that encompass whole industries, a much more plausible strategy today would be to develop specialized capabilities in particular stages of production.

In the case of RIB industries, new technologies are themselves the products. Therefore a development strategy that builds on technology transfer and imitation, assuming that both markets and products are known—and hence strategic planning is feasible—does not work. In our transformed world, states need to develop the capacity to innovate. Yet the point is that with the fragmentation of production, emerging economies now have many different entry points around which to innovate and develop their own unique industrial strengths, inspiring innovation with many different faces. Building on insights from the development state, globalization, and systems of innovation theories, I develop in this book a framework to explain both how different choices result in specific industrial systems and why the same state can both succeed and fail in different subsectors of the IT industry.

Following the neo-development-state theories, I contend that state-industry embeddedness is critical (Ansell 2000, Evans 1995, O'Riain 2000, 2004). However, I also contend that there are different modes of embeddedness, and that the process of becoming embedded is at least as important as the final structural result. Hence each mode and process of embeddedness leads to a different industrial system with diverse strengths, weaknesses, and relationships with the global markets. There is no one structural form to which all successful countries must adhere.

Furthermore, what influences the specific processes of state-industry interlinking, as well as the specific mode of interaction between the local and global IT industry and financial markets, depends on:

1. the ways in which the state acts to acquire the necessary knowledge and skills;
2. the ways in which the state acts in order to solve the inherent market failures in industrial R&D, specifically, by lowering the risk in order to spur private actors to enter the industry; and
3. the ways in which the state acts to interlink the local economy with the leading multinational corporations (MNCs) and the global financial markets, both within and outside its national borders.

These state actions, in turn, depend on the political processes behind state action. Hence while this book refutes the specific argument of Alexander Gerschenkron about the advantages of economic backwardness, it does urge a return to the fundamental Gerschenkronian insight. Since national economic backwardness equals powerlessness in the international arena, states do not, and should not, wait idly hoping that the miraculous power of the market will throw some economic growth their way. Hence economic development should be seen as part of the national building project, a rite of passage that many states must pass in order to preserve their independence (Gerschenkron 1962). Consequently, how and why states act reflect the ideals that their societies have of themselves and the role of the state within this vision; each state's interpretation of its fundamental security threats, both internal and external; and their position within the international system.

Before I fully elaborate on the theoretical framework and arguments of this book, I have chosen to present the three cases and follow with an open debate with the literature, which reveals how I reached the above arguments.

A BRIEF HISTORY

Ireland, Israel, and Taiwan were poor, peripheral, and technologically backward societies in 1950. They all had mixed track records of success in more traditional industries. At the end of the 1960s, state-led initiatives to develop indigenous high-tech industries appeared in all three societies. At that point, all three were very similar along most of the important economic dimensions, including size and population. All three had low skill intensity in their labor force (defined as the number and percentage of scientists and engineers in the population), a relatively low percentage of high school graduates, poor communication, and physical infrastructures and a high dependence upon agriculture.

All three states followed similar infrastructure policies. Each improved its educational system, leading to high rates of skill formation between the 1960s and the 1980s. All three improved their physical infrastructures and, after failed attempts at direct bureaucratic control, created public telecommunication companies that vastly improved their line-subscription penetration rates. Deregulation and privatization of the telecommunication market followed, leading to high rates of wireless and Internet penetration. Finally, unlike Japan and South Korea, all three countries based their growth on small and medium-sized enterprises rather than on big corporations.[3]

Despite similarities among their macro-level and infrastructure policies, however, their micro-level policies—those at the level of industry and firm— were distinctly different. Since the late 1960s Ireland has focused mainly on foreign direct investment (FDI)–based industrial development policies. Israel has focused on inducing industrial R&D activities through government grants, with project ideas originating solely in private industry. In Taiwan, the ruling party, the Kuomintang (KMT), mistrusted big private industry and feared the rise of competing powers. Hence it prevented the creation of overarching conglomerates, controlled the inflows and outflows of investment, and relied on such public research agencies as the Industrial Technology Research Institute (ITRI) and the Institute for Information Industry (III) to lead R&D efforts and diffuse the results throughout private industry.

Moreover, the structure of the state in all three countries had varied significantly. Ireland is a model of an English-style Weberian bureaucracy with its separation between engineering and management—that is, between industrial-domain knowledge and high-level bureaucrats and politicians (Rose 1981, 1986). Taiwan is a model example of a technocratic Weberian bureaucracy in the Japanese style (Kim et al. 1995). All high- and midlevel bureaucrats, as well as their ministers, have graduate educations in engineering and thus are quite versed in their industrial-domain knowledge. Israel has a much more chaotically structured bureaucracy. The key principle behind its establishment was to balance bureaucratic professionalism and the ability of politicians to implement their will. The result is similar to the American bureaucracy: elected politicians bring with them many of the top executives, including all the directors general of state ministries, from outside the state structure (Bowsher 1991, Deri 1993, Heclo 1977, Pfiffner 1992). These differences significantly influence the politics of industrial development in each country. Moreover, their existence severely weakens arguments that focus strictly on specific state structure.

It is important to underscore the critical role of the state in all three cases. For many years, the private market did not possess the necessary skills and capabilities to successfully create and manage R&D-based IT companies. Private actors—in particular, investors—shied away from even attempting to do so. Moreover, even after more than a few successes, such as the spin-off of UMC from ITRI in Taiwan or the several initial public offerings (IPOs) of Israeli firms on New York stock exchanges by 1989, private financial institutions were unwilling to invest in the IT industry. Thus the state was the only actor able and willing to start the process of skills and capabilities development in an attempt to spur the growth of the industry. Moreover, being small also posed significant challenges for all three states when they opted to develop their high-technology industries, challenges that larger countries like South Korea, India, and China did not face.[4] Lastly, while Israel, Ireland, and Taiwan are, on the aggregate, successful, they also had their fair share of failures. Consequently, looking at both hardware and software subsectors of the IT industry in the three cases gives us an added advantage of an in-case comparison and a fuller understanding of both failures and successes.

Today the IT industries of all three countries are undoubtedly successful.[5] Yet the three IT industries are markedly different in the way they work, the business models they use, and the way they relate to the global IT production network.

Israeli firms have succeeded in both the software and the hardware subsectors. The industry's role in the global IT production networks is one of a supplier of high-end new technologies (or of new products based on new technologies). Thus Israel's success is almost solely based on intensive R&D. The quintessential Israeli company is Checkpoint, the inventor and market leader of what has become the ubiquitous network security product: the firewall. Checkpoint was founded by three friends who, in the late 1980s (many years before the ascendancy of the Internet), realized that the move to large-scale networking computing would necessitate new security products. Understanding that the market was not yet ready for their invention, the three bided their time working for other companies until they joined forces to found NSK, later to be renamed Checkpoint, in 1993. Since its inception, Checkpoint has not only invented and created its own market niche but also organized international standard-setting bodies around its own technologies.

In Taiwan the software industry development has stagnated, and the IT hardware industry is embedded within the global IT production network in a very different way from that of Israel. Taiwan's industry bases its success on innovation in product design and manufacturing, and focuses on second-generation innovation R&D. The archetypal Taiwanese company is Taiwan's Semiconductor Manufacturing Corporation (TSMC). Similar to most of the leading Taiwanese semiconductor companies, TSMC began life as a research effort of Taiwan's public research organization, ITRI. ITRI's launching of TSMC has completely transformed the working of the global semiconductors industry, not by inventing new technology or products but by inventing a new way to organize integrated circuit (IC) chip production. The company, led by Morris Chang, the head of ITRI before resigning to become TSMC's chairman, was spun off to become the world's first pureplay foundry—that is, a company whose sole business is fabricating chips out of other companies' IC designs. Pureplay foundries receive codified designs from the design houses and fabricate their chips for them, thus accelerating specialization in both design and fabrication. By allowing small teams of designers to produce their own chips, the pureplay foundries have unleashed immense innovative potential, transforming the global industry as well as Taiwan's. Today TSMC, together with another ITRI spin-off, UMC, are by far the world's largest pureplay foundries.

In Ireland, even after more than forty years of industrial policies that brought MNCs to open manufacturing facilities there, the indigenous IT hardware sector growth has not been significant, and it is the local software industry that has risen to prominence. The prototypical Irish company is Iona. Created by four computer science lecturers at Trinity College, Dublin; boosted by the founders' ability to raise EU grants, Iona was established in 1991 to implement into products a new middleware standard, CORBA, which the group has been involved with. Iona's successful IPO on NASDAQ in 1997, at the time the fifth-largest software IPO on the exchange, has transformed the perception of the Irish indigenous software industry within and outside of Ireland. However, while Iona is at its core a product company, most of its revenues throughout its history have been generated by its services arm.

In all of these stories, politics plays an important role. In a similar way to Japan in the late nineteenth century and Germany before it, these three young societies faced a harsh reality in which a failure to build successful national industries would have meant the destruction of their societies as independent social units. Israel, Ireland, and Taiwan were all societies that had only recently gained the right to independent existence after long, bitter, and bloody struggles. The leaders who directed the three societies to their current success—politicians, civil servants, and businessmen and entrepreneurs—were all of a generation keenly aware of the price of failure.

Thus the ways in which Ireland, Israel, and Taiwan have been building their national IT industries, and shaping the relations of these with the global markets, can be understood only as part of national efforts. These have been endeavors in which Ireland, Israel, and Taiwan strived not only to stay independent but also to continuously win legitimacy as a coherent national unit, both internally and externally. Economic and industrial growth has been an important part of the national and international process with which these societies have been defining and redefining themselves. Analyzing the roles of the state in the growth of the IT industry, therefore, gives us another mirror in which to see how national sociopolitical identity is shaped in a globalizing world—a continuation of the constant sociopolitical struggle to define what it is to be Irish, Israeli, and Taiwanese.

In the bulk of the book I aim to show that politics—creating, choosing between, and acting on, different alternatives—has consequences. Accordingly, I have chosen to analyze how different policies in turn are structured and shape different national industrial systems. Equally important is how specific critical decisions were shaped, in part, as an element in this nation-building political process. Thus I will briefly explore how Ireland's economic policy was shaped within the context of its long dependency on Britain and its struggle to create itself anew; how science and technology policies were formed by both the Israeli-Arab conflict and the ongoing quest for a national Jewish identity; and how the Taiwanese IT industry has been shaped by its formal international political isolation and the need to craft and present a new and better model of "a China."

In this exploration, I have used the comparative case-study method in an inductive-iterative theory-building effort (Eisenhardt 1989, King et al. 1994,

Lin 1987, Ragin 1987, 1994, Van Evera 1997, Yin 1994). Hence the theoretical and research traditions from which this book arises are based on the assumption that only an intimate connection with empirical reality allows the researcher to develop a relevant and valid theory (Glaser and Strauss 1967). To this end, the data analyzed in this book come from a database of 482 interviews conducted between December 1999 and December 2003, as well as from official and industrial statistical sources.[6] The interviews were conducted with founders and executives of IT companies, top civil servants in all the developmental and science–and-technology industrial agencies, academics, and venture capitalists (VCs). All developmental agencies were visited at least once and their top officials interviewed. In addition, interviews were conducted with the specific labs and departments within each agency. For both the hardware and software sectors, a list of companies was compiled from public and official records. All the major Irish, Israeli, and Taiwanese companies in the two sectors were interviewed, together with a large sample of smaller companies chosen from companies that were not doing only bespoke development or consultancy. Finally, a snowball technique was used to tease out companies that were not included in the original lists but were deemed innovative by their peers. Thus our sample was intentionally biased toward the more successful and R&D-based companies, giving us, if anything, an overoptimistic view. In all company visits I tried to interview the top management, preferably the CEO-president and/or the firm's founders.[7]

THE STATE OF THE LITERATURE

No single strand of political economy literature offers a comprehensive answer to the puzzles that motivate this book. The first puzzle is the role of the state in the development of high-technology industries in less-developed economies, under the conditions of intensified globalization and fragmented production. The second puzzle is how such different development paths of the high-technology industry appeared, and whether they suggest that multiple developmental choices are available to emerging economies.

It was therefore necessary for me to develop a theoretical approach based on the arguments of several theories. For each question it was necessary to glean insights from a different body of literature. From the developmental-state and late-development theories I sought to understand the role of the state in economic growth in emerging economies; from globalization theories, specifically global production network and industrial fragmentation, I looked for a way to understand development in the radical new conditions caused by the rise of global production networks; and from the systems-of-innovation theories I sought to develop a fresh understanding of how different institutional systems affect the innovative capacity of industrial systems, and how different decisions about resources, industrial R&D, and industrial relations influence the dynamic creation of firms' capabilities. Systems-of-innovation theories also allow me to present a theory of how the co-evolution of state-industry interactions influences different development paths.

In this section I explore these theories and the answers they provide to the puzzles of R&D-based industrial development of emerging economies. Tying these answers together with research-based insights, I then present the full account of my approach in the concluding part of this chapter.

Late-Development and Developmental-State Theories

One prominent school of thought that attempts to explain the role of the state in emerging countries' economic growth is late development. This paradigm originates in the work of Alexander Gerschenkron on the industrialization of the "late developing" European countries—for instance, France, Germany, Russia, and Italy (Gerschenkron 1962). In *Economic Backwardness in Historical Perspective*, Gerschenkron presents an institution-based view of how a backward state's leadership can use the advantages of relative backwardness to attain rapid economic growth. He argues that the more economically backward a nation, the more state intervention is needed if it is to grow. An economic historian of Europe, Gerschenkron acknowledges that the task of economic growth should be positioned within the process of modern nation-state building. Late-developing states needed a more rapid industrialization than the pioneering nations, as economic backwardness equals political and military weakness.

One of Gerschenkron's main arguments is that states have different paths of industrial development built around different institutions, depending on the *timing* of industrialization. Gerschenkron points to the appearance of a new model of industrial banks in France and Germany and the transfer of this model to Italy and Russia as they reached their rapid industrializing phase. Advancing a linear theory of economic development that treats it as a process with specific stages, Gerschenkron contends that among the advantages of backward countries is that product markets are already developed and defined by the pioneering countries, which have already invested in the R&D to develop the manufacturing technologies.[8] A backward country, unlike a pioneering country, has the double advantages of knowing the market, and accordingly being able to predict needs fairly accurately, while at the same time having a clean slate with regard to manufacturing infrastructure, so that its industry can invest in the latest technologies. This allows backward countries to reach a scale and scope that the pioneering countries cannot match, as they have already invested in an array of smaller and older manufacturing facilities.

To use these advantages, backward economies need two institutional capabilities: planning capability (therefore a professional and capable bureaucracy) and access to large amounts of patient investment capital—that is, financiers willing to invest large sums for long periods of time. Under the adverse condition of a backward economy, this is more likely to occur with active state involvement. A relatively backward economy, if it manages to put these two together, can invest in large-scale factories with the latest manufacturing technology. It can achieve economies of scale and outdo the leader in manufacturing capacity and global market share. Gerschenkron stipulates the development of specific and new institutional systems, different from the institutional system of early developing countries.

The idea that backward economies have a specific path of development that depends on the *timing* of their industrialization is still prominent in the literature. For example, Alice Amsden argues:

> If industrialization first occurred in England on the basis of invention, and if it occurred in Germany and the United States on the basis of innovation, then it occurs now among "backward" countries on the basis of learning. The paradigm of late industrialization through learning generalizes to a diverse assortment of countries . . . but in all cases industrialization has come about as a process of learning rather than of generation of inventions or innovations. *Learning, moreover, has been based on a similar set of institutions.* (Amsden 1989, p. 4, italics added)

Even the most recent proponents of the developmental state theories bow to the notion that common timing necessarily means a common model of development.[9]

Gerschenkron's model provides the basis for a more recent version of the late-development theories, the developmental-state theory. Most writers in this tradition focus on the rapid growth of Japan after World War II and on the rise of the Asian newly industrialized countries (NIC), also known as the Tigers or the Dragons. The latter group of states has been described as late-late-developers. One of the pioneers of this approach was Chalmers Johnson

(Johnson 1982). Johnson situated the industrial and economic growth of Japan as a part of its national-political struggle and development process. In *MITI and the Japanese Miracle*, Johnson uses Gerschenkronian logic to argue that what enabled Japan to attain such rapid growth after its devastation in the Second World War was a unique developmental agency called the Ministry of International Trade and Industry (MITI). Johnson argues that MITI acted as a pilot agency, not only strategically planning the development of Japan, relying on the fact that both the technologies and the major markets for its final products were already well developed, but also using control over foreign exchange to encourage the entrance and growth of a few large conglomerates to compete in each of the strategic industries chosen.

Hence, Johnson argues, the fact that the Japanese state had a capable bureaucracy, and *a specific structure* with a pilot developmental agency, allowed Japan to become a plan-rational economy, enabling it to generate an export-oriented catch-up industrialization that became the basis for its "economic miracle" after World War II.[10] Some writers have applied Johnson's arguments to South Korea. Others claim that Taiwan also used a similar strategy even if in a less-state-controlled way (Amsden 1989, 2001, Amsden and Chu 2003, Cheng 1990, 1993, Fields 1995, Kohli 1994, Park 2000, Wade 1990, Woo-Cumings 1991).[11]

In sum, the developmental-state theories have built on Gerschenkron's theory of relative backwardness to present a model of development that emphasizes the role of the state in a national effort of creating an export-based industrial system and facilitating industries that excel in technology transfer–based catching-up. Thus they advance an argument about the need for *specific state structure* that enables emerging economies to utilize *a particular strategy* of development. This is a strategy of state-led development based on long-term industrial planning and the nurturing of a few large industrial conglomerates operating across a broad array of industries with some managed competition. This creates a system that tends toward large investment in the latest manufacturing technologies to reach scope and scale. Its underlying assumption is that industrial development is achieved by the growth of a few big vertically integrated firms that manufacture complete products and are not only competing among themselves but also able to directly compete with foreign companies in the world markets.[12]

The industrial systems built as a result of these policies are systems that foster industrial research that focuses on improvement in process and manufacturing technologies, and on incremental changes to products and technologies originally innovated and designed elsewhere. Moreover, this model of development is based on the assumption that advanced economies are willing to grant the emerging economies access to their market and to their technologies, even when their trade balances with the same emerging economies are deteriorating. In addition, a key element in all these theories is a particular model of professional elite bureaucracy, as was idealized by Weber (Weber 1952, 1958, 1999).

Yet none of the assumptions of this model holds in the case of R&D-intensive and rapid innovation–based industries. First, looking at the industrial landscape, the market is not already well developed. Therefore strategic planning by the state, based on the fact that both the products and their markets are defined, is not as useful. Second, the rate of technological innovation is so fast that industrial systems based on incremental innovations on technologies and products developed elsewhere find it difficult to compete and develop comparable products quickly enough. Third, products are no longer being manufactured by vertically integrated firms. Many of the leading MNCs in all industries, American as well as European, are shedding most of their manufacturing capacities and moving to manage a global production network where products are manufactured by stages in geographically distant locations. Finally, when the industry itself becomes the creation and rapid application of new technologies, a strategy that is based on catching up and massive long-term investment in large-scale manufacturing facilities does not grant such a big advantage.

Last, but not least, Israel, Ireland, and Taiwan, while developing at the same time and in the same industrial sectors, have profoundly different industrial systems and capabilities, employing different business models. Furthermore, their state structures and state-industry relationships could not be more diverse. Hence we need to develop a new understanding, a framework which would take the Gerschenkronian insights about the role of the state in industrial development but reshape them it into the new reality, where a linear model of development is not necessarily true, and where multiple options and state structures exist.

Indeed, some of these same concerns—especially the relative economic stagnation of many of the Asian NICs and Japan toward the end of the 1990s, their difficulties to succeed in more innovative industries, and the realization that under the new international conditions and the rise of China it would be difficult for other nations to emulate their growth strategies—brought a new version of the development state theories to the fore. Proponents of the neo-developmental-state theories, building on earlier research by critics of the strong developmental state theory, such as Richard Samuels, or on the revised theories offered by some of the developmental statists themselves, such as Peter Evans, proposed a re-structured theory of state-industry interaction in industrial development (Amsden and Chu 2003, Ansell 2000, Calder 1993, Chibber 2002, 2003, Evans 1995, O'Riain 2004, Samuels 1988, 1994). The adjectives describing this newly found category of developmental state proliferated. However, be it "the flexible developmental state," "the neo-developmental state," "the networked polity," "the developmental networked state," or "the embedded autonomy industrial bureaucracy," the same broad model is advanced. This model suggests that for a state to initiate successful industrial development, especially in a technologically intensive industry, it must cultivate interaction and a dynamic division of labor with the local industry. To accomplish this, the state needs to have and retain an ability to make and implement decisions in the national interest; be informed about the needs, abilities, and difficulties of the industry so that it can tailor its policies accordingly and refrain from policy initiatives that limit the ability of the industry to develop capabilities on which it can base long-term growth; and change its policies in tandem with the changing needs of the industry. Rather than long-term planning, the state needs a flexible structure that enables it to quickly change and implement different policies as quickly as possible when industrial conditions change.[13] In addition, the neodevelopment argument implicitly calls for the state to manage a process in which it lets the industry gain more and more power to decide its own future as it finds its feet and grows. Hence the state needs to be able to change its role from that of initiator and leader to that of a supporting actor.[14]

However, the neodevelopmental arguments are still structural and hence fail to take the new plurality of the world into account. The neodevelopmental writers all contend that if a state manages to have the *specific necessary state structure*, economic development will follow. The main difference between the various neodevelopmental statists lies in the specification of the necessary structure, not in the theoretical argument or causal mechanisms.

The neodevelopmental statists argue that in order to succeed in the developmental efforts in high-technology industries, the bureaucracy needs, first, to have multiple ties with, and embeddedness within, industry and finance, both locally and globally.[15] Indeed, recent writers in this line argue that the main attribute of a successful developmental state in the 1990s was its network structure. They argue that the ability of the state to successfully motivate industrial development stems from a structure in which different agencies are deeply networked into different social-industrial-capital networks (Ansell 2000, O'Riain 2004).

Nonetheless, they still view embeddedness as one specific option. Thus, within their framework, a state can either be a networked polity or not. The reality, however, is much more complex. There are many ways by which state and industry can interlink, and each one of them necessitates a different division of labor and gives rise to different industrial capabilities. Furthermore, the political process of becoming embedded itself has direct influence on both the success and the shape of the industry to be, in particular, when we take into account the duality of this embeddedness both within and outside the national borders. This is a critical point, which the neodevelopmental statists at best disregard.

Second, as soon as we discuss the need for a flexible bureaucracy that understands and quickly and correctly reacts to the needs of an ever more technologically sophisticated industry, the issue of skills comes into play. To be effective in the intricate dance of embeddedness and rapid innovation–based industrial growth, the bureaucracy needs skills that enable it to understand the complex and changing needs of a highly technological industry. This requirement, coupled with the need to deeply attach itself within the industry, means that we can no longer view the developmental bureaucracy as an ideal-type Weberian bureaucracy with long stable career patterns and skills and capabilities taught solely within the organization. In addition, if the arguments are that (*a*) the developmental agencies need to be able to act independently from other state agencies and (*b*) the developmental agencies need to be flexible and dynamic, constantly changing their policies in step with the needs of the *specific and different industries* each agency aims to nurture, it follows that we must also change our view of the state.

Thus, in contrast to the developmental- and neo-developmental-state arguments, we no longer can view the state as a unitary actor. The neodevelopmental theories themselves lead us to focus on specific parts within the organization of the state and analyze each one in line with the specific policy domains and industrial sectors we study. If we are to follow the neodevelopment arguments to their ultimate conclusion, the state itself is to be viewed as multiple groups of development bureaucracies, each with unique capabilities, structures, and powers, bundled and embedded within society. Indeed, even a cursory look at Ireland, Israel, and Taiwan reveals three very different bureaucratic structures and cultures, with very different politics of industrial development.[16]

Nonetheless, in much the same way as the old development statists, the new developmental-state theorists still portray the state as a unitary and underdefined variable: the state is portrayed either as a success, and therefore a flexible/networked/embedded developmental state, or as a failure, and hence not a neodevelopmental state. An example is Sean O'Riain's recent study of the Irish software industry, where he defines a flexible development state: "The flexible developmental state (FDS) *is defined by its ability* to nurture post-Fordist networks of production and innovation, to attract international investment, and to link these local and global technology and business networks together in ways that promote development" (O'Riain 2000, italics added).

The tendency toward a success-or-failure definition of states is the result of two common traits of recent studies. The first is the use either of a macro level of analysis of industrial development or of partial sectoral analysis looking at one specific industry or region and generalizing to the national level. The second trait is the tendency to focus on either successes or failures without attempting to analyze these at the micro level. This tendency can be attributed to the underdefined nature of the neo-developmental-state concept, which necessitates the classification of the cases studied using only a success-failure dichotomy. This is true even in studies that urge us to look at the different bureaucratic constellations of agencies and power.

Thus, for example, Vivek Chibber, comparing the development efforts of India and South Korea, argues that the Korean state was successful and that the Indian state was a failure. He does so even when arguing that Korean development efforts were successful because the Korean state had a "nodal" development agency with power not only over the industry but also over other agencies. Thus even with an argument locating the reason for success at the level of industrial agencies and constellation of power within the state, Chibber still treats the state as a unitary actor and industrial success as a binary success-or-failure variable (Chibber 2002).

I find this especially surprising because the neodevelopmental statists' arguments, in a very similar line of logic with our proposed framework, strongly suggest that the same state, having a structure where different agencies are embedded into different social-industrial-capital networks during their attempts to nurture diverse industries, can both succeed and fail in different sectors. It is quite possible that it is no longer the "state" that is neodevelopmental or not, but rather different parts of it. If indeed there are many ways to organize ties between the state and industry, many ways in which to organize R&D efforts, and no way in which to fully and strategically plan the industrialization process, then industrial systems that grow out of these diverse efforts will be different. The neodevelopmental statists, however, still propose one "best" model of development, focusing their explanations around specific state structures. Therefore their argument marginalizes the importance of politics.[17]

Another way in which the neodevelopmental statists diminish the role of politics in their theories is by not accounting for the dynamic process of co-evolution within which the state builds its "networked structure" and embeddedness. Even if the argument is that there is only "one" best way to be embedded, then it is important to explain how this embeddedness takes place.

It becomes crucial to explain this once the assumption is made that there is more than one way to be "networked" and that the different ways in which the state relates to industry have long-term consequences. Ignoring the politics of state-industry co-evolution is a significant oversight in the case of emerging economies. Since private industry lacks the skills, the capital, and sometimes the will to enter new high-technology industries, many times the primary role of the state is to directly intervene and create the industry. Hence it is imperative for sustained industrial growth that the state manages the dynamic political process of moving from a position of hierarchical power into a position where it acts more as the supporting actor. These processes are critical in molding the final shape of each particular industrial system, and as such they need to be accounted for. To be useful any theoretical framework needs to account not just for the idea of embeddedness but for the processes that lead, or fail to lead, to different kinds of embeddedness within and outside the state's border.

Since the old and neo-developmental-state theories are not focused on explaining the various outcomes of diverse industrial policy regimes, they do not supply tools to understand and predict these differences and to gauge their influence and importance. Instead, their main efforts are devoted to showing the importance of the state in industrial development and to distinguishing their model of state-industry interactions from that of the old development state theories. Indeed, "The State" might have been brought back "in," but only at the price of throwing politics "out" (Evans et al. 1985).

In order to understand how different policy choices lead to different industrial systems, we need to merge our insights about the plurality of embeddedness models with an understanding of rapid innovation–based industrial production. Although the neo-developmental-state writers claim to explain growth in post-Fordist industries, their argument proceeds without attention to the radical ways in which industrial production has changed since World

War II. Recall that the old developmental school was built around the coherent Gerschenkronian institutional theory of industrial development in relatively backward societies, and it was built on an understanding of industrial technology and production management. Thus the old developmental-state school not only explained but also predicted a whole set of complementary institutions seen in many successful NICs, such as high saving rates and the strategy of industrial conglomerates–based growth. In contrast, the neodevelopmental statists do not propose or integrate a theory of economic and industrial development. This explains why such writers cannot account for a particular set of institutions arising in a specific society or industry, nor for how certain institutions influence economic growth trajectories and behavior in global markets.

This is a major lapse in the neo-developmental-state arguments, as it also denies them one of the mainstays of the developmental-state theories: the intricate explanation of the specific ways in which developmental states' control over finance allowed them to influence industrial development (Zysman 1983). Many developmental-state writers have gone as far as to call control over finance the "nerves" of the developmental state; others have argued that answers to questions about financial resources and policies provide the best indicators for states' ability to realize industrial goals (Evans et al. 1985, Woo-Cumings 1991, 1999). It is a glaring omission that the neodevelopmental school does not have a coherent theory of how states' different financial initiatives shape the growth of different high-technology industries.

To summarize, by analyzing and debating the late-development school, we have gained an understanding of some of the components of the needed theoretical framework. Now we know much more about the need for embeddedness as well as what level of analysis we should seek. Moreover, we now understand that there is a need to gain insights into how different processes of embeddedness, influenced by the varying structures of bureaucratic skills and information and the different roles played by the state to interlink both locally and globally, lead to particular industrial systems. Lastly, we understand that to do so we have to gain a new understanding of industrial production, particularly in the case of rapid innovation–based industries.

Globalization as Fragmentation: Global Production Network Theory

The intensified movement of capital, trade, services, and, to some degree, people across national borders, starting in the 1970s, gave rise to a multitude of studies. Of particular interest among these studies is a specific line of research that tries to understand the international reconfiguration of industrial activities. Pioneered by economic geographers, these studies highlight two interlinked, novel features of the latest globalization: the growth of worldwide production networks, and the increasing fragmentation or "deverticalization" of the production process. Interestingly, this process is accompanied by a new pattern of geographical industrial clustering, that of similar activities of the production process (Arndt and Kierzkowski 2001a, Feenstra 1998, Gereffi 1994, 1996, Sturgeon 2000, 2002).

Today we see rising spatial specialization in particular stages of the product manufacturing chain and a rising international interfirm (not just intrafirm) trade in components (not only in final products). Within the electronics industry, for example, there has been a major transformation in the way final products are manufactured and sold. In the United States, new leading companies such as Dell, Sun, Cisco, or Microsoft's Xbox division do not even have their own manufacturing facilities but concentrate on R&D, high-level product design, sales, marketing, and, at most, final assembly. Old companies such as Hewlett-Packard (and Compaq before their merger), 3Com, and IBM have been shedding a large percentage of manufacturing capabilities and opting for manufacturing outsourcing. Even such components as hard-drives are now manufactured in discrete stages in different locations globally (Gourevitch 2000, Kenney and Florida 2004, McKendrick et al. 2000, Sturgeon 2000, 2003). In fact, a whole new class of high-technology companies—the so-called fabless IC design houses—took their name from their lack of facilities to fabricate their own chips.

Many writers use the term *product chain* to describe this growing "deverticalization." However, product chain may imply linear manufacturing processes of specific products from basic inputs to final assembly. The reality, in contrast, is of manufacturing processes built from multiple relationships between suppliers, each with a different power structure between actors involved in the production of numerous products. These products may be the final products and/or components for other products. For these reasons I prefer to use the term *production networks,* which implies many suppliers with different relationships producing multiple products. Especially in the case of the IT industry, the term *global production networks* describes reality much better than *product(s) chains,* with its linear implications.[18]

There are many causes of the growing fragmentation of production: lower transportation costs, lower telecommunication and information costs that in turn decrease the cost of off-site coordination and control, technological advances that enable the codification of component manufacturing and allow off-site manufacturing, and the de- and reregulation of trade. This fragmentation process has also been the cause of, and in turn is further expanded by, the delinking of the innovation, design, and marketing and sales processes from the production process. The delinking of production stages is now evident in almost every industry in the world, from textile to auto manufacturing, and from toolmaking to electronics (Fuller et al. 2003, Gereffi 1999, Gereffi and Korzeniewicz 1994, Herrigel and Wittke 2004, Sturgeon 2000, 2003, Sturgeon and Lester 2004, Yeats 2001).

The growth of the global production network raises questions about its effects on developmental strategies of nations and regions (Arndt and Kierzkowski 2001b, Bathlet et al. 2002, Berger 2006, Gereffi 1999, Gereffi et al. 2005, Henderson et al. 2002, Ruane and Gorg 2001, Sturgeon and Lester 2004). It is becoming more and more apparent that what are moving from country to country are specific phases of production rather than the production of complete products. Thus product-cycle theories, which predict that as products and industries become old and commoditized they will move from the more-advanced economies to the less-developed, are becoming less relevant (Akamatsu 1962, Cumings 1984, Vernon 1966).

This fragmentation occurs not only in production but also in R&D (Dunning 1994, Gassmann and von Zedtwitz 1999, Gerybadze and Reger 1999, Pearce 1999, Reddy 2000). A study by the MIT Industrial Performance Center analyzing the results of two surveys conducted in 1991 and 1999 on all the companies in western Europe, Japan, and the United States with R&D expenditures topping $100 million in 1991 current dollars (totaling 244) found a remarkable growth in the tendency of big companies to rely on external sources of R&D. While in 1991 fewer than 10 percent of American firms, 20 percent of European firms, and 40 percent of Japanese firms reported a high reliance on external sources for R&D, by 1999 the figure was above 80 percent for *all surveyed firms*. Moreover, the geographical range and distance of firms' sources of R&D had grown tremendously. The average in 1991 of the percentage of total R&D activity outside the home region was 26.8 percent for European companies, 24.3 percent for American firms, and 4.6 percent for Japanese ones; in 1999 European and American companies reported estimates of more than 33 percent of total R&D done outside the home region, and Japanese companies reported more than 10 percent (Roberts 1999).

There has been no study that systematically examines how product frag-mentation shapes the development of emerging industrial countries. Such an account would need to explain why some activities occur in specific locations, as well as clarify whether particular development strategies resonate better with specific stages in the global product networks. What the literature offers are only suggestions for research frameworks on the governance and power re-lations in different types of product chains, or case studies about particular in-dustries in specific locations.

For our purpose a promising point of departure is to look at the two dy-namic processes that reinforce fragmentation: production-stage specialization and capability building, and production-stage economies of scope and scale. These are the main reasons for the rapid diffusion of fragmentation and the growth of global production networks. If we can analyze these processes to gain an understanding of how different emerging countries' industrial policies give these countries advantages in specific stages of production, we will have the beginning of an answer.

Production-stage economies of scale and scope is the term I use to describe the process by which, once a specific production network fragments into discrete stages, suppliers in each stage, by pooling the demand of many customers, cre-ate economies of scope and scale that in-house manufacturing divisions can-not. These economies of scope and scale enable suppliers to become more ef-ficient and allow them to profitably operate on margins that are significantly lower than those achieved by in-house manufacturing divisions. This in turn allows them to further lower their prices while offering the same or even higher quality, further speeding the trend toward outsourcing of this stage's manufacturing activities (Sturgeon 2000, 2002).

Production-stage specialization is the term I use to describe the process by which product fragmentation leads companies to develop superior capabilities in particular stages or components of the product network. A recent example of this in the IT industry is provided by the pureplay foundries. Pureplay foundries, such as the Taiwanese TSMC and UMC, are semiconductor com-panies that deal solely in chip fabrication, and whose revenues come from fab-ricating chips according to the designs of their customers. Such specialization enables companies to become better and more efficient in this narrow set of activities.[19] It also helps them to acquire specialized capabilities and knowl-edge that more–vertically integrated firms could not. These capabilities, once acquired, enable these firms to excel in innovation around the particular production stages and set of components they focus on, using their superior skills and unique knowledge. Over time these two related advantages, in skills and innovation capabilities, grant these companies even more advantages vis-à-vis in-house division of vertically integrated companies. We observe this process both in high-technology areas—for example, in the manufacturing of specialized cards or chips for the PC, such as graphic cards or memory chips—and in more traditional industries, such as the bicycle, where the product network fragmentation allowed one company, Shimano, to become the innovator and market leader in drive-train components (Galvin and Morkel 2001).

The fragmentation of production and the growth of global product chains suggest that there are multiple entry points and ways to succeed, even in the same industry and even during the same time period. Global production networks allow emerging economies as many different innovation-based entry points to the global IT industry as there are stages in the global IT industry production network.

I argue that the decisive factors that influence the entry point of each national industry are:

1. the relationships of the industry with global markets, specifically with the MNCs that build, manage, and to a large degree control these product chains, and
2. the development of capabilities that enable the industry to excel in specific activities which are more or less suitable to specific stages of production.

Thus, focusing on the development and growth of global production networks, theories of product fragmentation enable us to formulate arguments as to how different states' science and technology policies build national industries that do better in different production stages.

Nonetheless, in order to complete our framework, we still need to account for how state-business interaction and the implementation of specific policy regimes translate into institutional systems that, through time, facilitate the development of particular capabilities and skills by private firms and motivate them to employ specific business models. We need to understand how different industrial innovational capabilities are created, maintained, and employed.

Systems-of-Innovation Theories

From the point of view of comparative political economy literature, the systems-of-innovation theories should be seen as part of the varieties-of-capitalism theories. Those theories assume many different models of national economies, each with distinct institutional systems. These systems confer different economic and industrial advantages and disadvantages on companies operating within them. As a result, these companies, in turn, behave differently even when operating in the same product markets and under the same international conditions.

Systems-of-innovation theories aim to explain how systematic differences in industrial as well as science-and-technology institutional systems give rise to industries with specific industrial technological-innovation capabilities. Systems-of-innovation theories were first developed in the 1980s by evolutionary economists (Carlsson et al. 2002, Edquist 1997, Freeman 1987, Lundvall 1992, Nelson 1993). The writers in this tradition build on Schumpeterian economics and on institutional economic theories. They argue not only that innovation is the main source of long-term economic growth but also that there is a major role for policy in R&D and science. Government has such a major role, they argue, for two reasons: first, the innovation process itself is iterative and cooperative in nature; hence there is a significant role for public actors (Braczyk et al. 1998, Cooke and Morgan 1998, Lester and Piore 2004, Morgan 1997, Piore et al. 1994, Piore and Sabel 1984, Teubal 1996, 2002). Second, building on Arrow's seminal paper, they argue that scientific research, especially industrial R&D, represents a clear case of market failure. This market failure occurs because the indivisibility, inappropriability, and high uncertainties of R&D lead private investors to allocate suboptimal amounts of finance to research under conditions of perfect free competitive markets (Arrow 1962, Schumpeter 1961 [1934]).[20]

Researchers in the systems-of-innovation tradition have argued that the different relationships between government, firms, research institutions, suppliers, and customers influence the ways in which new technologies are created and/or diffused throughout the industrial system. The relationships also affect the rates at which new generations of products using the latest technology are produced (Braczyk et al. 1998, Breschi and Malerba 1997, Lundvall et al. 2002).

These constellations influence firm behaviors via three main mechanisms. The first comprises the shaping of firm capabilities, especially their dynamic economic capabilities and innovation-production/absorption capacities—that is, their capabilities to produce new products and technologies or to infuse new technologies into their existing products and manufacturing systems (Carlsson and Eliason 1994, Carlsson et al. 2002, Cohen and Levinthal 1989,

1990). Second, institutional structures influence firm behavior by offering different opportunity structures and different resources which influence the profitability of certain activities (Carlsson 1995, Carlsson and Eliason 1994, Giuliani 2002, Morgan 1997, Teubal 2002, Teubal et al. 1991). Third, institutional structures influence firms' R&D behavior by infusing the system with specific research paradigms and business models that move certain R&D activities and procedures to the forefront and others to the background (Dosi 1982, Samuels 1994).

There are two main strands of systems-of-innovation theories. The American strand focuses more on the influences emanating from the different ways in which R&D is organized and financed (Nelson 1993). The European school, originated at Ålborg, has been more focused on explanations based on backward links between producers, and on the flows of information from users (or user sectors) to producers, and has a stronger emphasis on the role of the quality of demand on the development of capabilities; that is, greater attention is given to the correlation between the sophistication level of customers and users and the overall innovation capability of their suppliers (Lundvall 1992, Lundvall et al. 2002).[21]

Systems-of-innovation theories implicitly argue that three main variables explain the amount and intensity of industrial R&D of each system, all intimately connected to the fact that industrial R&D is a semipublic good. The first variable is the location of industrial R&D activities within the industrial system. The levels of industrial R&D sophistication and capabilities differ according to whether most of the industrial R&D is conducted by the firms themselves or by public and semipublic organizations like research institutions and universities. Systems-of-innovation theories contend that there are major differences between systems depending on the location (public or private) and the identity of the agents that typically conduct most of the R&D. While most writers do not deal with these issues in detail, the logical conclusion of their argument is that the more R&D that is conducted by private firms, the more private industry develops sophisticated R&D capabilities.

The second variable is financing. Different financing modes affect not only the location of R&D activities but also the focus (time horizons and product versus process innovation) and amount of industrial R&D. Again, systems-of-innovation theories do not fully elaborate their arguments on the subject but rather suggest that differences between public and private financing, the financial gains that investors are looking for, and the origin of the financiers directly influence the R&D capabilities and business models employed in each industrial system. The more resources that are available for innovative product R&D, the argument goes, the more R&D is conducted and the more sophisticated capabilities are developed. Similarly, the more there are sectoral limits on R&D activities, which inhibit the development of broader or multi-disciplinary capabilities and knowledge, the more the scope of R&D capabilities will be limited. Following the same logic, an implicit conclusion is that the more that financing is linked with global capital and exchange markets, the more investors will seek financial exits that allow them to channel the profits back home.

Accordingly, I argue that foreign or foreign-financed VCs will push firms into business models that aim at either going public on the leading stock exchanges or being bought by an MNC. As these tend to utilize a business model emphasizing new-product innovation, I contend that the more that the local industry is dependent on global venture capital financing, the more the industry will focus on product innovation and follow a business strategy aimed at foreign IPOs or merger-and-acquisition deals.[22]

The third explanatory variable highlighted by systems-of-innovation theories is the industrial-opportunity structure: the composition of the local industry, including the links among producers, between producers and customers, and between the local industry and the global production networks, in particular, with the MNCs that control them. Different opportunity structures affect the capabilities and business models employed by firms by giving different industrial systems access to different information and skills, as well as by giving each local industry different sets of customer focus, business prospects, and market-niche openings. A critical factor in this configuration concerns the local leading companies. In addition, as the main market for IT has always been the United States, and as American MNCs (with some exceptions) also control the global markets, a key to understanding the different opportunity structures is to look at the different relationships that the local IT industry has with these MNCs, both within and outside national borders. This has become especially true with the growing fragmentation of production.

MNCs (and leading local firms) are critical for the overall capabilities composition of each national IT industry in part because they are the main customers of new local IT companies. MNCs are also key actors in the transfer and development of two critical spheres of skills and capabilities. First, the

R&D labs of MNCs develop products and components on the technological cutting edge. Consequently, they are a major source of cutting-edge technological information and knowledge and, even more important, of world-level R&D-conducting capabilities for the industrial system in which they operate. Second, MNCs are the best organizations in the world in designing and developing new products. Therefore their R&D divisions diffuse into the industrial systems within which they are located the capabilities needed to design new products as well as better knowledge of the customers in the final market.

For these reasons, major differences in industrial-development patterns are to be found in IT industries with different leading companies and different relationships and links with the leading MNCs. If the MNCs' subsidiaries and leading companies within a specific country are conducting manufacturing activities with a focus on process and manufacturing innovation, then their outputs into and inputs from the industrial systems are significantly different than if most of the MNCs' subsidiaries and leading local companies conduct critical R&D activities. Thus the outputs that MNCs and leading local companies seek from local firms and the inputs they put into the local industrial systems, as well as the ability of local firms to sell their own products and services to these MNCs globally, vary depending on the activities MNCs perform locally.

For example, in the case of MNCs' manufacturing subsidiaries, local firms might find it easier to sell manufacturing services or become component suppliers to MNCs than to become suppliers of new technologies and innovations. The inputs of the leading domestic companies and MNCs into the local industrial system would be focused around manufacturing and process information and skills, including critical innovational capabilities around these activities. For the same reasons, local firms will find it harder to sell the same MNCs new technologies, and the MNCs will diffuse less R&D and fewer product-design capabilities into the local industrial system.

In short, the global production network and the systems-of-innovation theories give us a better understanding of the institutional underpinning of industrial development and innovation in a world of geographically fragmented industrial production. Using these insights, together with the lessons we have learned from late-development and developmental-state theories, we can now go back to our framework and develop a more comprehensive argument about the role of the state in the development of rapid innovation–based industries in emerging economies.

BUILDING THE THEORY

In this book I develop an approach to understanding the role of the state in industrial development in a world of globalized, fragmented production. I do so by presenting arguments about the roles and structure of the state in the development of high-technology industries in emerging economies. Hence we must identify first how states can organize and interact with private industry to promote the growth of innovative high-technology industry, and then the political process of this interaction. Second, we must understand how specific policies and state-business interactions produce different national industrial systems within the same industrial sector.

A New Model of Rapid Innovation–Based Industrialization Politics

From analyzing and debating late-development and developmental-state theories, we have learned that, in the development of high-technology industries, the state should act as the flexible facilitating agent, not as an overall commander. The state should no longer methodically plan the development of strategic industries by choosing specific products and product niches, forcing private companies to enter them and supplying some of the necessary finance and technologies. Instead, the state should concentrate on creating more broadly defined technological capabilities, and should focus on motivating private agents to work in these areas and to collaborate with one another and with the state. The state's role is no longer to make the decisions and compel private companies to follow them, but rather to motivate private companies to make long-term commitments to operate in rapid innovation–based industries and activities.

Furthermore, in the case of rapid innovation–based industrialization, the state needs not only to spur the creation of the industry but also to quickly grant the industry control if not full jurisdiction as it develops. At the same time, the state still needs to retain enough knowledge and skills to devise and implement policies that help the industry to grow and maintain its competitiveness in the world of constant technological change.

We should picture the state, therefore, as the national management consultant and central arbitrator and promoter of the industry, with the distinction between public and private roles and power becoming more ambiguous. State-industry relations, I argue, should be seen as a division of labor, of the tasks each side takes to reach the same national goal of economic growth. In this way the state is seen as embedded—that is, as an important agent but not the overall leader—in a network of private and public agents that together makes the industrial system.

In contrast to the neodevelopmental writers, I contend that in order to gain full understanding, we should fully account for the importance of sectoral politics. I argue that it is not enough to see embeddedness as the one final result. First, we need to explain how embeddedness develops in various industrial sector and the political process behind it. In addition, we need to confront the realization that there are multiple forms of state-industry networked relationships, each leading to a different industrial system. For example, we need to be able to explain why the Taiwanese hardware industry flourished while the software industry languished, although the two sectors had the exact same formal state-industry structures and rules of conduct.

Hence our framework needs to take into account the many differences between the developmental bureaucracies of different states, their policies, and the ways these policies are implemented. Furthermore, it needs to explain how these different modes of state-industry embeddedness and unique bureaucratic structures and cultures bring about different trajectories of industrial development. Failing to offer an explanation for these is a critical fault of the current developmental-state theories. In this book I explain these phenomena.

Lastly, we are missing a coherent framework that can help us to understand how and why, through the course of rapid innovation–based industrial development, a particular set of institutions emerges in a specific society or industry, as well as how certain institutions shape economic growth trajectories and behavior in global markets. The framework provided in this book rectifies this gap by utilizing insights from the systems of innovation and global production network theories.

There is a need for a new model that delineates the role of the state in the politics of industrialization. While this theoretical framework should be built on the neo-developmental-state arguments, it should take into account the multiple ways in which successful development can simultaneously take place within the same industries; accordingly, there are alternatives, with different consequences with which to create and from which to choose.

The idea of network development serves as the basis for my argument. My framework proposes that in successful cases of rapid innovation–based industrial development, state agencies will first aim at creating a set of firms and industrial actors, then seek to develop a thoroughly multiplexed network among

these actors, and between these actors and the international financial and production markets and networks (Ansell 2000, Locke 1995, O'Riain 2004,
Teubal et al. 1991).

In effect, successful cases of rapid innovation–based industrial development are the result of *different political processes,* in which the state's first role
is as a key actor in the creation of a network. At first, the network is hierarchical, but in the course of co-evolution I expect to find the network becoming denser and more heterarchial or policentric and international, with the
state moving from a position of controlling the network to a position of centrality—that is, becoming an important node within a bigger and much more
multiplexed, larger, and diffused network. Consequently, the state's main role
becomes more that of a facilitator-organizer than of an overall commander.
Further, I argue that the different ways local and sectoral politics shape the
development of these networks vastly influence the industrial structure and
capabilities.

Rapid innovation–based industrial development failure takes two forms.
The first occurs because of the inability or unwillingness of the state to facilitate and participate in the growth of this industrial sector. An example of that
kind of a failure would be the state's ignoring the industry, largely refusing to
participate in its growth or to channel the resources necessary to that effect.

A second kind of failure occurs when the state actively participates in the
creation of the network but then resists relinquishing its power, trying instead
to retain its position of power and control, aiming to maintain hierarchical relationships with private industry.

Overcoming these dangers is not easy and requires much more than state
will. Indeed, to successfully manage the dual-staged process above, the state
needs to acquire two assets: (*a*) sufficient technological and scientific skills,
knowledge, and information to make informed decisions in the case of ever
more complex industrial technologies development; (*b*) multiple relationships
with the industry that enable the development agencies to be constantly informed about the shape and needs of the industry, as well as to implement its
decision without resorting to coercion. Moreover, it needs to have and preserve its ability to make decisions independently. As I have noted, acquiring
these two assets, managing these transitions, and developing the needed
industry-state co-evolution processes suggest a model of the state that is incompatible with the Weberian model of the ideal-type bureaucracy. In addition, as there are many ways to acquire the needed skills and create embeddedness within the industry, as well as many ways to manage the relationship

with the industry, even within the same state, it follows that there are many different models of the new development state. The interventionist who looks for the recipe for success may be disappointed that there are multiple options available to the state. However, for the state that is striving for economic growth, the temporal and structural indeterminacy of solutions is a hopeful message.

We can now propose a new model of successful state efforts for rapid innovation–based industrialization. The new model suggests a bureaucracy that is less Weberian and isolated but much more fragmented. However, it is also more technologically and scientifically knowledgeable and skillful, as well as closer to industry. The state's structure must permit the developmental agencies to react quickly to the needs of the industry, allowing the state to nurture industrial development without itself seizing control over that development. While the old model conceptualized the state as a unitary actor with personnel recruited, trained, and indoctrinated within the bureaucracy, the new views the state less as a monolith and shifts attention to its different agencies. It follows that differences in the ways the bureaucracy is constructed, the social origin and educational background of its personnel, and its ability to shape the decision making process must be analyzed.

There are many ways in which the developmental bureaucracy can acquire the needed skills and embeddedness within industry (fig. 1.1). One approach is for the state to be involved as deeply as possible in the industrial R&D process, bringing the technology-creating agents into its own structure. Of the three cases, Taiwan's utilization of two state-controlled public research institutions—the Industrial Technology Research Institution (ITRI), and the Institute for Information Industry (III)—as the main impetus for IT industrial growth, is an example of such a strategy. A second approach is to create a development bureaucracy with porous borders and to employ a "revolving door" recruitment-and-training strategy, enabling scientists and industry leaders to move back and forth from state to private industry. Of our cases, the way in which Israel's main developmental agency—the Office of the Chief Scientist in the Ministry of Trade and Industry (OCS)—has been structured is an example of such a strategy.[23] The third approach is a variant of the second, in which the state attempts to preserve the cohesiveness and Weberian principles guiding the developmental agency by creating specific subunits, usually with a more limited or advisory role, in which regular recruitment and training procedures do not apply and into which industry insiders are recruited on a temporary basis. Of our cases, Ireland's utilization of such subunits, of which the

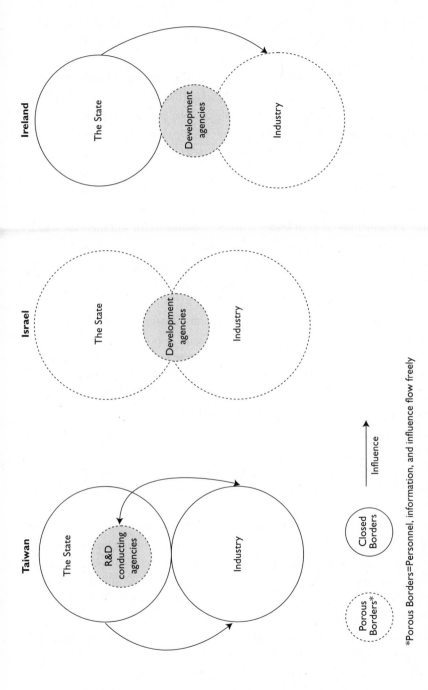

Taiwan

The State

R&D conducting agencies

Industry

Israel

The State

Development agencies

Industry

Ireland

The State

Development agencies

Industry

Porous Borders*

Closed Borders

Influence

*Porous Borders=Personnel, information, and influence flow freely

Figure 1.1. Three Modes of Local Embeddedness

National Software Directorate has been the most influential, within larger development agencies—the Industrial Development Agency (IDA) and Enterprise Ireland (EI)—that embody Weberian ideals, is an example of that strategy.[24]

The new framework differs from the old in the ways in which the developmental agencies create, conduct, and maintain their relationships with industry. In the old model the developmental state was portrayed as having strong relations with the leading big firms. While dialogue was maintained, the state had the authority and responsibility of guiding and controlling the industry's development. In the new model, the state aim is to become bundled within, and create tight relational networks with, the industry; industry-state dialogues are to be between equals; and the state's role is more of a facilitator than a planner and overall leader. However, unlike in the old theories, which described a fairly straightforward relationship and power structure, there are many ways in which the state can accomplish its roles and create the relationships that the new framework emphasizes. The shaping of these choices is done through a constant political process.

The choices available to the state can be conceptualized along two orthogonal axes. On one end of the first axis, measuring control, are attempts by the state to get maximum control over development and direct industrial R&D efforts, from basic research all the way to specific products. On the other end of this axis we have a state formulating high-technology industry–specific policies only after a few companies have already proven the growth potential of specific subsectors, with the state's direct assistance limited to more mature firms.

State decisions as to the degree to which it should target sectors and technologies can be conceptualized on a second axis. On one end are states that formulate policies down to the level of defining specific generic products and technologies. On the other are states that see their role mainly as assisting in the realization of decisions made by private firms, employing horizontal technological policies that are neutral with regard to technologies and sectors (Teubal 1983, 1997). In between there are states that target specific sectors— for example, software—but do not attempt to target specific technologies or define future products.

In our cases we have an example of the three main positions on these two axes, both extremes and the middle (fig. 1.2).

On the one hand we have Taiwan, where the state has been targeting specific technologies and products, authorizing and financing its public research

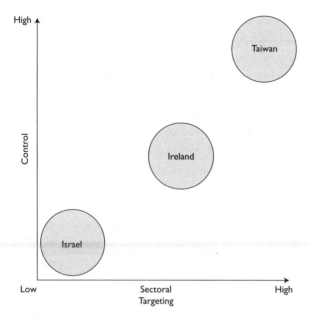

Figure 1.2. State Approaches to Technological and Sectoral
Control and Targeting

institutions to develop them to the stage of working product prototypes and
then either deliver the result to the industry or spin off the research teams as
companies to commercialize the results. On the other hand, we have Israel,
with a development agency that defined its role as fixing the market failures
associated with industrial R&D and maximizing product R&D activities.
The Israeli state followed almost ideal-type neutral horizontal technological
policies. It implemented a policy of giving R&D grants for product ideas developed by private companies and entrepreneurs in every industrial branch,
helping companies in all stages of development. In the middle is Ireland,
which did not have a specific industrial policy for rapid innovation–based industries until after the indigenous software industry achieved some success
globally. Ireland then restructured its development agencies and policies to focus on specific industries and tailored its financial instruments to companies
that, while still young, have already moved beyond the seed stage.[25]

The last dimension in which the new model of the state differs significantly
from the old is in its role in relation to the global industry and financial markets. In the old model the state had three main tasks. The first was to organize
and facilitate technology transfer deals from the leading MNCs to local in-

dustry. The second was to use its control over foreign currency to shape industrial development, granting it to chosen firms who were exporting successfully and denying it to others. The third task of the state was to prevent MNCs from gaining control of too large a percentage of the domestic market and crowding out local infant industries.

In our framework, the state's roles are much more complex. In a world of fragmented industrial production, vertical integration is no longer the sole option, nor necessarily the best one. Instead, there are many ways in which the local industry can become a part of the global production networks. In each of these, the local industry needs to develop specific relationships with the MNCs and with the global financial markets, and for each kind of relationship different technological and managerial skills are necessary. In addition, as the local industry is based more and more on indigenous R&D activities, the role of the state in strategically managing technology transfer, while it might still prove important in the early stages, is diminishing. These decisions relate to the heart of national politics: questions about national ownership, identity, and foreign relations, as well as financial security and independence.

Again, it is useful to think about state choices for enhancing the local industry's specific links with, and embeddedness within, the global industry and financial markets as two orthogonal axes. The first looks at the state's behavior toward foreign technology-based firms, in particular the MNCs that develop and control the global production networks. On one extreme, we have states that look at foreign firms as the main mode for industrial upgrading and focus on persuading foreign firms and MNCs to locate manufacturing facilities within their borders. They hope that these firms' subsidiaries, once established, will become embedded within the domestic industry. On the other extreme we have states that focus most of their efforts on persuading MNCs to locate their R&D labs within their borders, and that pay close attention to the development of specific relationships of local companies with their foreign partners.

On one extreme we have Ireland, which until the early 1990s focused its industrial policy almost solely on bringing MNCs to open manufacturing facilities in Ireland, without paying much attention to creating strong relationships between them and the local industry, within or outside Ireland. On the other extreme lies Israel. By generating collaborative projects between Israeli IT firms and American companies, the Israeli state has established relationships in which domestic firms focus on product R&D and their American partners focus on sales and marketing. Israel's developmental agencies have also been attempting to lure foreign firms to open R&D centers in Israel. Taiwan has chosen a middle course, first urging MNCs to open manufacturing facilities in Taiwan, but then goading them into buying a growing percentage of their components from, and outsourcing their manufacturing activities to, Taiwanese companies.[26] At the same time, Taiwanese developmental agencies have tried to help local companies produce more components and improve their manufacturing-and-design-services capabilities.

Relationships with global financial markets are better conceptualized along a second axis. On one end we have states that try to link their local industry with global financial markets. They court foreign investors not only to back local firms but also to be the financiers of the local VC industry, and encourage local companies to get publicly listed on foreign stock exchanges. On the other end we have states that try to limit, as much as possible, the financing of their high-technology industry to local investors, and try to limit, if not outright prevent, the public listing of local companies on foreign stock exchanges. In between, we have states that either are less active or aim to strike a balance between the two (fig. 1.3).

Of our three cases, Israel has done the most to lure foreign VC investors and urge public listing on foreign exchanges. State efforts have been a main cause behind the current situation: the vast majority of Israeli start-up financing, either directly or through local VC funds, is foreign. In addition, Israeli companies all aim to be listed on foreign exchanges, making Israel, with only six million people, the state with the largest number of companies listed on NASDAQ other than the United States and Canada. On the other extreme is Taiwan, focusing all its technology financing initiatives on the local investment community, and strongly advancing the Taiwanese Stock Exchange. Ireland has chosen the middle road: channeling European Union (EU) money to the local VC industry but creating the new funds mostly through local financial institutions.

Different Choices: The Varied Paths of
Industrial Growth

Conceptualizing the new model of state-industry relationships helps us to elucidate the different ways in which emerging states can structure themselves and their relationship with the local industry in order to nurture and support the growth of the high-technology industry. We can now consider how the different directions taken by states influence their high-technology industrial

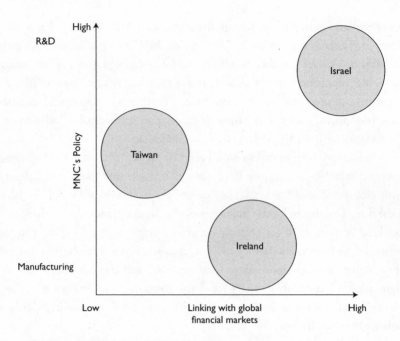

Figure 1.3. Local-Global Embeddedness Modes

development path. Using these insights we can explain how in the cases of Taiwan, Ireland, and Israel specific state policies and behavior have helped to spur the development of different IT industries and to generate the relative success and failure of each subsector within each of the three cases.

The spatial clustering of similar production activities and the underlying linked dynamics of production-stage specialization and production-stage economies of scale and scope point us to several domains of interest. First, specific industrial R&D, dynamic economic capabilities, and business models are more suitable for certain stages of the production process. Second, the analysis of the dynamics of production-stage specialization and economies of scale and scope indicates that industrial systems that specialized in a specific stage of production tend, if successful and with time and effort, to become ever more competitive and innovative in these specific stages. Consequently, if we want to understand the different evolutionary processes of high-technology industrial growth we need to understand, for each of our cases:

- how industrial R&D and dynamic economic capabilities are created, improved, and maintained;

- the growing utilization of certain business models; and
- the development of specific relationships that the local industry has with the global industrial and financial markets.

In effect, we need to analyze the development of industrial R&D capabilities, capacities, and opportunity structures in each of our cases.

In order to understand the growth of industrial R&D capabilities, we compare the different location of the R&D conducting agents, the R&D resources available and the way in which firms are financed, the scope and limits of R&D, and the industries' customers and relationships.

With regard to opportunity structures, infrastructural variables being more or less equal, two main variables—the industry's customers and markets and the ways in which the industry is financed—strongly affect the business models and strategies firms and entrepreneurs employ. This leads industrial agents to focus on the building of specific innovative and manufacturing capabilities. In a world in which most of the trade in IT is done through global production networks, there are two key factors in determining their opportunity structure: the relationships that local IT firms have with local leading firms and with foreign companies, especially leading MNCs; and the sources and forms of finance. One question is what forms of financing are open to technological entrepreneurs? Another question is whether the source of the capital is local or global and how deeply it is tied to foreign-exchange markets.

We can now focus on four critical decision areas to analyze how different behavior and structure of the state influences the development of the IT industry's R&D capabilities in each of our cases:

1. Decisions by the state on how to acquire the necessary R&D skills are influencing the identity of the agents conducting industrial R&D. The more the state bureaucracy encompasses R&D conducting agents within its structure, the fewer industrial R&D activities private firms are encouraged to take.
2. Decisions by the state over the level of control over the technological development path of the industry, including the decision of how, and whom, to finance, bear on both the R&D resources available to the industry and the scope of R&D activities taken.
3. State efforts toward developing the first local leading companies have long-term consequence for the industry's opportunity structure.
4. Decisions by the state concerning the involvement of foreign firms and investors within its national borders, as well as decisions about whether to

enhance specific relationships between local and foreign companies outside states' national borders, affect the resources, the particular feedback and information the industry gets from its main customers, and the diffusion and development of specific innovative capabilities.

It is my contention that private firms in the high-technology industry of emerging economies have more limited R&D capabilities when the state has tried to control the industrial R&D development path, has encompassed the R&D conducting agents within its structure, has supplied only limited resources, has refrained from urging foreign companies to conduct R&D activities within its borders, and has limited the involvement of foreigners as financiers.

Yet neither Taiwan nor Ireland nor Israel followed these idealized paths. In each case a particular mix of policies and initiatives across these different dimensions has been played out. Therefore the full answer requires a more refined level of comparison, fully elaborated in Chapters 2–4.

I have three goals for this book. The first is to expand our understanding of the role, and the limits, of the state in the development of rapid innovation–based industries in less-developed economies. The second is to explain how the different approaches taken by Israel, Ireland, and Taiwan shaped the IT industries, influenced the particular development path of and the particular capabilities developed by each industry, and moved each industry into a different position in the IT industry's global production network. Lastly, by showing that emerging countries have real alternatives with regard to RIB industrial growth, I argue that politics and the political struggles of crafting and choosing between these alternatives, as well as the politics of state-industry co-evolution, are important not only in explaining the difference between success and failure but in identifying the reasons behind the diverse paths to success. By shifting our explanations from timing and structure reasoning, I aim to show that both "state" and "politics" need to be explained if we want to understand both policy formulation and its outcomes.

Chapter 2 The Development of the IT Industry in Israel: Maximization of R&D as an Industrial Policy

Like old Soldiers, old R&D Projects never die.
There is always the sequel.

—*Brig. Gen. (Ret.) Professor Itzhak Yaakov, Israel's Chief Scientist, 1974–1978*

Israel's IT industry is an impressive success story. In less than twenty years, the country has emerged as a key player in global IT technology, with Israeli companies pioneering many hardware and software market niches, such as voice over Internet protocol (VoIP), encryption, printed circuit board inspection, antiviral protection, digital printing, and firewalls. This small country of only six million has, after the United States and Canada, the highest number of IT companies listed on NASDAQ. In 2000 Israeli IT industrial export revenues exceeded $13 billion and accounted for more than 71 percent of all industrial exports; the IT industry accounted for 70 percent of GDP growth, by far the highest percentage in the world. By 2004 the industry had shaken off the NASDAQ's dot-com crush, and revenues exceeded $15 billion (CBS 2000b, 2001, 2004a, IAEI 2006).

Looking at Israel today, with its strong science-and-research infrastructure, one can easily claim that its success in the IT industry was predictable. How-ever, nothing could be farther from the truth. Israel's industrial policy in its first two decades of existence resembled the model prescribed by the "old" developmental-state theorists. The state employed long-term planning and di-rectly intervened in the creation of specific sectors and industries, especially textiles and defense, without any thought given to the creation of high-technology industries (Levi-Faur 1998, 2001). In 1968, Israel's science-and-technology (S&T) industrial policies were based in public research institu-tions. R&D activities in the private civilian industries were almost unheard of. Israel's total R&D expenditures as percentage of GDP—less than 1 percent in 1965—were lower than any of the Organization for Economic Co-operation and Development (OECD) countries except Italy. The number of scientists and engineers was not low—10 per 10,000 employees—but it was still less than half the ratio of the United States (25) and Sweden (22) (Katchalski 1968, p. C-7). The absolute number of R&D personnel in the industry was minuscule, and most R&D activities and personnel were concentrated in the defense and academic research sector.[1]

What accounts for this enormous transformation and the success of Israel's IT industry? First, Israel's main competitive advantage has been its R&D ca-pabilities—its competitive edge originated in an existing defense sector and academic research system. The state's almost exclusive focus on the enhance-ment of technological cutting-edge R&D capabilities has enabled firms to de-velop novel products based on the latest technologies, the new technologies themselves, or new applications of these technologies. In turn this has led Is-rael's IT industry into its position as a supplier of new technologies to the global IT industry's production network. This development path brought the IT industry to success first in hardware and then in software; thus the soft-ware industry developed within an industrial system that was already centered around advanced product R&D activities.

Second, from the beginning of the 1970s S&T industrial policies focused almost solely on developing capabilities to create new R&D-based products. In addition, the state's R&D policies viewed private firms as the main agents of R&D; the state saw its own role as the grantor of capital for R&D activi-ties. It encouraged the development of R&D capabilities in the private mar-ket, diffused R&D know-how from the university and defense sectors to the civilian industrial sectors, and coordinated and provided public space in which private and public R&D agents could meet in order to enhance the flow of information and ideas (Breznitz 2005a, 2006). Thus in Israel the state's actions nurtured an institutional environment that stimulated private firms to develop advanced R&D capabilities and gave them the resources to do so.

Third, in the case of Israel the state forcefully advanced a specific division of labor between local firms and MNCs. The state advanced both a specific and prominent model of organizational development in the IT industry, and a specific model of embeddedness into the global IT industry's production networks. This division of labor allowed Israeli firms to specialize in product R&D and to utilize American (and later European or Japanese) MNCs as marketing channels.

However, the state's almost exclusive focus on promoting R&D activities and business models that are based on new innovations is also the source of the industry's most severe weaknesses. With management and business-development skills on the back burner many Israeli companies have difficulties in sustaining their initial success for the long term. Many market niches that were pioneered and controlled by Israeli firms no longer have any Israeli firms operating in them. More worrisome is that this is especially true in market niches that have grown in their importance and overall revenues. Indeed, for an industry with more than thirty years of global success, it is extremely rare to see market niches in which the Israeli industry has had long-term leadership.[2] Furthermore, the institutional setting of the industry, its strong imitation of the American start-up model and VC financing—and with it the need to focus on securing financial exits—exacerbates this problem. Meanwhile, it becomes increasingly apparent that Israelis no longer control a growing percentage of the Israeli IT industry. Therefore it is not at all clear whether it is Israel and its society that fully enjoy the fruits of the industry's success. In addition, the continuing decline of the rest of Israel's economy and its industrial productivity suggests that the IT-R&D sector is now disconnected from the rest of Israel's economy.[3]

In this chapter, I present a full view of the co-evolution of Israel's S&T industrial policies, the particular growth pattern of the industry, and the state's role in this growth. I first give an overview of Israel's early economic history as a background. It is important to show how the development of industry was profoundly influenced by the nature of the Israeli bureaucracy, national security concerns, and an ideology that privileged scientific research. In the next section I analyze the early years of the OCS, as well as the decisions that led to its creation. Following this account, I examine the growth of Israel's IT industry, first hardware and then software, by evaluating the intricate co-evolution process between state policies and industry development, the changing roles of the OCS, and the particular division of labor that evolved between the local and the global industry, and between public research institutions and private firms. In the last sections I investigate the industry's development in the 1990s, the influence of a new set of OCS policies, the ways in which these policies, in turn, were influenced by the industry's evolution, and the industry's current strengths and weaknesses.

HISTORICAL BACKGROUND AND THE
BEGINNING OF THE IT INDUSTRY

In the first two decades of Israel's existence, industrial R&D in general, and in private industry in particular, was almost unheard of. Nevertheless, a few factors that proved crucial for Israel's IT industrial growth were already in place. The three most important were the continuous growth of an educated workforce and a highly capable university research sector, a small but expanding defense R&D sector, and a national ideology that gave very high status to science and technology (with scientists having easy access to political leaders). Furthermore, the flexible structure of the Israeli bureaucracy made it possible for leaders within the civil service, who came to see the development of IT industry as a national interest, to devise and implement policies with relative ease.

The transformation of Israel's industrial policies, especially the beginning and evolution of S&T industrial policies, had little to do with the ability of the bureaucracy to conduct long-term planning and monitoring, or with its internal cohesiveness. It had more to do with the specific constellation of political leaders in positions of power in the development agencies and government, as well as their views on the proper goals for S&T industrial policy. The structure of Israel's civil service, with its porous borders and revolving doors between state, academia, and industry, eventually made Israel's IT industrial and financial elites not only look as one but act as one.

This structure reflects a conscious political decision to give political leaders power in shaping and implementing policies—in effect, designing the Israeli bureaucracy more in the American view of civil service than in light of Weberian ideals (Deri 1993, Heclo 1977, Sharkansky 1989).[4]

From Independence to the 1967 Crisis

From its 1948 independence to 1966, the Israeli state followed a protectionist economic policy coupled with an interventionist industrial policy. There were three goals: security and regional policy, industrial development, and the building of a private ownership–based economy. While waves of immigrants from less-developed countries lowered the average level of education, the institutional underpinning of Israel's education system and its research-oriented third-level education system was already well established and enabled Israel to quickly upgrade its workforce. New immigrants were channeled to new cities, located according to a security-based logic, not on a purely economic basis. The state anchored these new cities around privately owned, government-subsidized, large-scale plants. (The textile industry was the focus of this state industrial planning, but parts of the defense industry complex and various other industries were also enlisted in these aims.) The result was a quasi-private, large-scale, plant-based industrial sector, deeply dependent on, and actively lobbying for, government subsidies and aid.

The growing friendship and alliance during this period between two leaders of industrial and economic policy, Pinchas Sapir and Levi Eshkol, was to have an important long-term influence on Israel's industrial and economic development and the setting of S&T industrial policy until the mid-1970s. Each served as minister of the three main economic ministries: the Ministry of Development, the Ministry of Trade and Industry, and the Ministry of Finance. Eshkol was also the prime minister at a critical period of Israel's development between 1963 until his death in 1969, with Sapir serving as his minister of finance.[5]

This long-term alliance and friendship was critical for several reasons: first, the fact that these two strong political leaders remained in positions of influence for such a long period of time, gaining extensive and intimate knowledge of their domain, institutionalized specific patterns of state-industry relationship and gave the two an unusually high level of influence over Israel's economic development, even beyond the relatively high level of power that Israel's bureaucratic structure grants political leaders. Second, this long-term stability and influence over the key industrial-development ministries, especially the Ministry of Finance and the Ministry of Trade and Industry, enabled Sapir and Eshkol to follow a plan of professionalization, populating them with handpicked personnel. Many of the graduates of the Hebrew University Department of Economics (at the time the only one in the country) were recruited straight into the bureaucracy, sometimes even before they finished their studies (Levi-Faur 1998). Third, Eshkol and Sapir nurtured long-term personal relationships with some of Israel's key scientists and early IT entrepreneurs. These relationships were crucial for the start of Israel's S&T industrial policies.[6]

Ideology has also played a significant role in Israel's development, with social-democratic principles given cultural prominence, evident in the idealization of the kibbutz (Tsuk 2004). Nevertheless, the state, led by the Socialist Party until 1977, had also (surprisingly to some) used its considerable power to ensure that private ownership of the forces of production became the predominant form. The Labor Party's political leaders firmly believed that the future of the Israeli economy crucially depended on a strong capitalist industry led by private entrepreneurs. This tension came to a head in 1956 when the industrial conglomerate of the Federation of Labor Unions (Histadrut), Solel Boneh, was deemed too powerful for private industry to compete against, and the Labor Party's national political leaders moved briskly to break it up and force the resignation of its manager, Dan Hillel. The Labor-led government did so at a time when the party was controlling the Histadrut, with Hillel as a longtime party member. In a meeting of the Labor Party's members of Parliament during the Solel Boneh crisis, Minister of Finance Sapir's remark illuminated the economic belief behind these actions:

> When I spoke with Dan Hillel yesterday I realized that he has an interesting ideology. I think it is utterly destructive for the national economy, and I told him so. He says that there is no hope or future for private industry in Israel. Myself, I think that if there will be no private industry in Israel there will be no public industry in Israel. . . . The conclusion of the things I just said is that Solel Boneh is impeding the growth of Israel. I am utterly sorry for it, but it does not prevent me from seeing the reality. (protocol of the parliamentary Labor Party meeting of December 11, 1956, as it appears in Levi-Faur 2001, p. 179; my translation)

In 1965–1967, Israel suffered its first recession, which ended with the 1967 war. The war became a critical point in the development of Israel's science-and-technology industrial policy, thanks to the unexpected hero of the Israeli IT industry: French President Charles de Gaulle. Today, after three decades of close Israeli alliance with the United States, few remember that in the first two decades of Israel's independence, its main ally was France.[7] Israel bought almost all of its military equipment, including such critical systems as fighter jets and ships, from France, and Israeli engineers were working closely with French teams on the modification and specific systems R&D for various weapon platforms.[8] In 1967, on the eve of the June war, with Israel under a severe security threat, de Gaulle declared an immediate military embargo on Israel, due to France's decision to ally itself with the Arab world. That decision resulted in Israel's inability to buy critical weapon systems off the shelf anywhere in the world, while at the same time its enemies had access to the latest Soviet weapon systems and military aid.

The immediate reaction of the Israeli state was to shift large amounts of resources and R&D power to ensure the rapid growth of Israel's high-technology defense industry. A decision was reached that Israel should never again be completely dependent on a foreign power for military platforms. Starting in 1967 Israel's military R&D targets changed from developing niche weapon systems, the most sophisticated of which were radar-guided rockets, to developing its own weapon platforms, such as tanks, fighter jets, and ships. At least as important as the skills and product R&D capabilities these projects helped to develop in Israel was the rising demand for scientists and engineers. As we shall see, this demand and the accompanying higher wages and higher-status prospects for scientists and engineers in Israel created strong incentives in the Israeli labor and education markets to acquire these skills (Halperin and Berman 1990, Halperin and Tsiddon 1992).

The Seeds of the IT industry

While the official history of computing in Israel began in 1947 at the Weizmann Institute of Science (then known as the Sieff Research Institute), before the creation of the state of Israel, the 1948 War of Independence and continuing security threats propelled Israel's development of computing onto a different track. While academia, mainly the Weizmann Institute, continued to develop three generations of scientific computers called the Golems, the defense apparatus and the state bureaucracy quickly became the torchbearers of computerization development in Israel.[9]

Probably the first unit in the Israeli defense complex to develop and use computers was RAFAEL (the Hebrew acronym for armament development authority).[10] RAFAEL, the first, and for many years almost the only, body in Israel to conduct high-tech R&D, had already started to use computers in the 1950s. In 1956 RAFAEL built an analog computer, one of the first analog computers ever made and designed in Israel. In 1959 RAFAEL created a more sophisticated analog computer, Itzik, to enable larger-scale simulation. Later RAFAEL developed a few early digital computers.[11]

The way RAFAEL was organized is an example of the high esteem in which science was held in Israel and the way it was used in building a national identity. RAFAEL was organized until the early 1990s more as an applied academic institution than as a company. Its researchers were considered academics and were granted all the educational benefits of full-time academic staff, including a sabbatical every seven years, which most of them spent outside Israel at leading academic universities or IT companies. RAFAEL sponsored graduate academic education for its employees both in Israel and abroad, contributing to more than a few thousand graduate degrees in Israel and a few hundred in top U.S. engineering schools such as MIT and Stanford, to which these graduates returned regularly as visiting scholars. Thus, from the point of view of a national contribution and international scientific connections, RAFAEL acted as a small-scaled elite engineering university.[12]

RAFAEL played two other important roles, aside from being an important source of information diffusion in the areas of science and technology and R&D management, and generating spin-offs.[13] First, some of the scientists who founded RAFAEL, such as the Katchalski brothers Efraim and Aharon, formulated Israel's science-based industrial policy at the end of the 1960s. Second, RAFAEL was used by the state as an incubation center to "infect" other defense and civilian companies and organizations with IT R&D capabilities.[14] The most important of these were:

1. the creation of the Israeli military computer unit (MAMRAM) in 1960 (Breznitz 2005a, 2006);
2. the first attempt in 1962 to upgrade the Israeli Aircraft Industries (then known as Aircraft Maintenance Corporation) into a high-technology company with the relocation from RAFAEL of the entire project team that developed the Gabriel, the first Israeli sea-to-sea radar guided rocket; and
3. the creation in a joint venture with the Elron group of a high-tech start-up called Elbit in 1966, the R&D basis for which was created by the relocation of the entire digital computer development team of RAFAEL to Elbit.[15]

A second major computerization and software programming effort was conducted in the Ministry of Finance.[16] In 1960 the Deputy Income Tax Commissioner Emmanuel Sharon decided to computerize tax assessments.

Due to the absence of software programmers in Israel, a special course was arranged, similar in organization to the military's MAMRAM core programming course, on a one-time basis.[17] Graduates of these two centers later became the early leaders of the Israeli software industry.

While the state apparatus was generating future IT industry leaders, interesting parallel developments in the private sector occurred. Their importance is not just that they culminated in the first globally successful Israeli IT companies but also that they clearly show the differences between the co-evolution of state-industry relationships in Israel and that of Ireland and Taiwan. In Israel private entrepreneurs gave the impetus to critical policy decisions, including the idea of financing industrial R&D ventures. This was possible because of the porous and flexible structure of the bureaucracy and its early embeddedness within the industry. These early efforts of private industry were also critical for laying the foundation for the intimate relationship between the Israeli IT industry and the United States, fashioning not only their basis but also the specific form that they would take in the future.

While most of the banks and investment companies in Israel, like their Irish and Taiwanese counterparts, found investing in the IT industry too risky, there was one critical exception: Discount Investment. At the time, the group was called the Israeli Company for Investment and Finance and was headed by Dr. Augusto Levi. Italian born and educated, Dr. Levi decided to follow the export-oriented industrial investment model of Italian banks. At the beginning of the 1960s, Dan Tolkowsky, who left the military after commanding the Israeli Air Force, joined Discount Investment. Tolkowsky became instrumental in moving the discount group into high-technology investment. In 1961 he first met Uzia Galil, the founder of the Elron group. Elron was the first, and for many years the main, hub of IT NTBFs in Israel. Throughout the 1960s and 1970s, the Elron group and Discount became the two main sources of NTBFs in Israel. Elron, Elbit, and Elscient, all of which later had IPOs on NASDAQ, were created by Galil, with Tolkowsky, as the manager of Discount Investment, becoming their chairman.[18]

In 1965, without realizing it, Tolkowsky and Galil started the process that would culminate in Israel's first S&T industrial policy and development agency. Concluding that without state support there would be little hope for the industry's future, they came up with the idea of organizing a small industrial R&D grants program and presented it to the Ministry of Trade and Industry, arguing that the creation of "science-based" industry was important for Israel's economic future. At the time Aharon Dovrat, then a protégé of Sapir, was the manager of the industry department in the ministry.[19] In another example of the power Israel's bureaucratic structure confers on its politically backed midmanagers, Dovrat accepted the idea and was able to create a part-time position for a chief scientist to evaluate industry R&D-based new-product proposals for support from a very small fund. Thus the efforts of entrepreneurs secured the creation of the forbearer of OCS.[20]

Tolkowsky was also crucial at another decisive juncture for the Israeli IT industry, its development of relationships with the U.S. industry, financial markets, and stock exchanges. In 1971 he flew to the United States to interest the still young U.S. VC industry in investing in Israel. Knowing that on merit alone he would have limited chances, he approached Arthur Rock, who not only was one of Silicon Valley's most famous VCs (crucial in securing the financing for Fairchild Semiconductor and Intel, and later involved in Apple), but, even more important for Tolkowsky, was Jewish. Rock turned him down but introduced Tolkowsky to the other famous Jewish VC of the time, Fred Adler of New York. (Adler was involved in Applied Materials and Data Systems at the time.) Adler still remembers Rock's phone call:

> I got a phone call from Arthur about Dan Tolkowsky. He told me that Dan is seeking someone to invest in Israel. He then told me about Dan and his background: a fighter for the British RAF in World War II who became the commander of the Israeli Air Force. You must remember it was only three years after the 1967 war, and I must admit that it got me so interested in the man himself that I wanted to meet him just because of that. (interview, September 28, 2000)

Tolkowsky had better luck with Adler, who later visited Israel and became involved with Elscient. Realizing that he could not raise VC for the company, Adler decided to bypass the VC stage altogether and raise money through an IPO in the United States on NASDAQ. Adler assumed that after several IPOs had been successful, the Israeli industry would look more inviting to American investors. In the end this strategy would work, but it would take more than two decades and a critical state policy initiative.

Thus by 1972 the Israeli IT industry already had its first global success and foreign-listed IT company with leading American VCs on its board. Implementing its "self-reliance" ideology in the development of the high-technology defense industry, the state was gearing the accumulation of resources and skills toward a specific path of new-product innovation. Furthermore, thanks to the high esteem science and scientists enjoyed in Israel, and to the efforts of private industry, the pillars for what would become Israel's critical high-technology development agency had been established.

RESTRUCTURING S&T INDUSTRIAL POLICY ON THE SIDE: THE CREATION AND EARLY ACTIVITIES OF THE OCS

In May 1966, in the midst of Israel's first recession, Prime Minster Levi Eshkol convened a committee to look into the organization of government-backed research. The economic crisis convinced him that Israel's industrial policy had to change and that one of the only sources of growth for a resource-poor country was science. The second reason for convening the committee was that Eshkol faced a tough political challenge when the legendary leader of the Labor Party and Israel's first prime minister, David Ben-Gurion, decided to organize a new party and run against him, with the utilization of science in Israel at the top of his political agenda. Eshkol nominated his longtime friend Ephraim Katchalski-Katzir, then head scientist of the Ministry of Defense (as well as a university professor), as the head of the committee. Katchalski was a renowned scientist involved in the early development of defense R&D in Israel.[21]

Contrary to the common myth that credits the Katchalski Committee with the creation of the Office of the Chief Scientist in its present form, its original aim had very little to do with the OCS. It is true that its recommendations started the process that led to the institutionalization of S&T industrial policies in Israel. However, the reconstruction of the OCS had to wait, in what since has become a pattern, until Israel's political leaders nominated a powerful outsider to head and reconstruct the office.

The mission of the Katchalski Committee was to review the fourteen civilian public research institutions and offer recommendations for their restructuring and management. The committee was also asked to review the working of the Israeli R&D authority (the Israeli equivalent to the American National Science Foundation).[22] The committee met thirty times over the course of eighteen months and conducted the most extensive research ever done in Israel on the role of science in the modern state's economic life, the role of the state in the advancement of science for the use of the economy, and the workings of the public research institutions in Israel.

In December 1968 the committee submitted its report and recommendations to Prime Minister Eshkol in a very different Israel from that of 1966. In the intervening period, the country had decisively won a war on three fronts and, as a result, had much more faith in its capabilities; it had also begun a massive industrial defense R&D effort and had to deal with the Arab economic embargo.

Apart from its various recommendations for changes in the management of the public research institutes, the Katchalski Committee report had a long-term influence in two areas. The first was its recommendation of the creation of an official position of a chief scientist in each of the main ministries. The chief scientist was envisioned as the overall manager of the public research institutes and other R&D activities that related to the ministry's jurisdiction. The chief scientist was also to be the personal adviser of the minister for science-related issues. This recommendation gave formal governmental legitimacy to the activities already conducted in the Ministry of Trade and Industry. The chief scientist positions were specifically designed for outside consultants. This allowed the ministries to hire people outside the civil service and offer them better wages.[23]

The Katchalski Committee also argued that the ability to convert basic science into practical technology was the key to national economic success, and then sharply lamented the fact that in Israel there was almost no civilian industrial research. The committee urged the Israeli state to take responsibility and spur civilian R&D activities. It contended that the Israeli state should act through the creation and restructuring of the industrial R&D infrastructure and through the work of the public research institutes. This turned out to be its more lasting influence.

Thus the report not only led to the creation of offices of chief scientists in all of major ministries but also, on the basis of a comparison of Israel with other countries, crystallized a consensus that the national economic future depended on the creation of science-based industries. These industries were portrayed in terms of R&D leading to new products and technologies. This conceptualization, together with the extensive and highly successful defense R&D efforts and a realization after the 1965–1967 crisis of a need to change Israel's industrial policy, eventually led to the evolution of the OCS as an industry development agency.

From a Part-time Chief Scientist to Israel's
Pilot S&T Industrial Agency

Between 1968 and 1974 the OCS continued to work in its earlier format, as a part-time job for a university professor.[24] The OCS was inactive, and most of its industrial R&D budget was still channeled to the public research institutions. Even when companies came with proposals, they faced a heavy bureaucracy, at times waiting for more than two years without getting a final answer to their proposals. However, during that time, the Ministry of Defense was busily developing the R&D capability of the defense sector. Most of the data about those activities are still restricted. But it is quite clear that the defense industry stimulated the changes of the Israeli labor force's skill structure between 1967 and 1980. In that period Israel had the highest growth rate of scientists and engineers employed in the industry in the world: 260 percent, twice the rate of Japan's economic miracle age (Halperin and Berman 1990). The implementation of self-reliance in defense production doctrine was transformed in these years into major R&D efforts on almost all fronts and on almost all the platforms and equipment used by the military.[25]

Most of the decision makers in these years thought that there was a perfect match between the goals of establishing a strong R&D-based defense industry and the economic goals of the Israeli state, viewed as building a strong globally successful R&D-based high-technology industry. There is no doubt that the structural transformation of Israel would never have happened so quickly without the thrust given by the defense sector. This is especially true until the mid-1980s, when the negative effects—such as the crowding out of the private industry in the labor market—started to overwhelm the positive effects of this strategy.

While these activities in the defense sector were ongoing and an internationally renowned massively R&D-focused defense industry was created, very little happened with regard to civilian S&T industrial policy until the end of the 1973 war. By that time, two major transformations had occurred that would convert the OCS to an active development agency: first, Elscient's successful IPO on NASDAQ supplied a "proof of concept" and a model for imitation; second, with the 1973 war, the perception of the need to restructure the civilian industry became more urgent. In 1974 the Minister of Trade and Industry Haim Bar-Lev, a former chief of staff of the Israeli military, recruited Itzhak Yaakov as the first full-time chief scientist.

From 1955 to 1973 Yaakov had served in commanding positions within the military's R&D division. As head of the armament development department and then as the overall head of R&D in the military, he had been responsible for the management of the major transformation in defense R&D. Additionally, Yaakov's educational background, as an engineer with an advanced degree in technology management from MIT, and his international connections, not the least with the World Bank, made him uniquely suited to this role.[26] Yaakov was promised a free hand and sufficient financial resources, as well as the political backing that allowed him to transfer his ideas to reality.[27] This was the first example of what has since become a pattern of S&T industrial policy development in Israel. Managers within the bureaucracy, many of them recruited from outside, are given a free hand to formulate and implement policies and build programs and agencies.

On taking the position, Yaakov moved on four fronts. First, he formulated the goals and aims of the OCS. He prescribed an S&T industrial policy in which the state's role was to address the market failure in R&D by lowering but not eliminating the risk associated with R&D activities. The economic goal was the growth of industrial exports based on new science-based products. Private firms were seen as the optimal agents not only to conduct R&D but also to decide what projects to undertake and what technologies to develop. The logic behind this assumption was that private firms, deeply embedded within their markets, are far better equipped than the state or any other research institutions to formulate and devise successful product R&D projects.

Therefore the state's role was limited to motivate private entrepreneurs to conduct more product R&D. The main way in which this was done was through the central R&D fund, which granted 50 percent of R&D costs to project proposals submitted to and approved by the OCS in repayable loans. (The loans were repayable as royalties only if the products were profitable.) In addition, the bureaucratic processes were simplified, so, for example, a company could sign an agreement with the OCS within ten days of a proposal approval (OCS 1974, 1975).

Second, seeing private companies as the optimal source of R&D ideas and performance agents, the OCS also sharply decreased the support it channeled to the public research institutions, although it guaranteed that for joint ventures with private industry it would sponsor the institution's 50 percent of the project's cost (OCS 1974). This was a major break with the past, and since that day the importance of public research institutions to industrial development in Israel has been marginal.

Third, in 1974 Israel reached the upper limit of what the World Bank then defined as a "developing country." Yaakov, with the backing of Sapir and Bar-Lev, channeled the last World Bank loan to Israel into a program of national R&D projects, which allowed the OCS to give 80 percent grants to up to eight projects. In addition, after President Nixon's visit to Israel, an agreement was signed to create a cooperative R&D fund for Israeli and American firms

(OCS 1974). This fund, under the management of another outsider, Ed Mlavsky, later played a vital role in the development of the IT industry as the BIRD Foundation.

Yaakov also won approval for the OCS to grant the status of "approved factory" to science-based firms, giving them all the benefits provided under the law for the encouragement of capital investment, the same law used to grant aid to plants in the newly constructed peripheral cities.[28] That linkage became more important in later years, when MNCs with R&D centers that registered as a company in Israel were operating de facto under the same favorite tax regime they were granted in Ireland, and when Intel, National Semiconductor, and Tower applied for aid under its provisions when constructing silicon chip fabrication plants.[29]

Fourth, Yaakov transformed the OCS into an active industry-engaged agency. Very shortly after his nomination he initiated company visits throughout Israel and urged the companies' managers to come up with ideas. These activities by the OCS quickly bore fruit; by 1974 the OCS approved 70 million Israeli lire in proposals, three and a half times the amount approved in 1973. Yaakov recounted that some of his major problems involved changing the mindset of the agency:

> Civil servants thought that industrial R&D was a waste of money, that the money could be better used to buy meat in Argentina; it was, don't forget, the Ministry of Commerce and Industry. There was also this belief that innovation came from public research institutes. . . . I had cases where the office workers came to me and said: "This project has no use and there is no need for it." I'd usually send them back to the company that proposed the project to check it in person. More often than not they would return with their head between their hands because the company, operating in the market, knew better. I really wanted to get more industrial R&D activities in Israel off the ground, and I must admit I cut corners. For example, I went to the founder of Elscient and told him, "Bring me one R&D project which you want to conduct and you cannot for lack of capital, and I will declare it a national project and use the World Bank's finance to grant you 80 percent of cost." He thought about it for a day and told me that he decided that CAT scan is the future. [This is indeed the technology on which Elscient flourished during the 1970s and early 1980s.] I said, "Okay, I will give you a letter granting you up to half a million lire and within a reasonable time send me a proposal and I will make sure it is approved." Now because it was a World Bank project, I needed to assemble a prestigious research committee with a lot of academics. These professors wanted to show that they are smarter than the industry and argued that in Holland they already work on CAT scan technologies. I had no choice: I fired the whole commit-

tee on the spot and filled it with people from my office that did not have a vested interest to show how smart they are. (interview, September 28, 2000)

The same picture of the OCS at the time was reflected in the recollection of one of the OCS's first employees of that period:

During the Yaakov period we tried to create a dynamic of R&D activities—we wanted the industry to routinely conduct R&D and to create a dynamic that will infuse these ideas that R&D is something that should be done throughout the industry. To create a sort of paradigmatic change in the way businesses thought about what they are doing. Nobody in the industry even thought about R&D at the time; it seemed to them as a horrible risk, so Yaakov just started going around the country trying to convince managers to conduct R&D. We did not really care who, what, why, when, we just wanted to create an R&D dynamic. (interview, May 7, 2002)

Needless to say, this mode of behavior is far removed from Weberian ideals.

In early 1978 Yaakov left the office to become a consultant for the World Bank in Taiwan and then in South Korea, before turning to private business and joining the American firm Control Data Corporation (CDC). True to the revolving door between state and industry, he became instrumental again in the 1980s. Before he left, he submitted a series of policy papers formalizing the goals and aims of Israel's S&T industrial policy, the role of the OCS in achieving these goals, and the procedures that the OCS should use in order to achieve them. These policy papers defined the role and scope of the OCS for years to come as a quasi-independent agency and became the basis for the OCS operation, with many of their provisions incorporated into the 1984 law for the encouragement of R&D (OCS 1974, 1975, 1977, Yaakov 1974).

The most enduring legacy of these years, however, has been the ideological one. In a 2000 interview, Yaakov expressed his belief that industrial R&D remains Israel's only economic future:

From the national point of view, a failure in a research-and-development project is not a loss. This is especially true in the case of developing and resource-starved countries such as Israel. *This was my sole guiding principle when I gave grants to companies. This is the philosophy that guided me all the time,* and I had many arguments about it with the civil servants at the Ministry of Commerce and Industry. If truth be told, if you took the long term, there was almost no approved project that failed to deliver some tangible results from the national point of view in the end. This is another thing typical to industrial development. Like old soldiers, old R&D projects never die. There is always the sequel. (interview, September 28, 2000)

Over the years the OCS developed a core of professional, long-serving, high-level personnel with a special ethos and a strong identity. This is true even though a large percentage of its staff, including the chief scientists and many of its top advisers, has been recruited for a limited period of service from the private market. Nevertheless, the early recruitment processes of the OCS clarify more than anything the differences in bureaucratic structures between Israel, Taiwan, and Ireland. People who were deemed worthy were recruited to jobs at all levels of the organization disregarding formal channels. For example, a top executive of the OCS recalled the ways, and the reasons for which, she was recruited:

> Just before the enactment of the R&D law in 1984 the state comptroller came out with a report strongly lamenting the grant-giving procedures of the OCS. This was the reason I was recruited. It was quite amazing when I arrived. There were neither coherent financial procedures nor procedures of how to manage the relationships with firms and how to recognize R&D costs. My first job was to create some semblance of order in this mess; the chief scientist at the time was very thankful. He was quite worried and no one here had a clue what to do. (interview, May 7, 2002)

Looking at our theoretical framework we can see that by formalizing the OCS's role as fixing the general market failure associated with industrial R&D, Israel has become the first state in the world to employ as its main S&T industrial strategy a set of policies that are both neutral and horizontal in regard to industrial sectors and technology (Justman and Teubal 1995, Teubal 1983, 1997). The aim of horizontal technological policies is to stimulate a certain set of activities and capabilities throughout industry, without targeting particular industries or technologies. However, with the success of companies in certain sectors, the buildup of more focused capabilities, and the general trends of demand for certain technologies in the market, the system began over time to specialize in certain areas. The private market, not the state, determined the areas of technological specialization. In Israel, for example, we see a buildup of capabilities in IT, particularly in telecommunication and medical equipment.[30]

The Reaffirmation of the Local-International
Division of Labor: BIRD Foundation

In 1976, two years after the initial agreement between the governments of United States and Israel was signed, the Bi-national Industrial Research and

Development Foundation (BIRD) started operation. As with the reconstruction of the OCS, only after a strong-willed outsider was put in charge did
BIRD become the critical and active developmental agency it is today. The
idea behind the creation of BIRD was to encourage cooperation between
firms from the United States and Israel to jointly develop and sell new products. An endowment, later increased to $110 million, provided the financial
basis of the foundation. BIRD was put under the jurisdiction of the OCS and
under the auspices of the U.S.-Israel Advisory Council on Industrial R&D,
which consisted of senior scientists, officials, and businessmen from both the
United States and Israel.

At first, BIRD had no impact. Under its first director, Wade Blackman, an
MIT graduate recruited in the United States, BIRD did not manage to make
even one investment. Ed Mlavsky, then an American member of the U.S.-
Israel Advisory Council on Industrial R&D and a cofounder and executive
vice president of Tyco International, described these times and the chain of
events that led him to become BIRD's second director in 1978:

> I got a frantic phone called from Jack Goldman [then the vice president for tech-
> nology at Xerox]. "Ed," he told me, "we must find a new director for BIRD. Not
> even one single project has been started, Wade is leaving, and the Israelis are impa-
> tient." The council convened a committee to select a suitable candidate. We met in
> New York. The committee was filled with very impressive people. However, the
> candidates were not at all impressive. It was then that I made a fateful remark that
> just shows you that one has to take full and firm control of his mouth at all times. I
> said: "Gentlemen, this is horrible, even I can do a better job than any of them." Be-
> fore I knew it all these notable people, including Jordan Baruch [then the undersec-
> retary of state under President Carter], started to pressure me to go to Israel and
> check it out. I told them that they are insane, that there is no way I will do it. I even
> reminded them that I am married and my new family is not Jewish, that we have no
> emotional connection to Israel. In the end I agreed to come for two years. We put
> our U.S. furniture in storage, and I took a two years' Sabbatical from Tyco. (inter-
> view, June 12, 2000)[31]

Mlavsky came to Israel in June 1979, originally for two years, and stayed as
BIRD's director until January 1993, when he cofounded Gemini, one of the
first VC funds established under the OCS's Yozma initiative to encourage domestic venture capital. Under his management BIRD became an active organization that, like the OCS, did not follow the Weberian ideas for bureaucratic management and development. Mlavsky described this process: "We

just started to do things and crystallized a model after we had some cases to build on."

This model is still the cornerstone of BIRD to this day. BIRD funds up to 50 percent of a joint project in which two companies, one from Israel and one from the United States, agree to develop and sell a joint product and to share the revenues. BIRD's aim has been for the Israeli firm to concentrate on R&D and the American one on product definition and marketing.[32] BIRD coaches Israeli firms on how to approach, and cooperate with, American companies, a key skill that was not widely available to the Israeli IT industry until the end of the 1980s. BIRD also helps in the matching process and to that end maintains a database of American companies that might be interested in R&D, including their product R&D areas of interest. This database is gathered by visiting hundreds of American firms.

Starting in the early 1980s BIRD became prominent in luring MNCs to open R&D centers in Israel. BIRD helps, first, by exposing the American firms to Israel's R&D capabilities in a low-risk friendly environment. Second, BIRD actively convinces MNCs to open operations in Israel. BIRD employs two modes of operation, one assisting Israeli R&D executives who wish to come back to Israel, and the other approaching an MNC that participated in several successful BIRD projects and urging it to open an Israeli-registered R&D subsidiary. The financial benefit that BIRD offers is to recognize some of the R&D projects (starting with the first) of the Israeli-registered subsidiary as a BIRD project between the MNC's American headquarters and the Israeli subsidiary. Moreover, as the OCS also recognizes Israeli-registered MNCs' subsidiaries as Israeli firms for the purpose of R&D grants, these subsidiaries can enjoy both BIRD and OCS grants, enabling the MNC to start R&D operations in Israel at low cost. Both Dan Vilenski, who replaced Mlavsky as BIRD's director, and Dov Hershberg, who was the director until 2006, emphasized the importance that BIRD gives to luring American MNCs to open R&D centers in Israel.

As with OCS, BIRD's financing is in conditional repayable grants, with the grants repaid as royalties of 5 percent of sales of the product to third parties, and for up to a maximum 150 percent of the original grant. For many years BIRD has also been following the logic of neutral horizontal policy and does not limit itself to targeting only specific sectors or technologies. BIRD became a spectacular success and a model for other binational R&D funds both in Israel and abroad.[33] It supports up to thirty-five full-scale projects (a support of

$500,000 to $1 million over two to three years) and twenty miniprojects annually ($100,000) (BIRD 2000, 2004, various years). BIRD uses the royalty payments to increase the number of grants given. By the end of 2000 it had received a total of $64 million in repayments, of which $6 million accrued in 2000. The reuse of royalties by both BIRD and the OCS is another unique feature of the Israeli system.

Until the mid-1990s, when VC financing became available in Israel, BIRD and the OCS were the only two available sources of finance. Both of these institutions diffused a particular model of high-technology companies in Israel. This model views companies as R&D vehicles for the creation of new export-oriented products. The one and only high-technology industry model it stimulated in Israel sees the industry as consisting of companies selling novel products based on intensive in-house R&D efforts. By financially supporting only firms that followed this view, BIRD and the OCS were key factors in the creation of the particular model of the Israeli IT industry as a supplier of new technologies to the global IT industry production networks.

BIRD was also important in strengthening the R&D focus by enhancing a particular division of labor between Israeli companies and American MNCs. In this division the Israeli firms concentrate on R&D while their American partners participate in the product design stages and concentrate on marketing and sales. The relationship of Israel to the global IT industry's production network, in which Israel is a supplier of new technologies, was further reinforced by BIRD's activities, with OCS's support, in luring MNCs to open R&D facilities in Israel.

Furthermore, BIRD influenced the Israeli IT industry by enhancing its already existing propensity, after the success of Elscient, Elbit, and Scitex, to look on the United States as the main market for both products and finance. In an environment where other financial resources were lacking, BIRD's encouragement of this American orientation throughout the Israeli IT industry cannot be underestimated. For example, in an internal evaluation of its activities, BIRD found that 75 percent of the Israeli companies listed on NASDAQ in 1992 enjoyed the support of BIRD, with a large percentage of these companies building their business around the basis of their BIRD project.[34] Last but not least, apart from opening the doors of leading American companies to small Israeli businesses, BIRD infused the Israeli system with two key skills: (*a*) knowledge of designing new products for the American market and (*b*) knowledge of conducting business based on new-product R&D in the American market.

A remark by the founder and CEO of one company that received BIRD grants exemplifies these specific features of the foundation:

> For us BIRD was extremely important. We had a few BIRD projects. They enabled us, a company consisting of eight young people, who [had] just finished their military service, to collaborate with big successful American software companies. BIRD not only put us through the door so we could actually talk to them and see what are the needs of the American market from the best sources possible, but also enabled us to offer them a risk free model. They did not need to put a dime on developing the product, and if it was successful they distributed it using their channels. I see no other way in which an R&D team of eight Israelis could profitably sell so many copies in such a short time and also offer the needed customer support. Later when we decided to open facilities in the U.S., our BIRD experiences proved invaluable. Our first two American employees knew us from earlier BIRD projects, and they brought their friends. It would have been amazingly difficult for us, a godforsaken start-up from Israel, to recruit American employees of such quality otherwise. (interview, January 15, 2002)

As the creation stories of the OCS and BIRD show, unlike the Irish and Taiwanese cases, in Israel the policy was not built as a part of an orderly overall strategic plan. Both the policies and the agencies were built in a process of trial and error, which was managed at levels equivalent to a ministerial division head. In addition, proper bureaucratic procedures of orderly administration did not constitute a defining attribute in the creation and development of the Israeli industrial development agencies.

Nevertheless, there are a few firm principles that have always made up the backbone of Israeli S&T policies. These can be defined as Israel's particular variant of "technonationalism" (Samuels 1994). First and foremost was the belief that new R&D on the technological edge, with the aim to create novel products, is the sole and proper basis for Israel's high-technology industry. The second principle is a clear definition of the role of the state, limiting it to a role of promoter and facilitator of R&D activities. The state goal is to maximize industrial R&D demand in private industry and to lower the risk associated with it. As a result, throughout the specific co-evolution of state-industry relationships that was built on the basis of these ideals, private firms were seen as the loci of both R&D activities and ideas, a striking contrast to conditions in Taiwan.

With the formation of BIRD the Israeli state also started to advance a particular division of labor between the local and the global IT industries, where

Israeli firms and MNCs that opened facilities in Israel were urged to focus on the R&D stages and specialize in the innovation of new products. This specialization in R&D was further enhanced with the state's efforts to lure MNCs to open R&D subsidiaries in Israel, a very different policy from that followed by both Ireland and Taiwan in the same period.

THE RISE OF THE NEW INDUSTRY: THE
EVOLUTION OF THE IT INDUSTRY IN THE
1980s AND EARLY 1990s

After the 1973 war, Israel suffered multiple economic crises that lasted for more than a decade. Economic growth was almost halted, balance-of-payments deficits rose in alarming proportion, and inflation rapidly rose to more than 400 percent annually.[35] From 1977 to 1985 the first political transfer of power intensified the economic crisis. In 1985, a rainbow coalition government pushed a stringent stability plan. The plan succeeded in some areas; however, by the late 1980s, unemployment had become a problem, especially in the periphery.[36]

In the same years that the IT industry grew, the traditional and midtech industries, as well as agriculture, continued to decline. Already by 1988, 59 percent of Israel's industrial exports were high-technology products; by 1998 more than 71 percent of Israel's industrial exports were high-technology, and in 2000, the IT industry alone accounted for more than 70 percent of GDP growth, by far the highest percentage in the world (CBS 2001). At the same time, in direct contrast to the developments in Ireland, Israel's neocorporatist wage agreement regime had been crumbling, with labor union membership in rapid decline and the socialist ideology in rapid retreat.[37]

By the end of the economic crisis in 1985, an IPO on NASDAQ was a legitimate and well-trodden path for the more successful Israeli high-technology companies. However, the IT sector did not pass through the economic crisis unscathed, and with the collapse of the banking system, both the Elron group and Scitex were faced with their biggest crises to date.

During the 1970s the growth of the IT industry was slow, the OCS found it difficult to allocate its maximum annual budget, and not many new NTBFs were formed. The main inhibiting factor, as in Taiwan and Ireland, was the unwillingness of private entrepreneurs to take risk. This entrepreneurship failing was identified as acute in the OCS's annual reports:

It is evident that despite the opportunities described in this section on the one hand, and the massive government support on the other, too few new technology-intensive industries are being established. . . . Clearly we have here *a problem of technological entrepreneurship.* Despite opportunities and massive government aid, there are not enough people willing to take the risk. To reach the ultimate goal of industrial R&D, i.e., new increased exports, *particular attention must be given to this phenomenon as well.* (OCS 1975, italics added)

After Yaakov's departure, the negative side of Israel's more flexible and highly embedded bureaucratic structure became evident. The OCS lost some of its standing. Not anchored in law, it was to fight chronic budgetary battles. The OCS's image was tarnished: question marks over its capture by the industry appeared in the sociopolitical context of only a few relatively strong high-technology industrial groups with political sway, and few new entrants (Stigler 1971). This was particularly true following political lobbying by Elscient that ended with a tax-sanction law, aptly nicknamed the Elscient law.

Until the mid-1980s, when a decision was made to reduce defense R&D efforts and cancel the development of the biggest project—the development of a fighter jet (the Lavi)—the strategy of self-reliance in advanced weapon systems continued, and was implanted mainly in the R&D phase. In 1984, the year before the decision on the major budgetary cuts was made, the annual defense R&D budget stood at $750 million (in 1984 terms [Halperin 1987, Halperin and Berman 1990]). However, it is also important to remember that unlike the industrial defense sector, the military did not cut down on its in-house R&D operations.[38]

The intensification of the economic crisis gave another window of opportunity for the OCS to restructure itself and advance new programs, especially as it had the backing of two strong ministers of trade and industry, Ariel Sharon from 1984 to 1990 and Moshe Nissim until 1992. The approval of the R&D law in 1984, the recognition of software as an industrial branch in 1985, and the cancellation of the Elscient law in the same year marked a change in S&T industrial policies and the move of the high-technology industry to the forefront of Israel's industrial landscape. The period from 1984 until the beginning of the 1990s is the reconstruction period of the institutional basis of Israel's political economy.[39]

Under the new R&D law the OCS was quickly expanding its activities, together with BIRD's. Sanctioned by the R&D law, which designated the OCS as Israel's official S&T industrial agency, the OCS regained its independence and public image as a professional agency. Critically, until the mid-1990s the R&D law authorized the OCS's main R&D fund to finance all of the projects that passed its due-diligence process. These expanded financial resources significantly enhanced the ability of the OCS to create and sustain the industry's demand for R&D. Private IT entrepreneurship became more common, active, and successful.

The IT Industry in the 1980s and Early 1990s: The Growth of the Hardware Sector

Throughout the 1980s, with the available funds from OCS and BIRD reserved solely for R&D, two models of new company formation and growth emerged. Both of these models utilized the OCS and BIRD grants while answering two other financial needs: (*a*) the lack of working capital, especially for marketing and sales; and (*b*) the lack of expansion capital, especially acute during the first stages of international expansion.

Of the two broadly defined prominent organizational development models in this period the first was the creation of company groups. Successful entrepreneurs quickly found that they were being approached by other would-be entrepreneurs looking for organizational and financial help.

Probably the one group that was critical to the industry's development is the Elron group, founded by Uzia Galil. It was Elron that pioneered the NASDAQ model, created the first connection with the American VC community, and was influential in the creation and early development of Israel's S&T industrial policy. Many of the group's companies, such as Elron, Elbit, and Elscient, and even less closely held ones such as Zoran, grew to become leading companies in the industry and listed on NASDAQ.[40] The Elron group, unlike other groups, did not have a common technological sector but supported spin-offs and start-ups in areas that seemed to suggest to its management an opportunity at the time.[41]

One of the companies growing out of this organization model, Orbotech, is also one of the only cases of an Israeli company managing not only to pioneer its market niche—automatic optical inspection (AOI) systems for printed circuit boards (PCB)—but also to control it for a significant period. Orbotech's history also illuminates the wild competition and lack of planning in the Israeli IT industry in comparison with Taiwan and Ireland. Orbotech is the product of the 1992 merger of Orbot and Optrotech, two Israeli companies that between them controlled the global market (85 percent) in their niche during the late 1980s. Dr. Shlomo Barak founded Optrotech in 1981 with the backing of the Elron group. Orbot was founded shortly thereafter by a group of Israelis who first met in Boston, where some of them were MIT professors or students. Ormat, another of the first globally successful Israeli high-technology firms, backed Orbot, which commenced operation in December 1982.

The second model of organizational growth was to build a company on the basis of OCS and BIRD foundation projects (as OCS grants are given on a per-project basis, companies can win several of these grants). Among the most successful were Gilat Satellite, Comverse, and Mercury, all of which became globally prominent companies in their market niches. In the second half of the 1980s, the move of defense-oriented companies into the civilian market accelerated. The most successful of these has been ECI Telecom, which successfully transformed itself into a civilian company and listed on NASDAQ in 1982.[42]

During the 1980s the flexibility and reach of the "porous borders" structure of the Israeli bureaucracy were crucial in securing another source of finance: investor limited partnerships. These partnerships provided a classic example of state-business collaboration to achieve a common goal. The limited-partnership model was organized after Yaakov, at the time working for CDC, discovered the existence of R&D tax incentives in the United States. Yaakov (with others following him) collaborated with the OCS to create a specific set of legal entities to use the American tax shelter to channel finance into Israeli IT firms. Groups of U.S. investors were assembled to form limited partnerships investing in the R&D efforts of a preselected set of companies. The OCS then assisted these limited partnerships with additional financing that was classified as loans for tax purposes, maximizing the tax returns for the American investors and minimizing their risk exposure. The first limited partnership started to invest in 1980, and a few more followed, under the titles of Israeli R&D Associates (IRDA) or Israeli Technology Ventures (ITV). In 1985 the Reagan administration changed the tax regulations that were the basis of the limited partnerships. Activity continued until the late 1980s in those that had already raised their funds. All in all, the limited partnerships invested in twenty-five different newly created companies, the most successful of which were Technomatics, Comverse, Teledata, and Lannet. The main effect of these limited partnerships was to further strengthen both the R&D focus within the Israeli IT industry and its connection to the American financial markets.

In the late 1980s the growth of the telecommunication subsector of the Israeli IT industry helped another group of companies, RAD, to rise to prominence. The story of RAD is illustrative in several ways. Apart from the importance of the group itself, its growth marks a generational shift in the Israeli IT industry and with it the growing importance of graduates of the military R&D and intelligence units. Even more importantly, the growth and limits of the RAD group provide one of the best examples of the strengths and the weaknesses of the Israeli model: the ability to secure a technological edge and to react quickly to changes, on the one side, and, on the other, the relative lack of professional management, long-term planning, and business development skills.

The Zisapel brothers, Zohar and Yehuda, formally established the RAD group (or the RAD-Bynet group, as it is known in Israel) in 1981.[43] The Zisapels are engineers, and Zohar was a commander in one of the Israeli military's most respected electronic R&D units before he joined his brother in the civilian market. In 1985 the brothers decided to use their two companies as an incubator for R&D-based companies. Not having any specific plan or product in mind, they recruited Benjamin Hanigal, a young engineer who had just left the Lavi project, and the three started to search for ideas.[44] In 1986 Lannet was established and raised its first financing from the OCS and a limited partnership.[45] Just as Lannet was raising its limited-partnership financing, U.S. tax regulations were changed and Lannet managed to get only a third of the anticipated sum. As a result, the company quickly changed course, starting operations with a different and smaller project. During its first year of operation Lannet started a second line of products using the technology on which it would grow, Ethernet. A former Lannet senior manager argued that Lannet could develop a product that sold successfully worldwide because a large pool of engineers were users of local access networks (LANs) and could be asked to play the customers, helping in building the product specifications.

As Lannet had no other sources of capital, it needed to rapidly increase its revenues and became profitable at a very early stage of operations. In 1991 Lannet had its first public offering on NASDAQ, having already achieved an annual revenue stream of a few million dollars.[46] However, very quickly, the LAN market matured and started to consolidate. Lannet decided that it could not compete with the better-organized and more financially capable American firms. It merged with Madge, demerged, and was finally bought by Lucent. In the end Lannet's Israeli R&D operations became Lucent's R&D center in Israel.

Motivated by the success of Lannet, the Zisapel brothers expanded the RAD group and opened about thirty companies following more or less the same strategy, recruiting or backing engineer-founders with ideas for a new product within the telecommunication market broadly defined. From one point of view, RAD is an immense success story, with the group backing the largest number of companies listed on NASDAQ apart from Elron. From another view it is a perfect example of the limits of the Israeli IT industry, if only for the reason that none of the RAD companies managed to grow even to the size of the still–privately held anchor company, RAD Data communications.[47]

The story of Lannet and its end as Lucent's Israeli R&D center also symbolizes another trend that grew in importance in the 1980s, the R&D activities of hardware MNCs in Israel. The rise in the scope of MNCs' activities was so rapid that it caused a concern in Israel that the IT industry had become no more than a node in the MNCs' global activities, with most of the innovation and spillovers going overseas and with only few local spillovers (Felsenstein 1997). In the 1980s the MNCs that had major R&D operations in Israel were almost solely American semiconductor MNCs. The most important of these MNCs in the 1980s, apart from Intel and IBM (which, in 1972, opened its second research facility outside the United States in Israel; the first IBM research lab was opened in Zurich in 1956), were Digital, Motorola, and National Semiconductor.[48] All of these companies, apart from IBM, had VLSI chip design centers in Israel, with all except Digital also having manufacturing facilities in Israel in the 1980s.[49]

The relative importance of Israel as a supplier of new technologies is evident when we take into account that with one exception these Israeli R&D centers were the first that the MNCs had opened outside the United States. The exception was Motorola, but even Motorola's Israeli R&D VLSI center was the largest and most autonomous outside the United States, and in 1964, when Motorola Israel was established, it was Motorola's first fully owned daughter company outside North America. (R&D operations started in 1972, the VLSI design center in 1982.) These centers became crucial as one of the main training grounds for the technological capabilities that enabled the Israeli IC design industry to grow to become the fourth-largest in the world, and the most innovative after the United States and Canada, in the 1990s.

Thus MNCs in the 1980s already viewed Israel, unlike Taiwan and Ireland, as a preferred location for R&D and the development of new products and technologies. These R&D efforts were in some of the most advanced areas of research in the world at the time, such as microprocessors and applications of DSP technology. By the beginning of the 1990s, following the success of Israeli-based R&D operations of a growing number of MNCs, many more American MNCs started to look seriously at Israel and to acquire Israeli firms for their technologies. The fact that by that time both BIRD and the OCS were actively offering MNCs R&D-activities-related benefits served as a catalyst.

The importance of the OCS in that period, both in increasing the formation rate of new IT firms and in focusing their operations on new-product R&D, cannot be underestimated. Two prominent examples, out of a few hundred, are Comverse and Mercury Interactive, respectively the second- and third-largest software companies in Israel. The entrepreneurs behind both companies came back to Israel specifically in order to utilize the OCS's help.[50]

As is evident from the stories of ECI, RAD, and Comverse, this period brought the early rise of the telecommunication sector to prominence within the Israeli industry, a position it still holds, as can be seen in figure 2.1.

Changes in both the domestic and international market in the telecommunication industry completely transformed this industry and made it the fastest-growing IT industry worldwide in the late 1980s and all through the 1990s. These changes created a profitable market for niche companies with new technology, a category of firms in which the Israeli IT industry, with its strong focus on R&D and new products, excels.[51] The first change was the transformation in the regulation of the telecommunication industry and the worldwide move from a regulatory regime that viewed the industry as a "natural" monopoly to one that specifically aimed to spur competition, opening a market for small R&D-based companies to sell into. The second comprised advances in telecommunication technologies, specifically in wireless and data communication, both of which opened up new, rapidly expanding markets with big firms looking for new services to offer and new ways to manage their old businesses.

Israeli firms quickly excelled as suppliers of new technologies in all niches of the telecommunication subsector, pioneering, for example, voice over Internet protocol (VoIP) technologies, LAN systems and chips, DSP chips, urban networks, switches, routers, software, mobile phone technology, and Internet wireless and "last-mile solutions," among others.

However, even in this sector success and sustained growth necessitate not only a technological edge but also some access to management and business skills, as well as logistics and distribution resources. Acquiring these was not

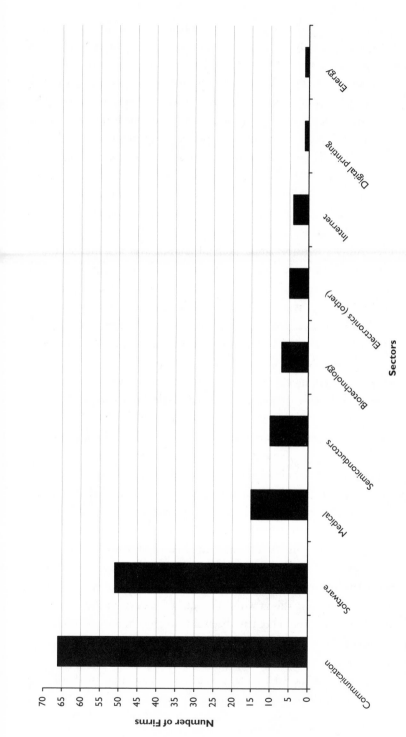

Figure 2.1. Israel's Internationally Publicly Traded Technology Firms: Main Product Niche, 1972–2001. *Source:* author's calculations

systematic and had more to do with good fortune and random effect. The story of Amdocs, the only Israeli company to date to become one of the top thirty software companies in the world, and its critical relationship with SBC, is such an example. By 1984 Amdocs, then called Aurek, became a leader in selling automated telephone directory systems (Yellow Pages) in Europe. This proved to be of immense strategic importance when on the first of April 1984, AT&T was divided into seven regional telephone companies that were desperate to buy reliable software systems from companies other than AT&T. Very quickly Southwestern Bell (now SBC) and Aurek started a joint venture to develop and sell automated directory systems. With SBC backing and with a few software systems all aimed at this market niche, Aurek soon became the global leader in this small niche.

However, Aurek's transformation from a leading player in a marginal market niche to one of the world's top thirty software companies came in the early 1990s and was prompted not by Aurek but by SBC. SBC asked for, and assisted Aurek in developing, a telecommunication billing system. In 1995 the new package, called Ensemble, was ready for the market. The former partners in Aurek, together with SBC and a few other investors, established a Channel Island company called Amdocs, a new holding company for all of the Aurek group companies. Very quickly Amdocs, with the clout of SBC behind it, became the leading provider of billing systems for telephone companies in the United States and later worldwide. In 1998 it went public on NASDAQ. Amdocs then showed remarkable strategic planning skills for an Israeli company and employed a strategy of mergers and acquisitions to become the leading supplier in another related niche—customer-relationship management (CRM) systems to the telecommunication industry. In 2002 Amdocs concluded its second strategic transformation by becoming a full-service provider to the telecommunication industry, offering integrated systems of billing, CRM, and order-management systems. At the same time Amdocs started to offer outsourced services, and a few companies, such as Nextel, turned over all their billing functions to Amdocs. While Israeli managers and engineers have been controlling and navigating this growth, without SBC's early guidance and constant support, Amdocs would not have been able to grow in the way it did, and probably could not even have recognized and realized the market opportunity in billing systems.

Thus the success achieved by many Israeli IT companies in these years should not make us disregard the weaknesses of the Israeli R&D-focused

model of development. The particular limitations of this model are apparent on both the micro company level, and the macro level of the industry as a whole, and may be attributed to an overemphasis on R&D and technological-engineering capabilities. This focus creates an Achilles' heel in other areas of management, from marketing and market research to planning and business development. The lack of these capabilities—in particular of managing sustainable long-term expansion and defending market niches against new entrants—leaves most Israeli IT firms vulnerable to competition from better-organized and -managed foreign firms.

The Beginning of the Software Industry: The 1980s and Early 1990s

In the late 1960s and early 1970s, while the seeds of the Israeli IT industry were planted and a few hardware companies achieved worldwide success, the software industry was practically nonexistent. The industry consisted of a few service-oriented data-processing centers and the IT units of government offices, including the defense apparatus and a few big organizations. However, the rapid expansion of defense R&D and the fast accumulation of IT skills by both university graduates and graduates of the military technological units created local demand for IT usage, the knowledge base to supply it, and a positive attitude toward this nascent industry.[52]

The first product-oriented software companies appeared only at the end of the 1970s and the beginning of the 1980s.[53] Unlike the first software companies in Taiwan and Ireland, they appeared within an industrial system that already had a few highly successful IT hardware firms that were publicly listed on NASDAQ, as well as an already well-developed local market that had many sophisticated users, most of whom were sponsored directly or indirectly by the state's defense R&D efforts.[54] Even more important, these software companies appeared in an industrial system where many R&D activities, both civilian and defense oriented, were taking place. Hence a critical mass of knowledge on the problems associated with IT usage, the IT R&D process itself, and software development was amassed in Israel, and a large market existed for software products that solved them. As problems in R&D and software development are similar worldwide, an Israeli software company that developed solutions for these had products that answered global needs. Moreover, the customers for these products, being engineers and programmers, are more sophisticated than the average consumer. Hence software products that were too complex and crude in their user interface to be sold to the consumer market could still be sold to these highly skilled customers.

It is not surprising, therefore, that the common thread of most of the successful companies established in these years is that their products offered solutions helping with IT development. As we usually categorize companies by industrial subsectors and not by their cognitive focus across sectors, some examples of the more successful companies are in order: OptiSystems Solutions, established in 1982, focused on optimization of computer systems; Magic, established in 1983, developed a rapid application development (RAD) tool for relational database applications; Cimatron, established in 1982, has been offering CAD/COM software for the tool industry; Nikov Haifa, now known as Attunity, established in 1988, moved away from its origins in ERP consultancy and started to develop RAD tools for reports programming, a product line which brought it to NASDAQ in 1997 and has since been abandoned; and Sapiens, established in 1982, has been focused on rule-based systems for RAD.[55] All of these companies were assisted, after 1985, by OCS R&D grants that enabled them to conduct large-scale R&D efforts, and each of these companies had an IPO on NASDAQ in the 1990s.

As venture capital to the industry was not available, the business model of many of these companies was either to create a joint venture with a more-established company that acted as the financial backer and/or the main customer, or to find their first customer before they started their development phase. A few also developed from an IT consultancy business, but not many of these managed to transform to a product-based business model successfully. In addition, as most of these companies could not secure enough capital to open an American branch, their first export market tended to be the European market.

Another common thread in this period is the importance of the state apparatus either as the origin of the entrepreneurs, the companies' first and main customer, or the source of the technology itself. Thus Amdocs had its origin in a team that worked for the Israeli Postal and Telecommunication Ministry and in a system developed as a joint venture with the company that had the license to organize and sell the telephone directory of Israel. A team of former officers of the military's central computer unit (MAMRAM) established Magic Software Enterprises, and its first breakthrough sale was to the Israeli military. In addition, the state was sometimes the source of the software product itself; for example, the Fourth Dimension (later known as the New Dimension) acquired from the Ministry of Defense a product for operations automation developed internally for the Air Force, in exchange for a promise to update and maintain it.[56]

In the late 1980s both the domestic factors described in the earlier section and external factors influenced the growth of the Israeli software industry. The external factors in these years that completely changed the software industry were the rapid diffusion of PCs, not only to the consumer and home market but also in the corporate market, and the growth of Microsoft's operating-software (OS) and programming platforms (first DOS and then Windows) as the dominant platforms and the de facto standards of the industry. The two most important effects of these technological changes on the Israeli software industry were: (*a*) the opening of new markets to the industry, while at the same time the cost of development declined, and (*b*) the manifold enlargement of the global need for platform crossover and conversion technologies. This was a demand that the Israeli software industry, already experienced in developing solutions for problems that directly relate to IT development, was well positioned to supply.

Thus during the second half of the 1980s and the beginning of the 1990s many software companies managed to enlarge their activities and penetrate foreign markets. Two examples of veteran software companies that took advantage of the growth of the global market and the new technologies are those of Magic and New Dimension. During the second half of the 1980s, the two companies managed to first secure critical sales in Israel and abroad and then move into the American market. Both went public on NASDAQ, in 1991 and 1992, respectively. Another development in the second half of the 1980s and the beginning of the 1990s was a new cohort of internationally successful companies. The common ground of all the Israeli software companies established in this period, differentiating the industry from that of Ireland and Taiwan, is that all these companies were developed by software programmers who were actively looking for product ideas that offered solutions needed in their own industry—software programming.

As was true of Israel's hardware companies, founders of these companies lacked business, management, and financial skills. This led many of them in the era before the advent of the Israeli VC industry either to join forces with other companies or to rely on luck and intuition in their early product development and expansion to foreign markets phases. Precise is an example. Established in 1990, Precise specialized in software systems optimization, and al-

most went bankrupt before it recruited Shimon Alon, a former manager of
Scitex. Under his management the company stabilized, listed on NASDAQ,
and was sold to the American software MNC Veritas in 2003.

The 1980s also brought the advent of the subsector in which the Israeli software industry truly achieved global fame—data security. In addition, more
than a few Israeli software companies have focused on the creation of new
software technologies or new applications of software technologies. The most
prominent subsector in which these companies operate has been the telecommunication market, which is also the subsector of strength of the Israeli hardware IT industry. A well-known example of that period is Vocaltec. Established in 1989 to develop speech recognition technologies, Vocaltec was the
first company to sell VoIP telephony products for the PC. Vocaltec went public in 1996 and was soon followed by a wave of Israeli companies in the same
market niche, such as Mind CTI, which develops VoIP billing solutions, and
Arel Communication, which develops video conferencing over IP.

These trends continue today, as we can see in table 2.1, which briefly describes the history and activities of the top ten public software companies in
terms of sales during 2001–2004.

INDUSTRY-STATE CO-EVOLUTION: THE
RESTRUCTURING OF S&T INDUSTRIAL POLICY

From the second half of the 1980s until the early 1990s the IT industry was
rapidly expanding, and Israeli companies, both hardware and software,
achieved growing international success. However, industry growth was limited by some severe weaknesses. Two in particular were venture financing—
especially at the preseed, seed, and the early sales and distribution stages—and
business management skills and capabilities. While the knowledge of how to
do business, and especially how to interact with the American financial markets, already existed within the Israeli industry, it was limited to the few firms
that had been successful, and there was no systematic sharing and dissemina-
tion of that knowledge.[57]

By the beginning of the 1990s the two bottlenecks of the Israeli IT industry had become evident. First, venture funds were not available to enable both
deeper and more consistent R&D activities, especially in projects that related
to the technological edge and, accordingly, necessitated longer R&D efforts
without any revenues. Second, management skills and knowledge were lacking, especially with regard to planning, marketing, and finance.

Table 2.1. Israel's Ten Leading Public Software Companies (USD millions)

Name	Short History and Primary Subsector	Revenues			
		2004	2003	2002	2001
Amdocs	Established 1982 by a team led by former employees of the Post and Tele-communication Ministry to create automated directories. Joined forces with SBC in the early 1990s to become the world leader in tele-communication billing, CRM, and automated directories.	1773.7	1483.3	1613.6	1533.9
Comverse[a]	Established in 1984 to create voice-recording systems for enterprises; in the 1990s developed to become a leader in voice mail, SMS, and MMS.	959.4	765.9	1270.2	1225.1
Mercury Interactive	Established in 1989 to develop software debugging tools, transformed itself in the late 1990s to become the global leader in software-systems optimization.	685.5	506.5	400.10	361.00
Checkpoint	Established in 1993 to pioneer firewall technologies, now a world leader in both the VPNs and firewall markets.	515.4	432.6	427.00	527.60
Formula Systems (1985)	Established in 1981 as Formula Software services, reincorporated in 1985 to become a software conglom-erate with business stretching from professional training and consulting to the holding and spinning off of product-based companies.	456.8	366.8	283.30	376.90

(*continued*)

Table 2.1. (*continued*)

Name	Short History and Primary Subsector	Revenues			
		2004	2003	2002	2001
NDS (News Digital Systems)	Established in 1988 as News Datacom Research to pioneer encryption technologies to allow pay-TV services. Joined forces with NewsCrop to become the world leader.	386.6	392.7	368.70	304.80
Ness Technologies	System integration and consulting services. Grew in the 1990s through acquisitions of smaller software business. IPO on NASDAQ in late 2004.	304.5	225.7	166.5	NA
Nice Systems	Established in 1986 to pioneer the Customer Experience Management systems (monitoring and recording of customer-service calls); currently a world leader of the niche.	252.6	224.3	162.50	127.10
Verinet Systems	Spun off from Comverse in 2002 to concentrate on products specializing in the analysis and capture of communication data for security and business-analysis purposes.	192.7	157.8	120.60	NA
Aladdin	Established in 1985 to develop graphology expert systems, ended up developing and pioneering software IPR security systems for the PC, a niche in which it became a leader. Transformed itself to a supplier of comprehensive Internet data-security suits in the 1990s.	69.1	59.7	49.50	46.60

Sources: Hoover's financial, companies' SEC filings.
[a]After spin-off of Verinet and Ulticom in 2002.

In 1989 the latest period in the development of the IT industry began. The USSR started to democratize and break up, and Jews, who had been unable to emigrate until that time, began the last large immigration wave into Israel. Because this wave brought the best and the brightest technologically educated workforce from the USSR to join the thousands of engineers who had been made redundant by the defense industry, the question of tapping this body of knowledge sprang to the top of the political agenda.[58] In addition, the Israeli government secured the United States' help in raising $10 billion in bonds to finance the settlement of so many immigrants (20 percent of the total population in less than one decade), giving it some financial resources.

Thus the political and bureaucratic apparatus of the Israeli state, knowing it had to act and having sufficient finances to do so, was very open to new initiatives led by the OCS.[59]

Starting in 1991 the OCS, led by Yigal Erlich and with the strong political backing of the then–Minister of Trade and Industry Moshe Nissim, initiated and implemented three new programs. The Ministry of Finance initiated another program, which proved to be a failure, aimed at the VC industry. These programs were devised through a process of analyzing the strengths and the weaknesses of the industry, both internally by the OCS and in conjunction with academics.[60] The aim of these new policies was the enhancement of the formation, survival and success rates, and R&D capabilities of firms. All of the programs have been following the logic of neutral horizontal policies. While the OCS's three programs, the Technological Incubators, Yozma, and Magnet, started operation between 1992 and 1995, they were all planned and approved in 1991, the year that can be seen as the high point of the latest political window of opportunity.[61] In 1991 two new programs started operations, each aimed at remedying a perceived market failure at a different development stage of NTBFs. From the macro level the main effects of these new programs have been twofold: on one side, increasing the R&D focus and usage of business models based around novel products, and, on the other, increasing the Israeli industry's embeddedness in and dependence on the United States and its financial markets.

The end of the 1990s marks another transformation. With growing public and political interest in the IT industry and the OCS, the institutionalization and public supervision on the OCS increased. The manifestations of this are many, from the establishment of a public committee process to recommend nominees for the position of a chief scientist to the growing supervision of the OCS by the Parliamentary Committee for Science and Technology. Indeed, of all developmental agencies in Ireland, Israel, and Taiwan, currently it is the OCS that supplies the most comprehensive and transparent information about its current and past activities.

THE NEW PROGRAMS OF THE EARLY 1990s

The Inbal program, proposed and implanted by the Ministry of Finance, was the first serious government attempt to induce the creation of a private VC industry in Israel. At that time only two VC institutions were present in Israel: Tolkowsky and Adler's Atena VC fund, a limited-partnership fund established in 1985 based on the American model, and Star, a private equity fund established in 1989 that became a Yozma fund after 1993. The Inbal program was an attempt to foster publicly traded VC companies by creating a government insurance company that guaranteed a minimum value, calculated as 70 percent of the value of their initial public offering, to new VC funds traded on the Tel Aviv Stock Exchange. As such, the program was similar to Taiwan's initiative, structuring the VCs as companies viewed not as an industry but as a pool of capital, with no attempt to foster learning, or to import and transfer professional VC skills and capabilities.[62] Four funds were initially established, but no follow-up activity was pursued, and the funds' valuation on the stock exchange tended to be low. The four Inbal funds also faced what their directors perceived as excessive bureaucracy and in the end left the program. Today all the funds are under the management of one holding company, Green Technology Holding (Avnimelech and Teubal 2004).

When the OCS initiated the Technological Incubators Program, in 1991, the program was presented as a solution to two problems. First, many technically oriented or scientific entrepreneurs were inexperienced and unable to become successful commercial entrepreneurs and find early-stage financing for their ideas. Second, many technologically skilled new immigrants from the former USSR had difficulty finding jobs and successfully integrating into a capitalist market. The idea was to open a network of technological incubators that would help entrepreneurs in their very early stages by giving them most of the financing and a large amount of professional business and management help.

The incubator program is also the latest example of the pattern evident in the restructuring of the OCS and BIRD: an outsider coming in as a manager and making the program a reality. However, this time the early crisis period was avoided. Yigal Erlich, the chief scientist at the time, realized the need for a strong leader and rerecruited Rina Pridor, Yaakov's right hand for many years, both in the OCS and afterward in CDC and the limited-partnership period. Her return is yet another example of the OCS's porous borders and networked structure. Under Pridor the program quickly commenced activities and grew in importance.

The goal of the program has been that after two years companies will be mature enough to secure private VC financing. In a similar fashion to the other OCS programs, incubation proposals had to come from the market.[63] Until 2001 (when specialized incubators were approved, even if none had yet started operation), the incubators operated on the principle of neutral horizontal policy. While some of the incubators became more specialized over time, overall the technological incubators network did not pick any sectors, and R&D projects from all branches of the industry were admitted. By 2005, according to the OCS reports, the distribution of projects by industry was as follows: electronics and communication 11 percent, software 11 percent, medical 18 percent, chemistry and materials 20 percent, biotechnology 20 percent, and others 23 percent.[64] Starting in 2003 a few established VC funds opted to buy and manage a few incubators.

Two of what may be the most important impacts of the program have yet to be considered and tested properly.[65] First is the major impact that the program has had on changing the preferences of technologically and scientifically educated personnel to become entrepreneurs. Second, as the technology industry crisis between 2000 and 2003 showed, the program is important in ensuring a minimum NTBF formation rate, which is independent of the volatile behavior of the VC industry in regard to the amount of investment, and the herd mentality and fashionlike behavior of VCs in their sectoral investment criteria.

A comparison with Ireland is striking. In Israel, to a great degree thanks to the OCS's programs, the annual formation rate of new companies remained above a hundred even after 2000. In Ireland, with the Irish VC industry managing record high levels of capital, in the whole of 2001 there were three seed investments, which together equaled $750,000, a sum which is slightly less than the support granted to two incubator companies. For a state like Israel that is economically dependent on the high-technology sector, securing this baseline is of critical priority.

In the same years that the OCS was busily developing and implementing new programs, new developments in the private sector were changing the IT industrial landscape in Israel. Before 1990 there had been a total of ten IPOs of Israeli firms on NASDAQ. In 1991 alone three Israeli companies went through IPOs, and in 1992 there were another nine. Moreover, unlike the low-valuation IPOs of the past, some of these IPOs resulted in a large enough market capitalization to allow a respectable exit for an American VC at the time. In addition, 1991 was also the year in which the first pure software companies went public on NASDAQ.

In 1992, learning from the failure of Inbal, the OCS initiated another program aimed at inducing the creation of a vibrant VC industry in Israel: Yozma. The aims of this initiative were fourfold: increasing the amount of venture capital available to Israeli firms, especially in their expansion phases; creating a professional VC industry that would possess the business skills that the IT industry was lacking at the time; injecting the Israeli high-technology industry with systematic knowledge of the American markets, both product and finance; and expanding what the OCS perceived as a too limited group of financiers.[66]

This time, in almost complete opposition to its policy in the past, the OCS, again led by Yigal Erlich as chief scientist, decided that the necessary skills and knowledge did not exist in Israel, and that in order to succeed an Israeli VC industry would need strong networks with foreign financial markets rather than with the Tel Aviv Stock Exchange. Yozma was created as a government VC fund of $100 million that had two functions. The first was to invest $8 million in a series of ten private limited-partnership venture funds, which would be 40 percent or less of the total capital, the rest to be provided by the other private limited partners. Second, a separate fund of $20 million started operation at the same time. In order to get this financing, the funds' managers had to secure investment and partnership from at least one established foreign financial institution and from at least one local one. Moreover, the OCS made a deliberate decision to pick one organizational model for the future Israeli VC industry, the American-style limited-partnership fund, and focused on early-stage financing VC.[67]

Unlike Inbal, Yozma became highly successful and was a model for VC-development policy worldwide. The precise construction of the program—in particular, its treatment of VC as an industry with specific skills to be acquired and capabilities to be nurtured, unlike similar initiatives in Ireland and Taiwan—had a few positive impacts. The first effect was the professionalism and education of the venture capitalists themselves. In Israel, with its already long history of the R&D-based IT industry, there was a growing pool of experienced technological entrepreneurs who successfully managed their companies, and this, together with the demand of Yozma to bring in a professional foreign partner, created a VC industry in which the typical background of the VC is as an entrepreneur or manager of an R&D-based IT firm. This VC profile is very similar to the ideal American background, and very different from the typical profile in Ireland and Taiwan, where most VCs do not have entrepreneurial or even IT management backgrounds. Second, the Yozma initiative itself sponsored and cultivated many venues of collective learning within the industry, which enhanced its capabilities (Avnimelech and Teubal 2003a, 2006a, 2006b).

The first Yozma funds had excellent returns on investment, thanks to the growing success of Israeli companies on NASDAQ, the presence on the Israeli landscape at the time of many high-quality NTBFs looking for capital, and the coincidence with the start of a period of rapid growth in demand for IT and the related financial boom. This success resulted in rapid investment of capital into the Israeli VC industry, most of which opted to use the limited-partnership organizational model. Thus, as can be seen in figure 2.2, by 2000 the American limited-partnership VC funds became the de facto standard of the Israeli industry. In turn, the existence and growth of the VC industry both accelerated the rate of company formation and, even more important, finalized the transformation of the Israeli IT industry into the image of the American one. Today the Israeli IT industry has the same focus on the American financial and product markets and the same milestones as in the American IT industry—either an IPO on NASDAQ or a merger and acquisition (M&A).[68]

As of 2006 the Israeli VC industry consisted of more than seventy local funds, with many of the top U.S. and global VC funds having local operations in Israel and with $2.3 billion available for investment. The industry has also shown its maturity and strengths by recovering from the technology bubble, raising $727 million in 2004 and $1.2 billion in 2005 without governmental interventions of the sort applied in both Ireland and Taiwan. The virtuous dynamics of a growing and successful IT industry co-evolving with a successful VC industry brought another facet of professionalism into the Israeli VC industry—a career pattern where successful entrepreneurs who managed to sell or publicly list one or more companies would later opt to become VCs.[69]

In addition, the success of Israeli companies in the United States in the 1990s transformed the IT industry's own networks. Lately many Israeli IT companies have raised capital directly from established foreign VCs and financial institutions in all stages of the companies' development. This is highly

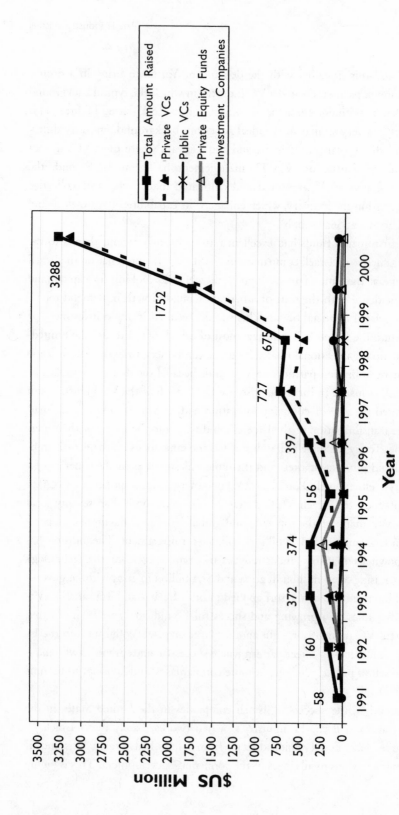

Figure 2.2. Venture Capital Raised in Israel, 1991–2000. *Source:* Israel Venture Capital Association, Avnimelech and Tuebal 2003a.

important for the Israeli IT industry, which to a large degree imitates the American mode of start-up growth, based on an expensive R&D phase, followed by an even more expensive buildup of marketing and distribution channels, during which the firm is hardly able to secure revenues from sales. Hence the creation of the Israeli technological VC industry, and the ability of the Israeli IT new-product R&D-based firms to secure venture capital abroad, make the Israeli IT industry different from those of Ireland and Taiwan in being able to compete successfully with the amounts of capital that American IT start-ups manage to secure.

The last initiative designed by the OCS in 1991, MAGNET, also started operations in 1992. Unlike the other OCS programs, MAGNET, the Hebrew acronym for generic noncompetitive R&D, aims to solve two problems relating to the later stages of development and maintenance of the long-term R&D-based competitive advantage of Israeli NTBFs. The first problem is the fact that in Israel a large number of companies work in the same technological space, all of them too small to be able to compete on the basis of cutting-edge infrastructural research activities that are crucial for their ability to sustain the competitive advantage against the bigger MNCs. The second perceived, if more debatable, problem was the underutilization of academic research done in Israel.

Similar to other OCS programs, MAGNET grants aid to programs initiated by private industry and operates on the principles of a neutral horizontal policy. However, as MAGNET aims to create a consortium to develop generic technologies, a consortium is created for a period of up to three years, and all IP outputs are shared among the consortium members, who also agree to license this IP to local companies at a cost that does not reflect monopoly status. A consortium, consisting of at least a few companies and one research-academic institution, applies in a competitive fashion to MAGNET and, if accepted, is granted financing to the level of 66 percent of cost. MAGNET financial aid is given as grants with no need to repay. A parallel process exists for users' consortia, with the aim of distribution and implementation of generic technology.

Again a comparison with Taiwan is illuminating. As we will see, in Taiwan, research consortia were created by the government in an effort to assist technological learning, upgrading, and catch-up en route to industry creation. In Israel the aim of the state in establishing research consortia was to help pre-competitive advanced R&D. Thus the national goals behind the usage of a structurally similar policy vehicle are as different as can be, symbolizing the different policy and development paths of the IT industries in the two countries.[70]

In addition to the new initiatives, the OCS's budgetary growth during the 1990s was quickly transformed into extensive investment in the industry. As can be seen in Table 2.2, the success of projects financed by the OCS in turn increased the amounts the OCS was able to channel to industry, even without an increase in the budget allocated to it by the government, creating a virtuous co-evolution cycle throughout the 1990s. It remains to be seen, however, whether the budgetary cuts imposed on the OCS in the past two years will limit its ability to continue this level of support or to open new programs in the future.

While the wave of immigration from the former USSR undoubtedly created the pretext with which the OCS was able to secure finance and political agreement to start these four programs, the Russian immigrants themselves have not, thus far, become successful technological entrepreneurs. They seem to play the important but lesser role of providing highly skilled labor. A preliminary analysis of an original dataset that I collected on the career paths of founders of Israeli IT NTBFs that went public on foreign exchanges did not find one new immigrant from the former USSR among the 151 founders on which comprehensive data were acquired.[71] This finding is reinforced by an analysis done by the Central Bureau of Statistics on the distribution of new immigrants in the IT labor market (Abouganem and Feldman 2002, pp. 27–28).[72]

In short, the industrial development agencies of the Israeli state proved quite able and flexible in advancing the overarching goals of creating science-based industry in Israel and advancing NTBFs as the cornerstone of this industry. The focus on R&D activities as the source of the competitive edge of the industry has been reinstated and even refined with two programs, MAGNET and the Incubators program. The aim of these programs was, however, narrower than the main R&D fund, as they specifically try to nurture R&D activities in both the early and the advanced stages of companies' lives. These goals were also strengthened with another policy initiative, Yozma, which treated VC as an industry with specific skills and a center anchored in the United States. The view of private companies as the source of R&D activity ideas was maintained, as were the dual principles of horizontalism and neutrality with regard to sectors and technologies. The division of labor between the local industry and MNCs that stresses the role of Israel as an R&D location was even sharpened by the Yozma initiative. The new programs, together with the continua-

Table 2.2. OCS Budget, 1988–1999

Year	(in 2000 $USD Million)				Paybacks (% of Investment)	Approved Grants to IT firms (n)
	R&D Grants	Paybacks	Magnet	Incubators		
1988	120	8	—	—	6.7	
1989	125	10	—	—	8.0	
1990	136	14	—	—	10.3	380
1991	179	20	0.3	3.6	11.2	460
1992	199	25	4.7	16	12.6	458
1993	231	33	4.6	23	14.3	481
1994	316	42	10	28	13.3	605
1995	346	56	15	31	16.2	559
1996	348	79	36	30	22.7	556
1997	397	102	53	30	25.7	517
1998	400	117	61	30	29.3	505
1999	428	139	60	30	32.5	506

Source: OCS 2000.
Note: Paybacks from each successful project are paid to the OCS throughout a several-year period.

tion of the older programs such as BIRD and the OCS's main R&D fund, fortified and supported the organizational focus of the Israeli IT industry on product R&D.[73] In addition, all these new programs were again initiated and implemented by the OCS with the agreement of the Ministry of Finance as "secretary general instructions," not anchored in law or in governmental decision. Only on April 7, 2005, did the Israeli Parliament enact a new industrial R&D law. This law repeated the pattern of the first (1984) industrial R&D law, anchoring in law activities that the OCS had already been successfully running for over a decade, and not prescribing future initiatives.

SUCCESS, GROWTH, AND ITS LIMITATIONS: THE ADVANTAGES AND DISADVANTAGES OF THE ISRAELI MODEL

The IT industry in Israel has experienced years of unprecedented growth. This growth was the result of changes in perception of the Israeli industry in the global IT markets, especially within the American industrial and financial communities, coupled with the dramatic growth in global demand for IT products and services, a related boom on NASDAQ, and the growth of a local

VC industry. However, while I briefly describe in this section the development of the Israeli IT industry, my main aim here is to illuminate the current strengths and weaknesses of the Israeli IT industry development model. Figure 2.3 shows the rapid growth of the industry's revenues.

The second half of the 1990s saw significant growth of old Israeli hardware companies that managed to transform themselves and achieve prominence in their chosen market niches. Israeli companies continued to operate in every subfield of the industry, from memory—in particular flash memory, where Israeli companies pioneered key technologies—to telecommunication, which continued to be the main area of operations of the global IT industry, especially in Israel.[74]

While the defense state-owned companies continue to be in a state of flux, many of the sector's graduates, from both military and industry, left to establish their own companies. RAFAEL again proved to be innovative in dealing with this trend, establishing the RAFAEL Development Corporation (RDC) as an incubation company with investment funds from Elron and Discount to commercialize ideas emanating within it. The lengthening history of industrial success also created another advantage for the Israeli IT industry: cohorts of young and middle-aged experienced managers and entrepreneurs who had passed through at least one cycle of company creation and growth. It is increasingly common in Israel to see serial entrepreneurs—entrepreneurs who specialize in the creation of new companies.

The software sector has been the site of the most spectacular wave of successes in the late 1990s. While the average age and education level of the entrepreneurs stayed more or less constant in the hardware sector, both the age and educational composition declined sharply in the software sector. Graduates of the military's technological and intelligence units founded growing numbers of software companies right after they completed their service. The number of foreign IPOs increased, and Israeli companies appeared in almost all of the industry's market niches, as can be seen in figure 2.4.

Toward the end of the 1990s, the growth profile of new IT Israeli companies became increasingly similar to that of technology-based new American IT companies, with IPOs and/or M&As by foreign MNCs becoming common. American semiconductor MNCs are still the most active in Israel, and in the past five years Intel, Motorola, and IBM, together with the Israeli universities, have been the biggest Israeli international patent issuers (TAF 2002). However, starting in 1995 with Siemens's decision to acquire Ornet, MNCs from other parts of the world and other sectors of the IT industry have also

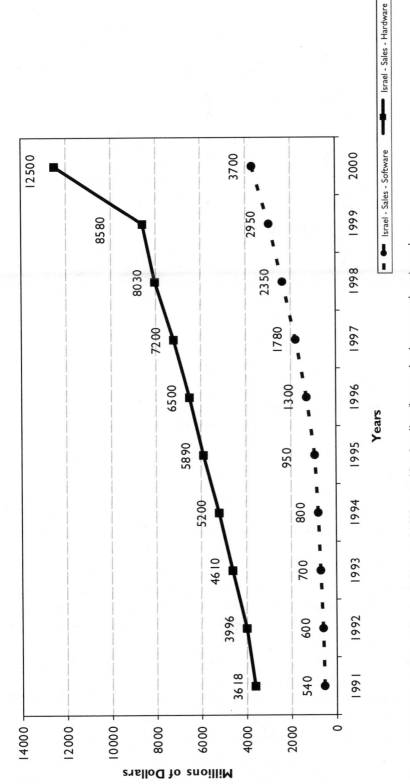

Figure 2.3. Total Sales IT, Israel. *Sources:* IAEI 2006, IASH 2003. *Note:* Israel's software sales data are underestimated.

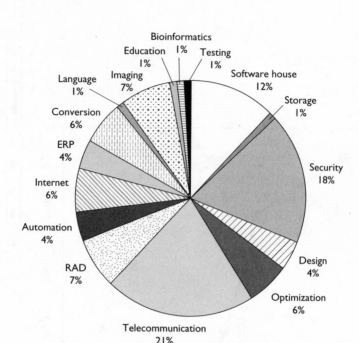

Figure 2.4. Israeli-Related Foreign Software IPOs by Main Subsectors, 1985–2001 (*N*=70). *Sources:* SEC filings, companies' Web sites and press releases. *Note:* for companies that are no longer traded, the main business line at time of IPO was recorded as main subsector.

been conducting more R&D activities in Israel and acquiring Israeli companies for their technologies.[75]

With the VC industry rapidly growing, the industry of creating, developing, and selling companies became almost as important as the sales revenues of the Israeli IT industry. The growing amount of VC finance, which necessitates "exits" in order to make a profit, enlarged both the rate of company formation and the trends toward the sale and public listing of companies. Even with the uncertainty of such statistics, it is significant that the official annual rate of new NTBFs in Israel grew steadily between 1990 and 1995 from less than a hundred to a hundred, and then with the rapid increase in VC financing between 1995 and 1999, the annual rate swiftly rose from one hundred to eight hundred (Avnimelech and Teubal 2003a, 2006a).

Nevertheless, a structural weakness limiting the ability of Israeli firms to achieve sustained growth also became more acute, a direct result of the Israeli industry's basing all its advantage on advanced R&D. By employing business models that rely solely on being either the pioneers or the technological leaders in a market niche, Israeli firms have a window of opportunity of between two and four years in which to secure their market position before facing intense competition from above and below. If successful, Israeli firms quickly face competition from above when better-organized and more financially secure MNCs and American start-ups enter their market niche. Additionally, as the technologies on which their products are based become commoditized and cheaper, Israeli companies face competition from less technologically advanced but cheaper competitors, many of them Taiwanese. Israeli companies imitating the American model—without the American infrastructure and MNCs, without the long experience and skills necessary to grow and maintain leadership under these conditions, without a local IT manufacturing industry with which to collaborate, and with the added disadvantage of being far away from both their markets and their subcontractors—rarely manage to sustain growth while staying in their original market niches.

The institutional weakness of the Israeli IT industry leads many companies whose managers do not believe they have the necessary skills to survive competition to choose one of two strategies. The first strategy is to quickly change niches and products with the first hint of intensified competition. If successful, this strategy allows the company to completely reinvent itself, moving from one technology trend to another; however, it also severely limits the ability of these firms to secure significant and sustained sales or to become market leaders. A perfect example is Attunity, which not only changed markets and products three times but also changed its name with each transformation. The second strategy is to agree to be acquired either by a leading MNC or by another start-up deemed to possess better management skills. A chief example of this was Galileo Technology, a NASDAQ-listed Israeli fabless communication company that continuously grew its annual sales by about 50 percent since being listed in 1993 and was seen as one of the most promising Israeli firms. In 2001 Galileo suddenly agreed to be acquired by Marvell technologies, an American start-up with a shorter history and smaller sales.

This structural weakness of the industry is glaringly apparent when we compare the Israeli IT hardware industry to the Taiwanese, and nowhere more so than in the IC design subsector. If the weakness of Taiwan's IC design industry is the lack of advanced R&D skills, its advantage is that it developed as a part of a virtuous co-evolution within a system consisting of both the world's leading pureplay foundries and original-design manufacturing (ODM) and original-equipment manufacturing (OEM) companies.[76] This enabled the Taiwanese IC design companies to utilize a model of competition from below, entering various market niches pioneered by Israeli or U.S. firms, gaining a controlling market share, and establishing long-term sustained growth (Breznitz 2005b, 2005c, 2005e). Israeli IC design firms are usually the pioneers in their market niches. Nevertheless, only two Israeli companies are now in the world's top thirty fabless companies by sales, and both are in the lowest third of that list. Thus while Israel's IC design industry is the fourth–most successful in the world, its long-term prosperity, its sustainability, and even the ability of its firms to imitate the success of the Taiwanese and become one of the world's ten largest companies in terms of sales are questionable.

The growth of the American-style VC industry and the growing reliance on it as the main source of finance might aggravate this institutional weakness. The positive effects of the VC industry have already been discussed. In addition, its contribution to the professionalism of the Israeli IT industry in the early stages of company life, and in acquiring more business and financial management skills, has been invaluable. However, the VC industry makes money through financial exits. Hence its main aim is to maximize the market capitalization value of firms in the shortest time with the minimum of effort, and then help to execute the financial transitions in which the VCs earn their profits. For VCs, careful building of sustained long-term businesses is a goal only as long as it increases the market value of the company. Accordingly, as long as it does not significantly lower the firm's value, VCs have an inherent incentive to ensure that their companies either conduct an IPO or agree to an M&A as early as possible. This is especially true for first-time VC funds that need to establish a track record in order to secure investments for their next fund. The Israeli VCs of the early 1990s consisted almost exclusively of first-time funds. Furthermore, if from the national point of view Israel might prefer that more of its companies stay independent, for VCs an M&A is usually preferable to an IPO. The comment of one Israeli VC is common:

> To be honest, I would prefer to have only M&As, especially cash M&As. I get my money quickly and have no further commitment to the company. I can then focus my attention on new deals. Do you know how much pain it is to go through an IPO process on NASDAQ? And why? As a VC it does not help me at all. The only reason I might go for an IPO is that many excellent entrepreneurs will avoid VCs that never back an IPO. (interview, August 20, 2000)

It is with regard to this key issue of the proper role of VCs in the IT industry's future development that the overembeddedness of the OCS in the industry is a source of some concern. Yigal Erlich, who stepped down in 1993 as chief scientist to manage the Yozma VC fund, also immediately became the chairperson of the Israeli Venture Association (IVA) and stayed in this position until 2002. Under his management the IVA became Israel's best-organized high-technology industry association and an effective lobbying group. In addition, of the five former and present chief scientists who are still active, three (including Erlich) are VCs, and the last private industry position of the current chief scientist was as a VC.

Additionally, the high involvement of MNCs in the Israeli IT industry has become even more pronounced. By now it is evident that MNCs control most of the productive parts of the Israeli industry, a large and growing share of the intellectual property created in Israel, and an ever-increasing share of the industry's revenues and profits. While this might actually improve the long-term sustainability of the Israeli industry, from the national point of view the growing loss of control, the fact that Israelis working for most of these MNCs will not acquire business-development and management skills, and the fact that a large percentage of the fruits of the industry success are not redistributed in Israel might be a concern.

The way in which most MNCs enter Israel has also changed; most now opt for acquisitions. The list of MNCs opting to buy an Israeli firm and convert it into the MNC's local R&D center includes all the major players, both software and hardware. Israel has truly become a key location for new-product R&D for these MNCs. A former vice president for business development in a leading U.S. MNC remarked,

> Our first acquisition of a company outside North America was of an Israeli company in 1999. In 2001, when I became VP of business development for the rest of the world, the company was very attracted to Israeli technology. We discovered that in every technology that we are interested in, there is an Israeli company developing something. When I became VP it was obvious that for the organization, Israel is the capital of the "rest of the world." (interview, May 9, 2002)

If there is one subsector of the Israeli industry that from a national industrial development point of view exemplifies the best and the worst of the development of the industry and the Israeli model since the mid-1980s, it is the software-data-security subsector. Throughout the 1990s this has been the most successful subsector of the industry (Teubal et al. 2002). In addition, it is the only sector of the software industry in which Israel, Ireland, and Taiwan all have companies that are globally successful and listed on NASDAQ.

Of the three industries, the Israeli had the best starting point. It had strengths in all the necessary technological areas for data security. The source of these strengths was both in the defense sector and within its universities—in particular, Professor Adi Shamir, whose research was central to the development of the public key infrastructure technology that became the global standard.[77] Israeli companies pioneered many critical market niches, such as encryption, authentication, intellectual property rights (IPR) protection, antiviral protection, and firewalls. On one hand, the industry has been a tremendous success, with five IPOs on NASDAQ and two data security companies, NDS and Checkpoint, among the five biggest Israeli software companies. Israel has also become a key location for the development of data-security technologies for leading MNCs. For example, CA acquired three Israeli companies to establish its data-security worldwide R&D center in Israel, and many other MNCs conduct their data security R&D in Israel, not least Microsoft's efforts in firewall technologies.

On the other hand, there are no longer any independent Israeli antivirus companies, while Taiwan's Trend Micro, starting in a far worse market position, managed not only to stay independent but also, with $602 million in revenues in 2004, to become larger than any Israeli data-security company. In addition, in the authentication and PKI fields, the Irish industry, with the success and subsequent failure of Baltimore and the continued success of Trintech, demonstrates that better business and market-analysis skills may be more important than a technological edge.[78] Among the more than twenty Israeli companies that existed long enough to secure significant investment and some sales, only three managed to remain independent and significant players in their own niche. Of these, one, NDS, managed to accomplish its sustained growth only after being acquired by News Corporation and with the help of its superb financial, market-penetration, and management capabilities.

A closer analysis of the growth of a few of the more prominent companies clearly shows all the strengths and weaknesses of Israeli IT industry discussed in this chapter. The industry's strengths have always been superior technology and pioneering R&D, its weaknesses the lack of market knowledge and, frequently, management skills, as well as the difficulties that even its leading companies have of growing into true leaders in the field. For example, the beginning of the data-security sector has been due more to a random event and good technology than to superior management and planning skills. Aladdin, the first globally successful data-security company, and one of only three that are now both publicly listed and independent, was established in 1985 in order to build an expert system for graphology.[79] The technological founder, Yanki Margalit, a young self-taught software programmer, was aware of the software piracy problem in Israel and developed an antipiracy software plug before commencing sales. By the end of the first year of sales, only two expert systems were sold, but so were more than two thousand copies of the antipiracy plugs. Good fortune continued to be the company's trademark even after the three partners other than Margalit left the company and Margalit's brother, Danny, joined the business, focused now on IPR protection. Completely innocent of any knowledge of how to start exporting, the Margalit brothers decided to buy a small ad space in *Byte,* the leading industry periodical of the time, without even knowing the tax procedures for export sales. European customers responded in earnest, and less than four months after that first ad, Aladdin had distributors all over Europe.[80]

Almost the same technological virtues, utter lack of professional management and financial capabilities, and pure good fortune are evident in the story of Israel's first antivirus software company, now turned technology investment house, BRM. The two original founders of the company, Omry Man and Yuval Rakavy, at the time computer science students at the Hebrew University, developed what was probably Israel's first antiviral software during one night of work trying to fix Omry's PC. They then distributed it for free on the Hebrew University campus. A couple of months later the two came up with the idea of developing a generic antivirus program, and the two joined forces with the Barkat brothers, Eli and Nir, to establish BRM.

For about a year the company survived without any substantial growth as the part-time hobby of the four partners, each of whom had either another company or a full-time job.[81] BRM's major turning point came when the founders met Hanina Brandes, one of Israel's leading lawyers at the time, who agreed to represent and coach them, and to defer payment for his services until BRM began to make a profit.[82]

The story of Checkpoint, Israel's premier data-security company, also shows some of the same weaknesses but also some progress in the management and market-analysis realms. Checkpoint has been the inventor as well as the market creator and leader for firewalls, now a basic security feature. Three friends, all graduates of the military's technology and intelligence units, founded the company. Unlike the stories of Aladdin and BRM, Checkpoint founders had a clear idea, gained from their service in the military, of what the firewall technology should be. Moreover, realizing that the civilian market was not mature, they waited a few years before commencing operations. The company was established in 1993 as NSK, and if only to show the relative lack of financial experience in the Israeli IT industry as a whole, it got its first seed finance (and some R&D help) from BRM by selling 50 percent of its shares for a $300,000 loan.[83] Checkpoint secured a strategic OEM agreement with Sun Microsystems that accounted for most of its early sales, and secured an important VC investment with a leading American fund, Bloomberg. In addition, showing the growing management savvy of the Israeli industry, Checkpoint established and led several industry forums that helped it in securing its technologies as the industry's standard. In 1996 Checkpoint went public on NASDAQ, and it has since aggressively been diversifying its products through both in-house development and acquisitions. However, with the growing success of firewall technology, Checkpoint is facing increased competition, not least from Cisco, Juniper, and Microsoft's Vista operating system. Hence its continuous growth and even its independence are not assured.

These structural weaknesses put the ownership and control of Israelis over the Israeli IT industry in question. Furthermore, they raise significant issues in regard to the distribution of the fruits of the industry's success and the connection it has with the rest of the Israeli economy. However, they do not put the continuous existence of Israel's IT industry in serious question. As long as the Israeli IT industry, MNC-controlled or not, can continue to come up with breakthrough innovations, its continuation is assured. A much more serious question mark will hang over the future of the Israeli IT industry if Israel's education system deteriorates and its ability to produce highly qualified R&D personnel diminishes. It is therefore worrying that Israel's education system, from K-12 to the higher education institutions, is indeed in crisis, with declining quality and standards in the teaching of math and science.[84]

It seems as if the future of Israel's IT industry is in danger due to two related factors caused by its own success. The growing success of the IT sector not only turned public attention away from the growing problems of Israel's education system, it also aggravated them by tempting many good researchers to leave the academy. These developments have occurred in a time of flux in the Israeli higher education system, with the establishment of regional colleges in the 1990s and the growing question marks over the long-term commitment of the Israeli government to building the academic R&D infrastructure and sponsoring university-level research.[85]

In this chapter I analyzed the development of the IT industry and the co-evolution of state-industry relations in Israel. Following the theoretical framework developed in the first chapter, we can see that the Israeli state has been active in the development of its local high-technology industry, but, as we shall see, it has taken an almost opposite strategy of that of Taiwan, and a very different one from Ireland's.

In Israel the state devised specific solutions, to the industrial R&D market failure and the questions of the skills-and-knowledge acquisition, by putting the loci of R&D firmly in the private market and opting for an active developmental agency with extremely porous borders between state and industry.

Defining its main goal as the development of novel product R&D-based industry, the Israeli state formulated its policies accordingly: it has been supplying financial backing to R&D projects developed and executed by private firms and entrepreneurs across the industrial range, without any attempt to direct the industry's technological development path. Furthermore, on the local-global front, the Israeli state pushed Israeli and foreign (especially American) companies to form partnerships in which the Israeli firms focused on R&D, the foreign firms on marketing and sales. Israel, uniquely in the less-developed world until recently, focused first and foremost on trying to persuade MNCs to open R&D centers, not manufacturing facilities, within its borders. The state was also actively linking both its companies and its VC industry to the foreign financial markets.

Of our three cases Israel's bureaucracy is the one farthest from the Weberian model, whether in its European or its Asian variant. Throughout the years there have been attempts to both professionalize the bureaucracy and follow the American model of "government of strangers," allowing politicians to have more control over their ministries by bringing with them many of their own people. The result has been a mixed-structure civil service with relative low status and workforce continuity. These features of the civil service, coupled with the porous borders of the OCS, led to a particular mode of embeddedness and state-industry co-evolution process, which is significantly different from Taiwan and Ireland's.

In Israel the hardware industry and the software, following its footsteps in a second stage of growth, became equally successful, with almost all firms following a similar strategy: industrial R&D leading to the development either of new technologies or of new products based on cutting-edge technology. Israeli companies positioned themselves as suppliers of new R&D inputs to the IT industry's global production networks. Israel has become one of the most prominent locations, if not the most prominent, in which foreign companies and MNCs open large-scale R&D centers.

In addition, our framework also makes clear that our ability to generalize lessons from the Israeli case might be limited. Since many commentators have looked to Israel as a case of success to be emulated, it is important to note that Israel's S&T industrial polices were all built around the notion of diffusion of top-notch R&D and technological capabilities that already existed domestically. Therefore it might be that the lessons other countries can learn from Israel are limited, helpful only in certain stages. Israel is a particularly useful case from which to learn when there is a need to diffuse throughout the innovation system R&D capabilities that have already been developed. However, states that do not already possess R&D capabilities should look to other countries as their model.

Furthermore, my analysis of the Israeli IT industry shows that it is not without some serious weaknesses. These weaknesses are a direct result of the Israeli industrial development path, with its sole focus on product R&D and its intimate connection with the United States—undoubtedly also the main sources of its tremendous growth. The first weakness of the Israeli IT industry is that the pull of the American market on Israeli NTBFs is becoming ever more pronounced. With not only their customers but also a growing share of their investors and shareholders being American, and with the Israeli market becoming less important, more and more Israeli companies feel the need to become as American as they can.

The second widely felt weakness of the Israeli IT industry is the still limited ability of firms to achieve sustained growth. This weakness is a direct result of the Israeli industry and state's focusing all their energies on securing advantages that are based solely on advanced R&D. Israeli companies are in fact imitating the American model, but without having the American infrastructure and MNCs, or the long experience and skills necessary to grow and maintain leading rapid innovation–based companies under intensified global competition. In addition, the Israeli IT industry adopts its strategy without the Taiwanese advantage of a local IT manufacturing industry with which to collaborate, and with the added disadvantage that Israeli firms are far away from their markets and their subcontractors.

In short, while Israel's model of development—with its R&D focus and particular division of labor between industry and state, as well as between local and global companies and markets—brought its IT industry to unprecedented success, it also makes the Israeli IT industry more vulnerable than the industries of Ireland and Taiwan.

Chapter 3 The Development of
the IT Industry in Taiwan:
Public Research Institutions
as Growth Impetus?

If you want to build something new where nothing was before, go to the
U.S. If you want to build something that would last for twenty years, go
to Japan. If you want to work successfully under always-changing conditions and changing regulatory systems, go to Taiwan.

—*A founder and manager of one of Taiwan's first IT companies*

Even within the world's most distinguished group of successful
emerging economies, the East Asian Newly Industrialized Countries (NICs),
Taiwan has one of the most inspiring stories. Taiwan is the only society in the
region that has, in many critical aspects, closed the gap in innovational activities with the leading Western industrial nations and with Japan.[1] Taiwan has
also developed a vibrant industrial system of indigenous new small and
medium-sized enterprises, a system that is not dominated by a few huge conglomerates or subsidiaries of foreign MNCs (Wu 2001, 2005). Taiwanese
companies have become a prominent force in the IT industry's global production network. During the 1990s Taiwanese companies pioneered the model of
the pure integrated circuit (IC) silicon chips fabrication (pureplay) foundry in
semiconductors, and more than half of the world's silicon chips are now being

fabricated in Taiwan. Designing and manufacturing products for the world-leading MNCs, Taiwanese IT companies in 2001 manufactured 70 percent of the world's motherboards, 55 percent of laptops, 56 percent of LCD monitors, 51 percent of color-display tube monitors, and 36 percent of digital still cameras.[2] In addition, with 225 companies and NT$147.8 billion in sales, Taiwan's IC design subsector is the second-largest in the world after the United States'. The total sales of the Taiwanese electrical and electronics industry in 2002 reached almost $88 billion USD, and on top of that the semiconductor industry added another $21.4 billion.[3]

How did this transformation happen? In Taiwan the state itself, acting as the technology-creating agent, has spurred the growth of the IT sector; the Taiwanese state acquired the necessary technological information and skills for high-technology industrial development policy by embedding the technology-creating agents within its structure. The main policy vehicle behind this achievement was the establishment of two public research institutions responsible not only for making the decisions on what R&D to conduct but also for implementing and executing them.

Nonetheless, the Taiwanese approach to S&T industrial policy was not without its limitations, in particular the stagnation of the software sector and the limited new product–innovation capabilities developed by the private industry. In addition, under the Kuomintang (KMT) as the governing party, the state purposely built a financial system with a severe scarcity of patient capital, in stark rebuttal to Gerschenkron and the developmental state models following him, specifically Taiwan's neighbors, South Korea and Japan (Amsden 1989, 2001, Gerschenkron 1962, Johnson 1995, Woo-Cumings 1999). Taiwanese companies' average equity-to-debt ratio has been as low as in the United States and, at times, even lower (Cheng 1990, 1993, Fields 1997, Gold 1986). This helped the Taiwanese economy to remain relatively unscathed from the East Asian financial crisis (Park 2000). However, it limits the ability of Taiwanese companies to compete in many IT manufacturing sectors (Fuller et al. 2003). Even in comparison with Israel and Ireland, the state has taken limited financial commitments (Cheng 1990, 1993, Pack 1993, Park 2000).

Taiwan has also followed a distinct policy with regard to MNCs and the shaping of the relationships between its local IT industry and global markets. Early in its industrial efforts, its policy goal was to become a supplier of components, systems, and design-and-manufacturing services to the global IT production network. Thus the story of the spectacular and unique growth trajectory of the Taiwanese IT hardware industry, and the less than spectacular growth of the country's software industry, stems not from massive investment of patient capital but from a distinctive institutional system of industrial innovation—a system built around public research institutions–led R&D science-and-technology (S&T) industrial policy, and a policy goal of attaining a defined position within the IT industry's global production network.

In this chapter I analyze the general growth of the Taiwanese IT industry and the Taiwanese S&T industrial policies. I pay special attention to the successful political processes of co-evolution between the Industrial Technology Research Institution (ITRI) and the private hardware industry, and the unsuccessful process of co-evolution managed by Institute for Information Industry (III) and the software industry. I also analyze the state's strategy in acquiring the necessary technological skills and information and its effects, and the state's attempts to control and plan the technological development path of the IT industry. Lastly, I inquire into the changing roles of the state in MNCs' activities in Taiwan, and their relationships with Taiwanese companies, within and outside Taiwan.

My conclusions are, first, that the success of the hardware sector and the relative failure of the software sector stem from the different politics of state-industry co-evolution in the two sectors. In hardware, ITRI evolved from being the initiator and leader of the industry to a position of a supporting actor, in the process instigating the move of the Taiwanese industry to leadership positions in semiconductor manufacturing and design, as well as in design and manufacturing of desktop, laptop, and other electronic systems and components. In software, from the beginning, III evolved to a position of a competitor to the private industry, doing as much to contend with it as to support it. III never managed to take a contributing leadership position in any software technology development project in the same way that ITRI did in hardware. Thus the Taiwanese software industry that developed did so in spite of III, not because of it. These differences originate, I argue, from the different positioning of the two institutions by the Taiwanese state, as well as from some inherent differences in the industrial sectors for whose development they were nominally responsible.

My second conclusion is that the institutional system of Taiwan, a system with strong division of labor between industry and public research institutions, limits the R&D capabilities of private firms by motivating these firms to concentrate more on development than on research. This system developed from the particular decisions of the state on how to acquire its own technological skills and knowledge. In this system the public research institutions decide which R&D projects should be pursued, conduct the lion's share of R&D, and only then diffuse the results to the private industry; accordingly, core R&D capabilities development is concentrated almost solely within the public sector. Thus in Taiwan, specifically because of this institutional system, the industry has focused on, and successfully developed, world-leading capabilities in second-generation, process, and manufacturing innovation, but not in new-product development.

My third conclusion is that the decision of the state to focus its attention on building a local supplier network for MNCs, coupled with the way it constructed its capital markets, paved a development path for an IT industry that concentrates on several complementary activities of the global IT industry's network: components development and design, together with manufacturing and OEM and ODM services. This development path correlates well with the IT innovation system, which has been developed around the private-public division of labor, with its strength in second-generation innovation and integrated design capabilities. However, it remains to be seen whether Taiwan can, or should, move to original new-product R&D activities in the future, the main declared goal of government policy in the past decade.

HISTORICAL BACKGROUND

Looking at the successful Taiwanese IT industry at the beginning of the third millennium, one can easily forget that in the 1950s Taiwan was a poor agriculture-based island with almost no industrial or technological infrastructure, ruled by what was for 85 percent of its population a foreign force, the defeated mainland China KMT. Taiwan's emergence as a democratic society has been equally remarkable since its politics started from foreign domination, including the KMT's organized killing of many of Taiwan's native intellectual elite (Gold 1986).

Much of the literature that attempts to explain Taiwanese economic growth depicts Taiwan as a "poster child" neodevelopment state. In almost all accounts, Taiwan is described as a society in which the state takes the lead in new economic activities—always, however, with the aim of spurring private entrepreneurs and always through interactions with private industry (Amsden 2001, Amsden and Chu 2003, Evans 1995, Fields 1997, Fuller 2002, Hong 1997, Hung 2000, Mathews and Cho 2000, Wade 1990, Wang 1995, WB 1993). In most accounts, Taiwan's industrial and innovation systems come through as a humming machine of industrial development, with a smooth and well-functioning division of labor between government and industry. It is this division of labor that is considered responsible for Taiwan's leading role in the global information technology industry. Indeed, from the point of view of the development of the IT hardware industry, Taiwan seems to be an exemplary case of a state managing to handle the complex, changing, and sometimes contradictory roles our theoretical approach argues that a state needs to handle in order to spur the growth of innovation-based industry.

Three recent accounts of Taiwan's high-technology industrialization exemplify this point by reaching an almost complete agreement on the ways in which the state and industry in Taiwan have co-evolved in developing the IT hardware industry since the early 1970s (Amsden and Chu 2003, Hong 1997, Mathews and Cho 2000). While each author has a different vocabulary, each describes a similar two-phase process. First, the state's research agencies acquire a technology from abroad, absorb it and improve it, and then spin off private companies to spur the industry. Second, after the private industry has emerged, the industry and state settle on a new division of labor in which the state's role is to locate and absorb new technologies, infuse the industrial system with them, and assist private firms with their own advanced R&D projects. However, the actual sociopolitical-economic history of these developments is far from smooth.

The 1960s: The World's Semiconductor Industry Going Global

Taiwan's modern IT industry dates to the 1960s.[4] At that time, the new semiconductor industry had evolved in the United States to become the first to have truly globally fragmented production. During the 1960s new developments made it feasible to geographically disconnect the heavily low-skilled, labor-intensive final assembly stages from the rest of the production processes. At the time Taiwan opted to follow an MNC–foreign direct investment (FDI) industrial policy similar to Ireland's, and the state marketed Taiwan as a business-friendly place with an unlimited supply of stable, reliable, hardworking labor and a growing market (Klintworth 1995). In these years, Taiwan had many of the same attractions for Western companies that mainland China now seems to possess.

With the help of the United States Agency for International Development (USAID), the Taiwanese state was actively targeting foreign MNCs, following the same tactics that were to become the hallmark of the Irish Industrial Development Agency (IDA) in later years. Extensive background work was performed on individual executives to create a feeling of personal connection. Executives of U.S. firms coming to Taiwan were treated like honored guests; they were ushered to personal meetings with ministers who were thoroughly briefed on the visitors' personal backgrounds and sometimes even managed to display symbolic pictures, emphasizing a common past, in their offices (Wade 1990).

As part of those early efforts at FDI attraction, Taiwan also established export-processing zones (duty-free manufacturing areas), again a striking similarity to Ireland's first attempt at FDI attraction to the duty-free industrial region around Shannon International Airport (Hwang 1991). The year 1961 marks the beginning of the transformation of global IT into an industry ruled by global fragmented production networks. In that year, Fairchild of the United States and Philips of Holland established their first semiconductor final-assembly factories in Asia, Fairchild in Hong Kong and Philips in Taiwan.

In 1964, after aggressive overtures by the Taiwanese government, General Instrument opened its first facility in Taiwan. In 1965 what the Taiwanese claim to be the world's first export-processing duty-free zone was opened near Kaohsiung, and between 1964 and 1966 twenty-four U.S. firms joined Philips and GI in opening manufacturing facilities in Taiwan.[5] These efforts also mark the beginning of the rise to prominence of Taiwan's two most influential S&T industrial policy leaders, the technologists-politicians Drs. Y. S. Sun and K. T. Li (Cheng 1990, Hong 1997, Mathews and Cho 2000, Wade 1990). In 1965, by creating Taiwan's first data-processing and software company—the China Data Processing Center—the state also pioneered what would later become a pillar of its IT industrial policy, the establishment and subsequent privatization of public firms in new technological areas.

The FDI-based IT industrial policy proved, at first, to be very successful. Exports of electronics boomed at 58 percent annual growth rates between 1966 and 1971. However, relatively quickly it became apparent that the U.S. semiconductor companies had no intention of locating any higher-skilled operations in Taiwan. The sustainability of this first success in semiconductor and advance electronics relied on relative low wages (Amsden and Chu 2003, Wade 1990). With wages rapidly rising as a result of the early economic success, it became apparent that unless something was done, this success in semiconductors would be temporary.

In the same period, and even earlier, the electronics-manufacturing industry in Taiwan was rapidly growing. Here, the Taiwanese government policy sharply diverged from that of Ireland. The Taiwanese state, taking a more nationalistic approach toward ownership, started to demand that a large and growing percentage of the components used for final assembly in Taiwan by MNC subsidiaries and joint ventures be locally manufactured.[6] The policy proved to be successful in breaking the enclave positions of MNCs. This was especially true in the case of the Japanese MNCs, which aimed to sell to the local market and hence were more susceptible to the new local-components requirements. By 1971, 37 percent of all components used by the electronics industry in Taiwan were manufactured locally. Moreover, the first original-equipment manufacturing (OEM) relationships between Taiwanese companies and foreign MNCs started in these sectors, becoming prominent first in the manufacturing of color televisions (Amsden and Chu 2003).

This policy had far-reaching impacts on the future of the Taiwanese IT industry and S&T industrial policy. The KMT's early political aim was to prevent the emergence of competing centers of power. This goal led to the creation in Taiwan of a financial system that specifically limited the use of large investment of long-term capital and the accumulation of debt. That in turn led to a particular vision of the future of the Taiwanese IT industry. Accordingly, the first goal of the Taiwanese S&T industrial policy was to spur the growth of a local IT industry that supplies many of the necessary components, especially the higher-value ones, to the global IT production network. The second goal was to develop a local IT industry that provides manufacturing (and later design) services of increasing sophistication to the world's leading MNCs. It has never been the goal of the Taiwanese state to create big vertically integrated national champions in the same way that other Asian NICs, such as South Korea, did. Nor was it ever the goal to create cutting-edge innovation-based firms similarly to those of Israel or the United States. Of our three cases, Taiwan was by far the most persistent in its efforts to convince MNC manufacturing subsidiaries to embed themselves more deeply within the Taiwanese industry, and in urging them to transfer more and more responsibilities over a growing span of activities to local suppliers.

For these reasons, by the time the economic and political crises of the 1970s hit Taiwan, its electronic industry was already geared toward a specific relationship with, and embeddedness within, the global IT industry production network. Moreover, the Taiwanese innovation system and industrial policy were already centered around components manufacturing, thus on manufacturing and process innovation, not on the generation of R&D-based new products.

The Crisis of the 1970s and the
Crystallization of the Public Research
Institutions–Based Industrial Policy: The
Creation of the Semiconductor Industry

In the early 1970s the global economy in general and Taiwan's economy in particular went through several waves of severe economic and political crises. In 1971 the Bretton Woods system was dismantled; in 1973 the first oil shock resulted in a steep rise in the price of oil, and many of the advanced industrial economies started to suffer from stagflation. Taiwan's exports, then mainly textile, footwear, and low-level electronics, started to face competition from less-developed countries and protectionists' measures in their target markets. In addition, with the reemergence of China on the global political scene and the derecognition of Taiwan in the United Nations in 1971, the country had started a long period of formal political isolation. It was under those conditions that Taiwan reformulated its S&T industrial policy. Nonetheless, for years many politicians and bureaucrats did not view the IT industry as a primary source of growth. As we shall see, the overall budget of ITRI's semiconductor technology–development efforts has been minuscule in comparison with the amounts dedicated to other industries by the Taiwanese state and with the investment of other states in their semiconductor industries.

By 1973 some Taiwanese-owned subcontracting firms for assembly and packaging of semiconductors appeared; however, there were still no direct forward or backward linkages, and the semiconductor industry was still an MNC enclave utilizing relative low labor costs and focusing on low-skill final assembly stages. In January 1973 Yun-Hsuan Sun, then the minister of economic affairs and later the premier, oversaw the establishment of ITRI near Hsinchu, a strategic location close to Taiwan's two leading engineering universities, National Chiaotung University and National Chinghua University. ITRI was created through the merger of three existing governmental labs. Using his considerable political power, Sun managed to transfer the responsibility for electronics R&D from the Ministry of Telecommunication laboratory to the newly formed ITRI. However, as was the case initially with Israel's OCS, ITRI was not at the time considered to be a major policy initiative, and its overall financing was negligible from the point of view of the state's overall industrial policies.[7]

The idea behind ITRI's creation was to form one main national lab, which would be responsible for the upgrading of Taiwan's industrial technology through technology transfer, development, and diffusion. The objective was that the government would take it upon itself to solve the risky and more challenging part of the R&D process and would then diffuse the results to the industry, which would concentrate on final development and manufacturing. Thus the state had opted to bring the R&D-creating agents within its own structure, developing a particular division of labor between the industry and the state. This division of labor, which after a few successes became prominent in the innovation system of Taiwan's semiconductor and electronics industry, has had significant influence on the kind of capabilities private firms developed, and on the kind of business models and business strategies that gained paradigmatic hold in Taiwan.

In August 1974 Sun met his friend Dr. Wen-Yuan Pan, a Chinese-American engineer working at RCA's David Sarnoff Laboratories in Princeton, New Jersey. The two agreed on a plan to formulate an S&T industrial policy geared toward the creation of a semiconductor industry in Taiwan. Pan subsequently established a group of mostly Chinese-American engineers working for leading American semiconductor companies in the United States. The group regularly convened at Princeton as the Technical Advisory Committee. The committee submitted specific recommendations for the establishment of a specialist lab in ITRI that would act as the focal launching point for the industry. In September 1974 the Electronic Research Service Organization (ERSO) was established in ITRI, with its main first goal being the development of technological capabilities to spur the growth of a semiconductor industry.

ERSO started to look for sources of IC fabrication technologies. However, it did not manage to find any suitable partners until, through Pan's influence, in 1976 RCA agreed to transfer its obsolete technology to ITRI. RCA had decided to get out of the semiconductor industry and saw this as an opportunity to earn royalties from its abandoned seven-micron complementary metal oxide semiconductor (CMOS) fabrication technology. This technology was already far behind the world limit of two microns. A group of forty engineers, many of whom later became the leaders of the semiconductor industry in Taiwan, spent almost a year in RCA's facilities in the United States, and ERSO built its first IC fabrication plant with RCA's guidance. In 1977–1978 the first trial wafers were produced, and the Taiwanese team started to test its own experimental designs. In 1979 the ERSO team advanced to such a degree that it had better yields than RCA's and started to sell small quantities of chips to supplement its financial resources.

At the same time, the Taiwanese state was establishing the physical and business infrastructure needed for the semiconductor industry. It is here that Kuo-Ting Li's leadership over Taiwanese S&T industrial policy became crucial. Li was minister of finance after serving as the minister for economic affairs. In 1978 Li organized a special conference on Taiwan's economic and scientific future. The result of this well-attended event was the document "The Science and Technology Development Program," which was adapted by the cabinet and called for the creation of (a) a special permanent advisory body for science and technology, the Science and Technology Advisory Group (STAG), which would be chaired by Li and report directly to Premier Sun, and (b) an infrastructure focused on the needs of science-based advanced industries.

The latter project was championed by the president of National Chinghua University, S. S. Hsu, who urged the creation of a science-based industrial park next to Taiwan's three prominent engineering institutions in Hsinchu to duplicate what he perceived to have happened around Stanford University in California (Hong 1997).[8] The park, named Hsinchu Science-Based Industrial Park, was put under the jurisdiction of the National Science Council (NSC) and launched in 1980.[9] Hsinchu Park became an extremely important factor in Taiwan's subsequent success in the semiconductor industry. Hsinchu Park has been accepting only firms with significant R&D operations, for which, apart from providing specialized infrastructure, it has been granting special subsidies, such as tax holidays, duty exemption on equipment importation and commodity exports, low-interest loans, and matching R&D funds.

However, it was not private industry that established the first leading firm of the Taiwanese semiconductor industry, as well as many of the subsequent ones. In the late 1970s, facing what seemed to be large initial investment with high uncertainty, no private entrepreneur, industrial group, or investor was willing to invest capital in commercializing the technologies developed in ERSO. Under these conditions both Sun and Li decided against the establishment of a fully state-owned company and chose to create a joint private-state venture. In 1978 the head of ERSO, together with one of the forty engineers who went to RCA, proposed a plan for the establishment of a private-state company. The ministry of economic affairs (MoEA) accepted their proposal and invited some of Taiwan's biggest companies as investors.[10] At first, none of the companies invited agreed to join. MoEA then used its direct influence and organized a coalition of local companies that finally agreed to invest in the project, and between them, 51 percent of the shares of the new entity, United Microelectronics Corporation (UMC), were distributed. The total sum invested stood between $14 million and $20 million USD.[11]

Apart from receiving all of its technical staff and technology from ERSO, UMC was also granted technical assistance from, and the use of, ERSO's fabrication plant, a source for many subsequent conflicts of interest. UMC quickly engaged in another series of fund-raising and built its own first fully owned fabrication plant in the newly established Hsinchu Park in 1982.

DIVERSIFYING AND DEEPENING THE TECHNOLOGICAL BASE OF THE SEMICONDUCTOR INDUSTRY: ERSO'S STRATEGY OF PARALLEL CAPABILITIES DEVELOPMENT

ERSO's preeminence over the development trajectory of the Taiwanese semiconductor industry did not end with the spin-off of UMC. On the contrary, the successful launch of UMC encouraged subsequent formal and less-formal spin-offs, as teams of engineers left to establish their own companies. Following the establishment of UMC, ERSO itself slightly changed its focus. At the urging of American advisers, ERSO made a few important decisions. The first was to stay clear from what would become an extremely capital-intensive market niche: memory chips, specifically DRAM.[12] The second was to base the Taiwanese semiconductor industry around capabilities that would allow it to competitively and quickly design and manufacture custom-tailored (application-specific integrated circuit—ASIC) chips, and not just around specific products. ERSO argued that by developing this technological capability Taiwan would, first, strategically differentiate itself from Korea and Japan, which had embarked on a strategy of high-volume rapid-generational-upgrading hardware such as memory chips, which necessitate extremely deep-pocketed companies of the kind Taiwan did not possess. ERSO further argued that this strategy would enable Taiwan to focus on the consumer industry, where Taiwanese electronic manufacturing companies were already globally successful and realized substantial revenues using relatively simple technology. ERSO rightly contended that by developing these capabilities, Taiwan's semiconductor industry could innovate across the whole spectrum of the IT industry (Wade 1990).

The Taiwanese semiconductor industry developed capabilities that both (a) strengthened the IT hardware OEM and ODM industry and (b) allowed it to excel in the market niches opened to it by the existence of Taiwanese OEM and ODM firms. In other words, the decision by ERSO to prompt the development of strong ASIC capabilities in the semiconductor industry positioned the industry perfectly to take advantage of the opportunity structure offered by the successful IT design and manufacturing subcontractors industry, and strengthened the competitiveness of that industry in turn. As I shall show, this in turn has reinforced Taiwan's embeddedness in the global IT production network as a supplier and innovator of components and design-and-manufacturing services and processes.

As part of its strategic decision to focus on ASIC technologies and capabilities, after UMC's spin-off ERSO pursued a dual-capabilities development strategy. The strategy focused on developing both ASIC capabilities and the fabrication technologies needed to manufacture them. ERSO managed to move its own fabrication capabilities to 4.5 microns in 1981 (still far behind the world's technological edge at the time at 2 microns), and to acquire and develop complementary technologies that would enable Taiwan to excel in ASICs. In the early 1980s ERSO expanded its capabilities in design, testing, and several other stages of IC production, including masking. It was in this early stage that many teams of ERSO employees started to leave ITRI to open IC design houses that utilized ERSO's and UMC's fabrication facilities, one of the first being Syntek in 1982 (Chang and Tsai 2002). Hence, even before the establishment of the pureplay foundry model by another ERSO spin-off—Taiwan Semiconductor Manufacturing Corporation (TSMC)—more than a few design houses were operating in Hsinchu Park, and within a year after the establishment of TSMC their number was estimated at forty.

TRANSFORMING THE GLOBAL
SEMICONDUCTOR INDUSTRY: ESTABLISHING
THE PUREPLAY FOUNDRY MODEL IN TAIWAN

The pureplay foundry business model, pioneered by ERSO and spun off as TSMC in 1986, developed as part of ERSO's efforts to infuse the Taiwanese industry with very large–scale integration (VLSI) capabilities. ERSO's foreign advisers, who did not view the progress to 4.5-micron technology as fast enough to close the gap with the world's technological leaders, urged these efforts on. In 1981 STAG, chaired by Li, argued that Taiwan should achieve VLSI capability of 1 micron or better, the technological frontier at the time.

A political battle immediately ensued, as this view was attacked from almost all quarters in Taiwan's economic development bureaucracy, including the Ministry of Finance, the Council for Economic Planning and Development, and a large percentage of ERSO's personnel. However, with the backing of now-Premier Sun and Li, a decision was made to go forward with a VLSI 1-micron technology development project simultaneously with ERSO's other activities. In 1983, $72.5 million USD was allocated to a five-year program on various semiconductor projects, a larger amount than provided before but still insignificant in both international terms and in comparison with other Taiwanese industrial policies. The goal was to reach 1-micron capabilities by 1988. Once again, ITRI was leading the private market.

The decision on the implementation of the VLSI research project was a continuation of the earlier strategy of a division of labor in R&D between public institutions and private companies, with the public institutions commencing most of the research and the results diffused to private companies that focused mostly on development and design. After a battle with UMC, which argued that it should be responsible for the development of the VLSI technology, ERSO was again the chosen agency, in part to prevent an overconcentration of power and capabilities in one private company (Fuller et al. 2003, Hong 1997, Mathews and Cho 2000, Meany 1994).

This time ERSO decided to follow a joint-venture technology-development strategy and did not pursue technology-transfer contracts. The chosen party was Vitelic, a small Silicon Valley firm founded by Chinese-American engineers in 1983. The R&D phase was successful, with a DRAM chip developed by June 1986. However, at the time, neither the government nor the private sector in Taiwan was willing to supply the necessary manufacturing facility, and as a result Vitelic sold its technologies to various Korean and Japanese companies (Meany 1994).

This awkward situation politically strengthened those who argued for more direct state intervention in the building of VLSI fabrication facilities in Taiwan (Hong 1997). In addition, by the end of 1986, with many of the new design houses in Hsinchu Park opting to follow Vitelic and selling their technologies to Korean and Japanese firms, it became obvious that there was a wider demand for VLSI fabrication facilities.

In the same time that ERSO developed VLSI technologies, UMC developed its own similar technology, utilizing both in-house development and joint-venture agreements. This technological competition was straining even more the conflict of interest between ERSO and UMC, especially as Morris Chang, the head of ITRI, was also serving as the chairman of UMC. Chang also epitomizes another important trend in Taiwan's rise to prominence in the semiconductor industry, the returning immigration wave of graduate level–trained engineers from the United States.[13]

Taiwan has one of the highest numbers of engineering and science students who immigrated to the United States to get advanced engineering and science degrees. For most of the period until the early 1980s, these Taiwanese expatriates did not see any opportunity to employ their skills profitably in Taiwan, and most of them stayed on in the United States. However, with the creation of ITRI, and even more so with the growing success of the semiconductor industry, a large percentage came back or established cross-country businesses. This so-called reverse brain drain has been one of the most important factors in the rapid growth of the semiconductor industry (Saxenian and Hsu 2001).

However, while the influence of the returnees has been important, we should remember that this pullback started and strengthened only after many of the émigrés saw an economic opportunity in Taiwan, not vice versa. Moreover, while returnees established many companies, locals founded most of the key companies.[14] In addition, while the sizable return from Silicon Valley is celebrated, the influence of returning immigrants from other parts of the United States, notably the large contingent coming back after long stints in Bell Labs and IBM, has been at least as important, a fact that our interviewees repeatedly noted during our research trips to Taiwan (Amsden and Chu 2003, Saxenian and Hsu 2001).

In 1986, after some internal debate, a decision was made to move forward with the privatization of ERSO's VLSI efforts and the construction of a VLSI fabrication facility employing an innovative business model—the pureplay foundry. This decision marks a turning point not only for the Taiwanese semiconductor industry but also for the global industry. As at UMC, the decision was to commercialize and privatize the VLSI project by creating a joint public-private company, TSMC. Again the Taiwanese state faced a similar investment landscape as with UMC. Although by now the success of UMC and the growth of the industry was proof that the semiconductor industry in Taiwan could be profitable, the private market was still unwilling to commit to a leading investment.

This lack of will by Taiwanese investors ironically proved to be a boon for TSMC, as Philips, the Dutch MNC, agreed to provide 27.5 percent of TSMC's initial capital and became its leading private shareholder, with another 48.3 percent of the investment coming from the China Development Corporation, an investment arm of the ruling KMT party (Fuller 2002, Fuller et al. 2003). Apart from securing some business from Philips, having the MNC as its main shareholder gave the new venture legitimacy; even more important was a full patent swap agreement, which was critical in the beginning in protecting TSMC from legal actions.[15]

The pureplay model had a major revolutionary influence on the global IT production network, on Taiwan's embeddedness within it, and on the reshaping of Taiwan's semiconductor industry. The pureplay foundry model is one of the best examples of an organizational innovation that enabled new levels of fragmentation of the semiconductor industry's production network—an innovation spurring a rapid process of advances in production-stage specialization and product-stage economies of scope and scale, consequently in stage-specific innovation. Before the establishment of TSMC and the pureplay foundry, the semiconductor industry consisted mainly of companies that utilized the business model of integrated device manufacturers (IDM). The IDM model calls for the creation of large vertically integrated firms that perform both design and fabrication in house. The leading semiconductor firms were all IDMs that built their own dedicated fabrication plants. The industry also consisted of design houses that were smaller and marginal and that needed to secure their fabrication capacity from IDMs with no standards for information transfer, and with the added risk of sharing their IP with potential competitors. Moreover, the process was lengthy and cumbersome, putting the design houses at a distinct disadvantage.

The pureplay foundry model calls for the creation of companies whose sole business is fabrication. Pureplay foundries receive codified designs from the design houses and fabricate their chips for them. Thus they enable stage specialization in both design and fabrication. In 1986 the viability of the pureplay foundry was still unclear, as the technology for full codification of the designs was not yet developed. However, in the particular case of Taiwan—(a) the industry's growth limited by the political choice of a financial system that restricted the use of long-term financing and debt; (b) the already growing number of design houses in Hsinchu Park; (c) the political pressure arising from the lack of VLSI fabrication capability that brought many of these design houses to sell outright the IP to foreign firms; and (d) the political constraints that the existence and lobbying of UMC put on ERSO—the pureplay foundry model seems to be worth the commercial and technological uncertainties that still exist. An additional advantage of the model was that a pureplay foundry could also learn from its customers. Many of TSMC's early customers passed on their technologies to TSMC so that it could fabricate their chips. They were willing to do so only because TSMC's pureplay foundry model allayed their fears of its becoming their competitor. Consequently, TSMC has been using customers' feedback to refine and expand its fabrication method (Fuller et al. 2003).

For a few years, TSMC's growth was slow. Nevertheless, even then its effect on the Taiwanese semiconductor industry was immense. Its services enabled a growing number of fabless companies to profitably commence operations. This unleashed the commercial potential of the Taiwanese industry's ASIC specialization and skills. By 1994 there were already sixty-five design houses in Taiwan (ITRI 2003, various years). In that year the design-codifying and transfer technology was fully developed, and since 1997 the pureplay foundries have been fabricating the lion's share of chips in Taiwan, with many of the IDMs, including UMC, converting to the foundry model or being bought by pureplay foundries in need of more fabrication facilities.

Pureplay became the prominent production model in the global semiconductor industry, completely transforming it in several ways. First, the pureplay model enables groups of engineers to quickly bring innovative designs to market with only limited financial resources, fostering even more rapid innovation cycles in the semiconductor industry. Second, the lower cost also enables groups of engineers to profitably utilize the business strategy of offering cheaper chips in already developed niche markets using second-generation technologies. Third, the pureplay model transformed the industry by creating virtuous cycles of internal innovation and growing efficiency that make it even more profitable, vis-à-vis the IDM model. Today, thanks to their head start, the Taiwanese pureplay foundries TSMC and UMC are the global market leaders, with sales in 2004 of just less than $8 billion USD and just more than $4 billion, respectively. TSMC and UMC are the main reasons behind the growth of the Taiwanese semiconductor industry to its current status as the world's fourth-largest IC producer.

Apart from UMC and TSMC, ERSO was also responsible for a few more of the leading Taiwanese semiconductor firms before it was closed and the Computer and Communication Lab (CCL) became ITRI's sole semiconductor technology division. The Taiwan Mask Corporation (TMC) was spun off ITRI in 1989, culminating the successful development of the masking technologies project at ERSO, which had begun with technology transfer from the United States in 1977. TMC successfully grew in the years since, and in 2000 it bought Innova, Taiwan's second masking company.[16]

Two other important spin-offs from ERSO were Vanguard and Winbond. Vanguard was the official spin-off of ERSO's submicron project that culminated in an industrial-size fabrication plant in Hsinchu Park. It was auctioned in 1995, with TSMC becoming its main shareholder. While Winbond is not an official ERSO spin-off, its history makes its connection to ERSO clear. In 1987, after the launch of TSMC, ERSO was still in possession of its first pilot fabrication plant and its personnel. The plant manager, Dr. Ding-Yuan Yang, engineered an MBO, secured with financing from the Walsin Lihwa Corporation, launching it as Winbond. Unlike other Taiwanese companies, Winbond has been following the OBM model and has stayed as an IDM company, moving into both memory and logic. In 2004 Winbond's sales were slightly less than $1 billion USD.

FROM OEM TO ODM: THE TECHNOLOGICAL
UPGRADING OF THE ELECTRONICS SUPPLIERS,
AND ITRI'S ROLE AS A SUPPORTING ACTOR

Taiwan's ODM-OEM firms are as important to Taiwan's success in the IT industry as are its semiconductor firms, if not more so. Taiwan's OEM-ODM firms are successful in all sectors of the IT industry, employing many different business models. The range of strategies moves from more focused OEM-ODM companies—such as Quanta or Inventec, which design and manufacture most of the world's laptops, and Asustek, which does the same in motherboards—to more flexible OEM-ODM firms such as Sampo, BenQ (formerly part of the Acer group), Tatung, and Mitac, which operate across a wider array of products.

The existence in Taiwan of local world-leading OEM-ODM companies also propelled the growth of the semiconductor industry in a particular trajectory. The existence of ODMs has given the Taiwanese IC design industry a competitive advantage and a unique opportunity structure focusing on second-generation innovation. These opportunity structures are not available to Israeli, Irish, and American IC design companies. The OEM-ODMs, in turn, have been strengthened by the success of the local IC design industry, which caters specifically to their needs and helps them to improve their quality while lowering their costs.

ITRI and the Taiwanese state have been as important to the success of this sector as they were to the semiconductor industry. However, while ITRI was the first and, for a long time, the only actor in the field in the semiconductor industry, in the case of the OEM-ODM electronics, ITRI's main goal has been to technologically upgrade existing firms, some of which, like Tatung (1918), have been around since early in the twentieth century. This sector gives us an excellent example of how the Taiwanese state has pursued the same goal —developing a local IT industry that supplies many of the necessary components and manufacturing services to the global IT production network, applying the same division of labor in R&D, while using a different mechanism as the state-led research consortia. In addition, the case of OEM-ODM enables us to follow another angle of the co-evolution of industry-state relationships.

As has been vividly argued by John Mathews, the main goal of the Taiwanese R&D consortia has comprised technological learning, upgrading, and catch-up as part of attempts at industry creation (Mathews 2002). This is a very different objective from the strategy of Israel, described in Chapter 2, of constructing a special program to sponsor collaborative R&D efforts in an attempt to enable smaller Israeli firms to successfully compete with MNCs on the basis of their own developed cutting-edge technologies.[17] Like Israel, the Taiwanese state recognized the handicaps of its IT industry—in this case, that the smaller size of Taiwan's manufacturing-oriented companies, with their lack of sophisticated in-house R&D capabilities, hinders the ability of the industry to upgrade and compete in global markets. The solution was to assemble a series of ITRI-led research consortia. From the start of this process, the same division of labor in R&D that had been used in the case of semiconductors was applied, with ITRI conducting the R&D and the private companies concentrating on manufacturing and final product development. Even in more recent research consortia, in which private companies have assumed leadership roles, this division of labor has been maintained.

The first few consortia, and some of the most significant ones, were developed as part of ITRI's multiclient projects in the early 1980s. These projects assisted in the creation of a PC development-and-manufacturing industry in Taiwan. The first such project started after Apple clamped down on the thriving Taiwanese Apple II cloning industry in late 1982. The industry, then a highly fragmented one with no prior experience with IP protection laws, came to MoEA and ITRI for help.[18] ERSO already possessed some experience working with Intel processors, and ITRI advised the industry to concentrate on the new IBM Intel-based PC instead of Apple (Noble 1998). The real activity started after February 1983, when Acer approached ERSO with a request to develop a PC.

After various halts and requests from other computer-manufacturing companies, ERSO devised the project as its first multiclient project, with the title of MCP-1. A decision was made to limit the number of participants to nine. By the end of 1983 Taiwanese companies had started manufacturing PC clones, hoping to ship them to the United States in time for Christmas sales. However, IBM counterattacked, claiming that ITRI's basic input-output system (BIOS) was infringing on its IP.[19] ERSO engineers rewrote the code, but by the time IBM agreed that the new version was legal, it was already May 1984. By then, most of the project's participants had either sold their PCs in less IP-strict markets, such as Europe and Asia, or followed Acer and used a different BIOS (Noble 1998).

Although this project was deemed less than satisfactory, as soon as IBM announced its new PC AT system in August 1984, ERSO announced its intention to launch a new multiclient project. This time the participants were limited to three, including Tatung, which used this project as an entry into the computer business. The prototype was transferred by ERSO to the companies by July 1985, and soon thereafter the companies started to bring their own products to market (Chang et al. 1999, Mathews 2002, Noble 1998). This project was considered a great success and paved the way to a series of related multiclient projects. From this point onward the projects were run by the newly established Computer and Communications Laboratory (CCL) and were more formally viewed as consortia, not as ITRI's multiple-clients research projects.

By 1990 the Taiwanese industry was firmly established in desktop computers and other related products; nonetheless, its technological capabilities were still far behind what was needed to succeed in the lucrative new laptops market. CCL formally drafted the project as an R&D consortium with the aim of developing a set of key components to become the standard on which the different companies would build and develop their products. The biggest computer-manufacturers trade association in Taiwan was involved and recruited as a joint coordinator. In July 1990 the Taiwan Laptop Consortium, with forty-six subscribing companies, was officially announced with capital of $2 million (USD; Mathews 2002). The project was concluded quickly, and by the end of 1990 Taiwan achieved the status of the world's leading supplier of laptops. This time CCL not only transferred prototype machines but also constructed extensive training programs, and many of its staff moved to private firms. The main problems of the project were oversubscription and a too tight division of labor. The companies, given an almost complete product that had been developed solely by CCL, were unable to differentiate and further develop their products, leading to a relentless price competition among the Taiwanese companies. These lessons were learned, and throughout the ITRI-led consortia in the 1990s, private companies were given slightly greater R&D responsibilities, or at least slightly more-flexible prototypes. In some of the projects one of the declared aims was the creation of R&D, or at least integrated-design capabilities, within the participating private companies.

As the Taiwanese industry has grown to become globally important, many of the leading MNCs have happily supported many of ITRI's consortia. The MNCs have hoped to spur the growth of an industry based on their technology, and find it easier to deal solely with ITRI than separately with every private company. The best examples of such a project was NewPC, which was based around the PowerPC processors developed jointly by IBM, Motorola, and Apple (Dedrick and Kraemer 1998, Mathews 2002).

However, in the key area of developing the R&D capabilities of private companies, the research consortia are still far from successful. A top official of CCL bitterly described the situation:

> Technology transfer from CCL is very important in Taiwan. The companies use us to train their people, take our technology, and create some products. After which they go to their customers, show them the products as a proof that they can do OEM, sign some OEM contracts, and just do the same things for a couple of years down the road. Our aim is to help and spur them to routinize R&D and product innovation. However, the end result is that they do not do it, a main reason being that they can more cheaply rely on technology transfer every time they need to upgrade their skills, which allow them to operate as a pure OEM. (interview, May 24, 2001)

The state also has used the research consortia mechanism not only to develop and create new IT products industries but also to upgrade the Taiwanese electronic components industry, following its strategy from the early 1960s of trying to localize the creation of key components.

One of the most illuminating such projects was the CD-ROM project, which evolved from MoEA's decision in 1992 to view CD-ROM as a strategic product. As a result of this project, by the end of 1999 Taiwan moved from being a supplier of less than 1 percent of the world's CD-ROMs to supplying more than 50 percent, with almost 49 million units sold (Amsden and Chu 2003, p. 104). This project evolved into a series of consortia and moved on to DVD technology.

From the point of view of our argument about opportunity structure, it is important to note that one key subcomponent that none of the consortia managed to develop was the IC chip. By 1997 the development in the CD-ROM industry, along with ITRI's inability to develop the needed IC chips, created an ideal market opportunity for a new IC design company, and MediaTek was spun off of UMC. MediaTek succeeded where ITRI's consortia failed and quickly developed chips for the CD-ROM industry, breaking the monopoly of Japanese companies in the area. MediaTek's technologies moved together with the industry's, first to CD-RW and then to DVD.[20] In the process, MediaTek became Taiwan's most successful IC design company and the world's fourth-largest in terms of sales since 2002.

Nevertheless, even in the IT hardware sector not all of the Taiwanese state's initiatives have been successful. In parallel with ITRI, the Taiwanese government has sponsored and expanded an even bigger pubic research institute—Chungshan Institute of Science and Technology (CSIST)—Taiwan's defense-technology research institute. Apart from funds received through the defense establishment, CSIST was, as late as 1999, the receiver of the second-largest amount of funds, after ITRI, from MoEA's Department of Industrial Technology (Hsu and Chiang 2001). Little information is available on CSIST, but while ITRI's efforts resulted in significant commercial success for relatively low investment, those of CSIST, often working on similar technologies with vastly larger resources, did not achieve even one commercial success in the semiconductor industry.[21] This compares poorly not only with ITRI but also with Israel's experience. The main difference between CSIST and both ITRI and Israel's RAFAEL is that CSIST does not maintain close relationships with the private industry and instead prefers to work in isolation and secrecy.

THE DEVELOPMENT OF THE SEMICONDUCTOR
INDUSTRY IN THE 1990s: THE GROWTH OF
THE IC DESIGN SUBSECTOR

Of the many subsectors of the global IT hardware industry in the 1990s, the IC design (or fabless) subsector was one of the most innovative and most successful.[22] By the early 2000s Taiwanese IC design houses were the only non–

North American companies to reach the top ten positions in terms of world-wide sales. As a matter of fact, Taiwan and Israel are the only non–North American countries to have any companies at all among the top thirty companies. By 2003 the Taiwanese IC design industry was already the second-largest in the world in terms of sales after that of the United States. The IC design industry was the focus of attention for the Taiwanese state in the 1990s and has been key in the attempts of the Taiwanese state to spur more cutting-edge innovational activity.

As can be seen in table 3.1, between 1991 and 2002 the Taiwanese IC design industry experienced a remarkable growth. From an industry that consisted of 57 companies in 1991, the industry grew to 66 companies employing 2,109 people in 1995, and to 225 companies employing 11,800 in 2002. This rapid growth, with sales of more than $6 billion USD in 2003, made it one of the three biggest IC design industries in the world (ITRI 2003, various years).

Looking at the largest ten companies by sales in 2002–2004 (table 3.2) and the thirty largest fabless companies in 2002–2003 (table 3.3), we see that the industry's skills are quite developed and flexible, as attested to by the ability of Taiwanese IC design firms to excel in almost every subsector of the semiconductor industry. In addition, it is apparent that these successful companies have built their businesses around the opportunity structures offered by the existence of the large OEM-ODM companies in Taiwan and ITRI's efforts to develop local manufacturing of key components. For example, MediaTek's core business has been the PC's CD and DVD industries; VIA is developing PC chipsets for motherboard and PC manufacturers; ALi's main business is laptop chipsets; and Sunplus is catering to the consumer markets, especially to toy OEM-ODMs.

Another common trait appears if we analyze the strategy of the leading companies: none of them develops completely new innovative products that are first to the market. Furthermore, even the most innovative firms, those that manage to develop some brand recognition for their products, such as VIA and ALi, rely on developing secondary innovations on the basis of technologies developed by the leading American MNCs. This tends to leave many of them in a weakened position, where changes in technology or in the behavior of leading MNCs can rapidly deteriorate their market position.

The story of VIA, the largest Taiwanese IC design company in terms of sales until 2002, is a case in point. PC chipsets are VIA's main product line. As long as Intel's Pentium 3 was the leading PC CPU, VIA gained global market

Table 3.1. Size of the IC Design Sector in
Taiwan, 1991–2002

Year	Number of Companies	Employees
1991	57	
1992	59	
1993	64	
1994	65	
1995	66	2,109
1996	72	2,141
1997	81	3,349
1998	115	4,200
1999	127	6,000
2000	140	7,600
2001	180	9,800
2002	225	11,800

Source: ITRI 2005.

share at Intel's expense, reaching almost 50 percent, in part because of Intel's decision to stick with the more expensive Rambus technology. With the move to Pentium 4 technology, Intel attacked VIA on multiple fronts: it did not license VIA its P4 technology, and it took VIA to court over patent infringement allegations in October 2001. As a result of these moves, all first-tier PC manufacturers, such as Asus or Gigabyte, refrained from using VIA's chipsets, fearing legal action from Intel. VIA countersued Intel for both patent infringement and usage of monopoly status, and the legal battle was fought in five jurisdictions. In April 2003 the two companies reached a settlement that includes a patent swap agreement and a licensing agreement. By that time, however, VIA had lost substantial market share and revenues. Moreover, because it agreed to pay royalties to Intel, it can no longer retain the profit margins it enjoyed before. Although in 2001 VIA was the biggest Taiwanese IC design house, with about $1 billion USD in sales and control of almost 50 percent of global market share, in 2002 VIA was only the second-largest Taiwanese IC design house, with sales down to $729 million and global market share of less than 25 percent. In 2003 VIA's sales continued to drop, and its sales were only $600 million (AFX 2001, FT 2003a, 2003b, 2003c, Hille 2003, Hung 2002).

Another example of the vulnerability of the Taiwanese IC design industry position within the global production networks is the fact that this legal battle

Table 3.2. Top Ten Taiwanese Design Houses by Sales

Rank				Sales (NT$100 million)			
2004	2003	2002	Name	2004	2003	2002	Main Products
1	1	1	MediaTek Inc.	400	380	295	Optical storage
2	2	2	VIA	193	203	252	PC chipsets
3	3	4	Sunplus Technology	189	110	86	Consumer
4	4	5	Novatek Microelectronics Corp.	175	109	67	Consumer
5	—	—	Silicon Integrated Systems	106	167	158	Multimedia/ chipsets
6	9	—	Himax	100	45	NA	LCD Drivers
7	5	3	RealTek	93	92	92	Networking
8	7	8	Elite Semiconductor	87	53	34	Memory
9	10	—	Etron	63	44	30	Memory
10	6	6	Ali Corp.	65	60	61	PC chipsets/ DVD player IC

Sources: ITRI 2003, 2005, ITRI various years.

was fought after VIA had already changed its ownership structure to placate Intel's demand. In order to do so VIA separated itself from its main shareholder, First International Computers (FIC). This restructuring was done because Intel viewed the combination of motherboard producer, FIC, and chipset producer, VIA, as a threat.[23]

As can be seen from the rapid growth of the design, or fabless, subsector after 1996, the main impetus for growth had been the establishment and rapid growth of the pureplay foundries. Both major foundries, TSMC and UMC, have taken leading roles in the development of the design subsector. Both established exclusive foundry-IC design house relationships with what they term club members, which they also assisted financially. Many of the top IC design houses, such as MediaTek and Novatek, were spun off from UMC when it turned its business model from IDM to pureplay foundry.

Table 3.3. Top Thirty Fabless Companies by Global Sales

Ranking							
2003	2002	Company	Country	2000	2001	2002	2003
1	1	Qualcomm	U.S.	1,215	1,395	1,942	2,510
2	2	Nvidia	U.S.	699	1,275	1,915	1,835
3	4	Broadcom	U.S.	1,096	962	1,083	1,595
4	3	Xilinx	U.S.	1,560	1,149	1,125	1,265
5	5	MediaTek	Taiwan	411	447	854	1,170
6	8	ATI	Canada	520	480	645	1,135
7	10	SanDisk	U.S.	602	317	493	930
8	7	Altera	U.S.	1,377	839	712	830
9	11	Marvell	U.S.	135	275	482	780
10	9	Conexant[a]	U.S.	—	646	1,942	650
11	6	VIA	Taiwan	909	1,009	729	620
12	12	Qlogic	U.S.	362	357	415	520
13	18	Globespan Virata[a]	U.S.	348	265	229	360
14	16	Sunplus	Taiwan	201	195	250	320
15	23	Novatek	Taiwan	121	124	193	311
16	24	Silicon Laboratories	U.S.	103	74	182	310
17	15	RealTek	Taiwan	174	214	265	300
18	17	SST	U.S.	490	259	244	250
19	21	PMC-Sierra	Canada	695	323	213	245
20	20	ICS	U.S.	195	155	228	237
21	19	Lattice	U.S.	568	295	229	218
22	29	Zoran	U.S. (Israel)	68	100	141	213
23	22	Genesis Microchip	Canada	56	126	196	211
24	28	SMSC	U.S.	163	128	145	202
25	—	Zarlink[b]	Canada	—	—	—	201
26	25	Ali	Taiwan	98	159	176	200
27	13	Cirrus Logic	U.S.	729	534	304	198
28	14	ESS	U.S.	303	271	273	180
29	32	DSP Group	U.S. (Israel)	85	88	125	170
30	26	Semtech	U.S.	215	170	170	160
		Others	—	3,512	2,504	2,210	2,514
		Total		17,010	15,135	16,795	20,640

Source: IC Insights 2004.
[a] Conexant and Globespan Virata merged in 2004.
[b] Became fabless in mid-2002.

Structure, Development, and Business
Models in the Taiwanese IC Design Industry

Taiwanese fabless companies employ one main business model, apart from the few cases in which a Taiwanese company manages to sell its own branded products to final customers. This business model is based on the utilization of the unique advantage that the Taiwanese IT industry's structure offers: the co-location of both the world's biggest and most advanced pureplay foundries and of some of the largest OEM-ODM companies.

Most of the Taiwanese IC design houses employ two variants of the same strategy: to supply the Taiwanese (and more recently the Chinese) OEM-ODMs with the chips they need in order to supply finished products at competitive prices and of sufficient quality to OBM MNCs. The Taiwanese fabless companies rely on the proximity of the world's biggest pureplay foundries. This geographical proximity enables them to produce cheaply and speedily large quantities of newly designed chips and to inspect and assure quality in almost real time. All the Taiwanese IC design houses whose personnel we interviewed specialize in chips based on second-generation technologies with the aim of lowering costs and increasing reliability; they also do some process innovation. Apart from an unsuccessful attempt by ICreate, a subsidiary of Etron, to develop and market advanced chips in a joint venture with the Israeli company Zoran, no Taiwanese IC design house at which we interviewed tried to develop original products, new technologies, or products that are based on cutting-edge technology. Figure 3.1 provides a graphic representation of the main differences between the market relation and information-and-communication flows of the Taiwanese industry in comparison with the Israeli and U.S. industries.[24]

The Taiwanese fabless companies' business model has two variants that are not mutually exclusive. In the first variant, the design houses custom-design chips to clients' specifications (a local OEM with specific contracts with an OBM), test and quality-assure them, and then manufacture and deliver them using a pureplay foundry for fabrication. In the second variant the IC design house builds "standardized" chips for OEM companies and other customers, manufactures them using a pureplay foundry, and sells them either directly or through distributors. Representatives of the firms whom we interviewed claimed that as the market for standard chips is vastly larger, revenues using the second variant with successful products are much higher. However, because custom-designed chips have the advantage of a secure customer and

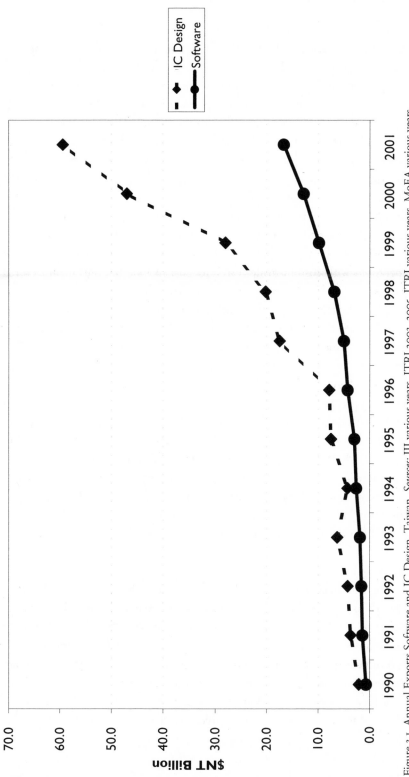

Figure 3.1. Annual Exports Software and IC Design, Taiwan. *Source:* III various years, ITRI 2003, 2005, ITRI various years, MoEA various years.

higher profit margins per fabricated chip, a significant number of companies use both business models.

As the customization-based business model also has lower costs and companies can secure quick revenues, until recently it has been the preferred mode of operation for new companies. The story of Sunplus, consistently one of the top four companies in term of sales since 2000, is illuminating. Sunplus was established by a group of former ERSO engineers who left ITRI to join Silicon Integrated Systems (SiS) and left SiS after its restructuring in 1989. The idea of the founders was to focus on the consumer market, especially toys; thus reliability and price have always been much more important than the latest technology and features. Using their own money to seed the company, the founders immediately sought revenues to supplement their capital and started operations with custom-made ASIC designs. In 1994 Sunplus manufactured its first standardized chip, a microcontroller for toys with LCD monitors, from which it branched out to other multimedia-related chips. Currently, Sunplus uses the customization-based business model for its entire gift and toy business and the standardized-chips business model for the rest.

Most of Sunplus's revenues now originate from its standard chips; however, as there is fierce competition in the multimedia mass market, a large percentage of profits come from the smaller custom-made-chip division. Sunplus realizes that even though it does not use cutting-edge technologies, in order to excel, it must keep abreast of new technologies and be able to implement them quickly once their prices go down. In order to do so, Sunplus employs a few strategies similar to those of many successful Taiwanese fabless companies. First, it maintains a close relationship with ITRI, especially with its CCL lab, using ITRI as a channel for new technologies. Second, Sunplus has established its own investment arm, which invests in foreign and local start-ups in fields that Sunplus thinks it might need in the future. Third, Sunplus directly licenses technologies.

The Taiwanese IC design houses rely not on in-house-developed cutting-edge IP to give them market advantage but on their ability to deliver moderately sophisticated products more speedily, cheaply, and reliably than their competitors. This is true even for companies that pass through the new government-sponsored small-business innovation research (SBIR) program and/or ITRI's incubation center. For example, one interviewee told us: "Our game plan is to focus on the China market. The U.S. is far too technologically advanced for us."[25] Another interviewee, a serial entrepreneur, the founder of a company that was then still in ITRI's incubation center, added, "The customers we aim to have need good chips but not state-of-the-art chips. They care more about reliability, mass production, and unit costs than cutting-edge technology. They are not looking for new innovations." Two other interviewees, from two of the most technologically advanced communication Taiwanese fabless companies, were even more pessimistic about the status of innovative activities in the industry:

> There is only one place in Taiwan that develops new technology and cutting edge products: ITRI. I sometimes miss being there. The only reason I left is because I wanted to get rich.

> I do not know about any real R&D-based company in Taiwan, apart from ITRI, of course. Everybody is interested in revenues and profits. MediaTek is the biggest model of success. The biggest problem for any R&D-based model to work is the stock options–bonus regulations. These pull all the talent into the big manufacturing companies. (interviews, January 30, 2003)

This is equally true for all the companies that have been established by returning immigrants from the United States, including those that have successfully founded and managed new product–based IC design houses in Silicon Valley. Hence the decision to utilize only the second-generation innovation business model has less to do with skills and capabilities than with the institutional structure of the Taiwanese industry and its links with the financial markets.

In sum, the fabless chip sector evolved around a particular business strategy that has relied on the unique institutional features of the Taiwanese IT industrial system as a whole. The main three features are (*a*) the existence of large OEM-ODM companies that sell in foreign markets, which creates a large demand for chips based on second-generation technologies; (*b*) the close proximity of the world's largest and most advanced pureplay foundries; and (*c*) an innovation system with a division of labor between ITRI and the private sector that excels in quick technology transfer and second-generation innovation, while continuously infusing the system with the most recent foreign technologies.

Utilizing this strategy, the IC design subsector provides complementary assets to the Taiwanese OEMs and pureplay foundries. First, it supplies the pureplay foundries with a constant stream of orders in a variety of IC designs, helping them to stay profitable and to extend and maintain some of their own technological capacities. Second, it supplies OEM-ODM manufacturers with the chips they need either to profitably offer solutions for Western OBMs or to compete successfully with Western and Japanese OBMs by lowering their cost structure.

The development of the IC design subsector thus enriches the Taiwanese IT industry with positive feedback, strengthening the Taiwanese position as mid-level supplier within the global IT product networks. Each part of the Taiwanese IT hardware industry—OEM-ODMs, pureplay foundries, and IC design companies—strengthens and is in turn strengthened by the existence, outputs, and demands of the others. Despite this virtuous cycle, or maybe because of it, the IC design industry is unable to develop alternative business models for capturing the higher rents that come from original innovative designs.

We should not, however, discount the magnitude of Taiwanese achievements in IC design. Taiwan, a small and until recently technologically backward society, developed the second-largest IC design industry in the world, far surpassing the South Korean, Japanese, and western European industries. The industry is not only growing but also enhancing the overall competitiveness of the Taiwanese hardware industry. Whether or not there is a move to innovative products, the industry's growth seems secure in the near future.

THE TAIWANESE SOFTWARE INDUSTRY

If the story of the hardware IT industry is one of impressive growth and successful policies, the software industry offers a less sanguine tale of industrial policy and growth. Official statistics are inflated, but even they show the one major failure of the Taiwanese software industry: it is mostly a domestic-oriented industry. Official figures present a picture of rapid growth in sales from NT$22 billion in 1991 to NT$149 billion in 2001, but exports in 2001 amounted only to NT$16 billion, or a little more than $490 million USD, less than 11 percent of total sales. For comparison, the annual export figure for the whole of the Taiwanese software industry is just slightly higher than the quarterly sales of Amdocs, Israel's largest software company. These figures are tiny in comparison with those of the hardware sector, or even with those of the IC design sector alone (for example, MediaTek's sales alone are more than twice as large as even the official export figures of the software industry). Moreover, the annual sale revenues of two of the three largest Taiwanese software product companies, Ulead and Cyberlink, were around $30 million USD in 2003, too small to put them in the league of medium-sized IC design houses in Taiwan, or large software companies in Israel or Ireland. Figure 3.2 compares the rapid growth of exports of the IC design sector, the smallest and latest subsector of the semiconductor industry, with that of the whole software industry, putting this failure in perspective.[26]

The relative failure of the software sector is even more puzzling if we take into account the amount of high-level software development critically needed by the hardware industry, especially the IC design sector. Thus the success of the hardware sector in the development of what is usually termed embedded software, coupled with the global success of a few Taiwanese software companies, shows that the cause of this failure cannot be explained by lack of software programming skills in Taiwan.[27]

With this in mind we can understand why a high-ranking official in MoEA mused in one of our interviews, "Look where we are and where other countries like India, Israel, and Ireland are with their software industry. Nobody heard about them thirty years ago. I must admit that we [the Taiwanese] are not doing very well with software" (interview, May 30, 2001).

In striking contrast to the electronics and semiconductor industries and the positive role played by ITRI, the Institution for Information Industry (III) has no stories to tell of ERSO-like successful spin-offs or any other initiatives spurring the creation of an industry. III has had little positive role in the development of the software industry. Indeed, III can be seen as one of the main obstacles to the industry's development.

K. T. Li provided the impetus behind the establishment of III in 1979. Li hoped that III could play a similar role in software to the one played by ITRI in hardware, and he remained influential behind III for some years after its establishment. Thus III and ITRI were structured in the same way. Moreover, they were established within six years of each other and under the same political leadership. If the structure of the bureaucracy and its policies were the key variable, we would expect a similar industrial outcome. In fact, though, the political process of sectoral industry-state co-evolution moved III and the software industry on a divergent path from that of ITRI and the hardware industry.

Unlike ITRI creation in relation to the development of the hardware industry, III was created after some of the early leading software firms had been established. The private sector, in contrast to the semiconductor industry, was active in the software sector. The agenda and the funding granted to III by the Taiwanese government were vastly different from ITRI's. First, III was asked to promote the software industry. Second, III was given the task of promoting

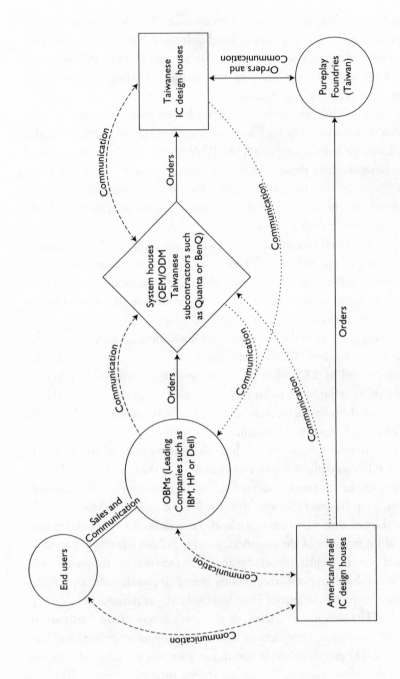

Figure 3.2. Market Relations and Communication Environment of the Taiwanese IC Design Houses

the use of IT and software throughout Taiwan and was asked to help the government with its own computerization. Finally, III was also asked to generate enough revenue to cover most of its activities. The different agendas proved to be in conflict, with the end result that III transformed itself into one of Taiwan's biggest IT consultancies and software houses and has been competing directly with private software firms.[28] Hence the political positioning of III has spurred it to see itself as a "profit center," while at the same time giving it the regulatory and political backing to disregard the needs and lobbying of the Taiwanese private software industry.

The responses of many software firm executives to our questions about the role of the state in the industry's development offer the view of III as the biggest hindrance to the industry's growth. The response of a founder of a financial software company is typical: "The state does not have any positive role; as a matter of fact, III is our greatest competitor. They also compete unfairly. I need to sponsor my R&D from my revenues. They have all their R&D covered by the state" (interview, January 17, 2003). A founder of another software company observed:

> In our seventeen years we had direct conflicts with III only once, so I am very lucky. However, I do not think III is good for the industry. They get government money to help the industry and nothing happens. III do not really care about the industry—they just talk and talk but do not do anything for the industry. They do not even properly do the more simple and straightforward task of consulting the government on policy issues, so policy making is all tangled up. Even in the basic task of changing the perception of the software industry in Taiwan they do nothing. Customers think software and software companies should not be paid because they do not see software as a "real" product. (interview, November 6, 2003)

This view of III is shared not only by those we interviewed in private firms and in industry associations but also by officials of other developmental agencies. One official of an industrial R&D agency responded to a question about the role of III in the software industry's development: "III is a funny organization. It both competes with and tries to assist the local software industry. On a charitable estimate I would say that they compete at least as much as they assist" (interview, January 29, 2003). Another official, a head of a different department, gave a similar response: "I agree that III is a very problematic institution. I think that the problem of III is the confusion or the strange positioning that they are in. They try to compete and help at the same time" (interview, November 4, 2003).

III is well situated to play a role as a facilitator of collective action and organizer of consortia. However, even in this role both researchers and industry leaders criticize III. Noble claims that even in the crucial case of agreeing on a standard for Chinese-writing input-output and internal conversion—a basic need for the software industry's growth—III's actions fostered distrust and hampered the industry's efforts to reach agreement. In the end an international body, on which Taiwan had no influence, settled the issue almost a decade later (Noble 1998, pp. 123–147). This impression of the failure of state efforts is strengthened by our analysis of the software industry. As we shall see, the most successful subsectors are those in which III never intervened.

Structure, Development, and Business Models in the Taiwanese Software Industry

The structure of the Taiwanese software industry reveals a divide between older companies, which are focused on the development of software applications for big organizations and fiercely compete with III, and a newer cohort of companies developing software technologies, most of which were founded after the success of the hardware IT industry in Hsinchu Park. This division tempts one to contend that there are in fact two Taiwanese software industries. However, the reality is more complex.

As we have seen, it is extremely hard to gather precise sales figures on the software industry in Taiwan. Most of the bigger companies, faced with intense competition from III, have branched out into sales and distribution of hardware and even into completely unrelated fields at times of severe need. Even public game-development companies, such as Summit, earn much of their revenues from bundled sales—the sales of their products on top of sales of DVD and other entertainment electronics. Estimating software sales in Taiwan is also complicated by the fact that PC manufacturers have been for many years some of the biggest software developers.

Nevertheless, the picture that emerges is of an industry in which until a decade ago most of the Taiwanese software companies merged both IT consultancy and bespoke development, as well as the sales of specific software systems (such as automation or finance) that were developed as part of earlier work with customers and then packaged. Most of the PC manufacturers were also successful software producers, especially in the 1980s, when each manufacturer had its own slightly different version of the Chinese input-output system, and when most of the classic PC software packages from Western companies, such as spreadsheets, were unavailable in Chinese.

Because III had captured the big governmental contracts, and the big global IT companies were competing directly on big projects, the industry was unable to develop big software houses specializing in customized development. A remark from a founder of one of the companies that managed to survive these times is illuminating:

> Competing with III is like competing with Microsoft. If you compete, you get killed on the spot; if you cooperate, you get less money and you might be killed later, but at least you get some work. However, III always wins more contracts than they can program themselves, so they then subcontract some of them. They will pay me less than what I would get if I could compete on the project in the free market, but I prefer to cooperate with the Microsoft of Taiwan, and not get killed by it. (interview, November 6, 2003)

As a result, most of the industry has evolved around a particular market niche that was neglected or considered too small by III, such as international banking or securities-trading systems. Today many of these companies are realizing that their future lies with mainland China. And here they find that their former relationships as subcontractors of American MNCs in Taiwan are an important asset. For example, a CEO of one of Taiwan's oldest software companies described his decision to move to China:

> The funny thing is that we never wanted to go to China, but our American MNCs partners asked us to come, both HP and Oracle. The best example is HP. They won the whole IT systems project for a big new plant, and they asked us and three other Taiwanese companies to open a China branch and do subcontracting for them. We did that, and before we knew what happened, Oracle asked us to do subcontracting for them when they won a big Chinese state-owned company contract. I think that without the mainland, my company would not have been able to grow at all in the last three years. Only because of China we have a chance to survive. (interview, November 4, 2003)

For the most part, the industry has not been able to develop unique products or strong enough brands to guard their own products when the big software MNCs launched Chinese versions of their products. Thus when Western companies such as Microsoft localized their products for Taiwan and China, Taiwanese products were wiped out of the market.

The one sector that evolved differently is the PC game industry. Unlike other sectors of the software industry, the video game industry had four tremendous advantages that allowed it to thrive in Taiwan. First, III was not at all interested in this sector. Second, video games, unlike many other software products, benefit from certain cultural traits, and Chinese-born gamers were keen on playing "Chinese" games. For example, almost every Taiwanese game company has had a strategy or fantasy–role playing (FRP) game based on the classic tale of the Three Kingdoms. Third, the costs of game development were very low for many years. Most video game companies either started by sponsoring teams of high school students, who developed the games as a hobby on a cost-only basis, or had a mixed development strategy of in-house and semi-independent teams. Fourth, with 7-Eleven and similar popular chains in Taiwan selling local games on the corner of every block, video game companies have had distribution channels that reached every Taiwanese on a daily basis.

It is not surprising that until 2000–2001, video games were deemed by many in both the private and public sectors to be the most successful part of the software industry in Taiwan. All the medium- and large-sized companies, such as Softstar, Summit, Gamania (formerly known as Full Soft), Interserv, and Soft-World, had gone public on the Taiwanese stock exchange in the 2000–2002 period. Since then, the industry has been hard hit, and in 2003 most of the companies that we revisited had either retreated from original game development or were cutting down their development activities to the bare minimum. Apart from the worsening economic situation in Taiwan, the two changes that transformed the business environment of the Taiwanese video game companies were technological: the wide diffusion of CD-read-and-write technology and the rapid emergence of online gaming.

These two technological changes have significantly and swiftly lowered the revenues coming from the sales of PC games, with most but not all of the leading companies reporting sales of tens of thousands of copies of their new games at best, instead of hundreds of thousands of copies. These developments coincide with the maturation of the international gaming industry. The quality and technological sophistication needed to make competitive game titles has drastically raised the costs of development per title. In addition, the Korean gaming industry, for many years the poor and unsophisticated cousin of the Taiwanese industry, was the first to develop online FRP games, winning market share and financial backing and overtaking the quality and technological sophistication of the Taiwanese industry at a critical moment. At the end of 2003 all but one of the extremely successful massive-multiusers-online FRP games running in Taiwan were developed by non-Taiwanese companies.

The Taiwanese video game industry, without the financial resources of the Korean and Western industries, finds itself technologically backward and stuck with business models that are based on low-cost development. It has been unable for the most part to compete. Individually, video game companies do not have the financial resources to regain the technological lead vis-à-vis the Korean industry, and as the industry is widely fragmented, it has been unable to coordinate collective action. A few industry leaders approached III and asked for leadership or help, only to be rebuffed until October 2002. A CEO of one of the biggest companies recounted a tale of a failed attempt to cooperate with III in late 2002:

> The worst of the worst is III. A representative of the video game industry approached the president of III, the new one who promised to change III for the better and help the industry, and asked him to help our sector. Mind you, we are the only sector that was really successful in the Taiwanese software industry. After a few talks his answer came back from his secretary: "This is not III core business; therefore we are not interested." I ask you, "What the hell is their 'core business'?" They say their goal is to help the software industry, not to make profits, but they do not give a damn about anything but making money. (interview, January 20, 2003)

This failure by III is even more surprising because starting in October 2002 the Taiwanese government declared digital content as a high-priority technological area, specifically targeting online games as one of the more promising digital-content sectors. However, both government officials and industry leaders see the digital-content initiative as a failure so far. According to one of the industry's representatives in the initiative:

> This is the latest government fad. They finally realized IP is important. So we sit there for a year, so many important people and so many people from the government, and talk and discuss for hours every week and nothing happens. It is running for over a year now and still nothing happened. Elections are coming in six months' time, so nothing will happen until after the elections because the civil servants are waiting to see who will be their master and are afraid to do anything. (interview, October 30, 2003)

This criticism of the progress of the digital-content initiative for online games was echoed by the responsible minister of state, who contrasted efforts so far with government efforts in the hardware sector: "Nothing much is happening with online games. We basically did nothing; we do not even have a budget. We have to admit that a lot needs to be done with software and digital content. However, we [the government] still think that Taiwan's future is more in hardware" (interview, November 7, 2003).

By the end of 2003, most of the Taiwanese video game companies were already fast retreating from game development. From an industry whose leading companies had operations and sold their own published products throughout the greater China region, the industry was transforming itself to an industry whose core competency is game distribution and resale. This does not mean that two or three of the leading companies will not continue to prosper and grow and develop original games. However, the number of Taiwanese game-developing companies is declining sharply, with no new entrants coming.

In the past few years, a cohort of software companies with new business models have emerged and succeeded. These companies are much more technologically oriented. Their products deal either directly with software technology itself or with new applications of IT technology, like antivirus, optical-character-recognition (OCR), or systems-recovery applications. These companies appeared after the success of the IT hardware industry in Hsinchu Park; indeed, many of them are tightly connected to the industry. There are two types of operations: (*a*) firms supplying the Taiwanese hardware industry with software technology that enables it to add features to its products, differentiating them from the competition, or supplying critical software that the hardware industry would find difficult or prohibitively expensive to get abroad; and (*b*) companies producing products that are directly associated with the software industry itself, such as antivirus products or application-development tools.

One prominent example of a company focusing on software technology itself is Trend Micro, which develops corporate antiviral protection products. In 2006 Trend Micro continued to be one of the largest software security companies in the world, with revenues of $618 million USD in the 2005 fiscal year. Trend was established by Taiwanese, grew in Taiwan, is run by Taiwanese, and still conducts a large share of its activities in Taiwan, but its management felt that it needed to leave Taiwan in order to be globally successful. In 1998 Trend moved its management team and headquarters to Japan and reestablished itself as a publicly traded Japanese company; it is also traded on NASDAQ.

The two most successful software companies that followed more closely a business model of alliance with Taiwan's hardware manufacturers are Ulead and Cyberlink. In 1989 three friends who worked together at III left the institution to try out their own ideas for software development and established Ulead with finance from the Taiwanese scanner manufacturer Microtek. Ulead's first business was to supply OCR and image-processing software to the fast-growing Taiwanese scanner industry. The scanner industry was facing difficulties in securing critical software from American companies. A few years later, realizing that there was no true-color-imaging processing editor for the PC (Adobe was selling its Photoshop software only for Mac at the time), Ulead launched its own product called Photostyler. In 1992 Adobe bought the company that held the copyrights for the technology Ulead was using. Since then Ulead has come out with its own product for the midrange user.

Hoping to use the same OEM model it used with the scanner industry, Ulead wrote software for video imaging for the video-capture-card industry. The Taiwanese video-capture-card industry never took off, but ironically, this proved to be a boon for Ulead, which started to work with foreign manufacturers. Today, apart from its image-processing products, Ulead also develops video- and DVD-processing and authoring software. Ulead sells either directly to private users or through OEM agreements with hardware manufacturers. In 1999 Ulead became the first software company to go public on Taiwan's stock exchange. By 2002 Ulead had sales of more than $30 million USD and operations on all five inhabited continents. In April 2005 Ulead, at the same level of revenues, was bought by InterVideo, a Silicon Valley DVD-multimedia software company founded by Taiwanese immigrants. It is striking that one of the three most successful software product companies in Taiwan has had such small total revenues.

The latest globally successful Taiwanese software company is Cyberlink. Cyberlink directly employs business techniques that its CEO, Alice H. Chang, learned as a top executive at Trend Micro during Trend's rapid growth and IPO period. This is a clear case of diffusion of learning and economic capabilities in the industry. Cyberlink is also the most successful company to be spun off directly from a Taiwanese university lab, attesting to the growing capabilities of Taiwan's computer science academic research.

Jau Huang, Alice H. Chang's husband and the cofounder of the multimedia lab at National Taiwan University, established Cyberlink in 1994 together with four of his students.[29] Encouraged by Chang, then the executive vice president of Trend Micro, the team decided to develop a software product instead of a hardware product. In 1995, using self-financing, Cyberlink was formally founded. The company finished developing its first product, a video (VCD) decoder, in November 1996. In January 1997 Chang stepped in as

CEO and embarked on a strategy of OEM sales to Taiwan's VGA card manufacturers, the world's largest.[30] These OEM agreements gave Cyberlink immediate market recognition, and the company went on to develop a complete
suite of DVD products that now accounts for about 50 percent of the world
market in the PC's DVD multimedia tool niche. Currently Cyberlink sells
multimedia management tools and development tools for electronic training
(e-training) and e-learning solutions. In 2000 Cyberlink went public on the
Taiwanese stock exchange. In fiscal year 2002 Cyberlink had sales of more
than $35 million USD, reaching $75 million by 2005. Most of Cyberlink's
sales originate with its DVD products produced through OEM agreements
with PC and notebook manufacturers in the United States, Taiwan, Japan,
and Europe.

In short, the Taiwanese software industry today seems to have a dual structure. On the one side are the older private companies dealing with business
solutions that need to directly compete with III, which has become the biggest
business software solutions provider. On the other side are the younger and
more successful companies that are much more technologically oriented, developing in market niches in which III has no dealing, with a few of them beginning to have true global reach. Overall, the Taiwanese software industry is
still mostly oriented to the domestic market. Only a few companies possess
the necessary capabilities and skills to develop products and services for the
global market. Relative to the Taiwanese hardware sector or compared with
software in countries such as Israel or Ireland, Taiwan's software industry is a
stark example of a stage 2 failure—the inability of the state to change its roles
in tandem with the industry's growth.

GOVERNMENT ACTIONS, INSTITUTIONS, AND
MARKET STRUCTURE IN THE DIVERGENT
GROWTH OF THE IT HARDWARE AND
SOFTWARE SECTORS IN TAIWAN

We can now position Taiwan on our explanatory framework to gain understanding of the institutional systems in which the Taiwanese industry evolved.
First and foremost, we notice that the Taiwanese state has opted to deeply intervene in the IT-industry development path by encompassing the R&D-
creating agents within its bureaucratic structure, as well as by trying to in-
tensely influence the industry's technological development decisions. The
Taiwanese state initiated policies with a clear division of labor between private

industry and the public sector. The public sector has been conducting the lion's share of R&D and then diffusing the results, developed to the stage of working prototypes, to the industry. The state also sees itself as the proper locus for making decisions on which R&D projects to pursue and which technologies to develop and obtain. This is almost in direct opposition to the role played by the state in both Ireland and Israel. A recent example is the current system-on-chip (SoC) development program.

The SoC program is the last in a long tradition of technological capability upgrading programs. It is organized in three discrete stages.

1. The government focuses on specific products it thinks that the Taiwanese IT industry needs to be able to manufacture in the midfuture.
2. The universities and ITRI are asked to propose which intellectual property and technologies are necessary to develop these products, and how they are going to develop these technologies and transfer them to the industry.
3. The universities and ITRI implement the development and transfer planned in stage 2.

Hence, in a way similar to the past, the envisioned role of private industry in this innovation capability–development program is limited to one of developing products decided upon by governmental officials using technologies developed by the public sector.

The SoC program also exemplifies the different role for universities envisioned by the Taiwanese state.[31] Whereas in Israel the universities have for many years been geared toward academic research and have been given wide academic freedom in defining and pursuing their goals, in Taiwan the universities have been viewed mainly as skilled labor–creating mechanisms. This view is especially evident in the new career-path and tenure regulations.[32] Recently the envisioned role of the universities has somewhat changed, and the government has realized that the university system should be seen as a key agent in the development of new technological and innovational capabilities.[33] Nonetheless, the overarching technological goals of Taiwan are still defined by the state, and academia is seen as a subsidiary tool that is used to achieve these aims. The universities, therefore, are urged to develop their faculty and departments in accordance with the state's S&T industrial policies. Part of the SoC program is a detailed development of the technological capability of the university sector, sponsoring eighty-five new faculty positions in predefined subfields of specialization.[34]

Another example of the state's direct intervention in the industry's technological development path is the R&D tax-incentive program of one of the main governmental investment vehicles, the Industrial Development Bureau of the Ministry of Economic Affairs (IDB). This program gives tax incentives and other benefits only to companies that make products that are specified in extensive detail by the IDB itself. The products are gathered in a list based on market research by the IDB every two years. Therefore the list does not include truly innovative technologies whose market is unpredictable or does not yet exist. Moreover, the program specifies that the tax incentives are to be given only to companies that control the whole production chain—that is, from the design to the manufacturing and sales—and only with products that, according to an official, "are not in niche markets that are so innovative that we cannot predict the future so we cannot really help" (interview, May 28, 2001).

Various other government programs finance industrial R&D. In fact, several of our interviewees from the major developmental agencies complained that Taiwan has too many small agencies and programs, each with its own bureaucracy, resulting in a policy hodgepodge and confusion. Of these programs the three that have been most relevant to the IT industry are the SBIR, the Technology Development Program (TDP), and the Leading Product Development Program (LPDP), all of which are sponsored by MoEA Department of Industrial Technology (DOIT). Aside from SBIR, most programs assist mainly in the development of products that are based on some R&D effort, disregarding whether they are new to world markets or not. Most of the grants to IT hardware companies assist them in pursuing second-generation product innovation and do not provide incentives for a riskier approach.

Moreover, although DOIT has been leading the way in fostering more R&D activities in the private sectors in the past three years, it started to channel grants directly to private companies only in 1998. DOIT started to channel a small percentage of the funding formerly given to the public research institutions (ITRI and III) directly to the private industry only after intense lobbying.[35] Both the SBIR and the TDP are staffed with ITRI personnel who are seconded to the programs. Indeed, according to our interviewees, around one-third of the IT companies that are funded through SBIR also have contract research relationships with ITRI.

These constraints are still more severe in the case of software R&D. For example, thus far software is not even included in the IDB's tax-incentives scheme. During the interviews many software company executives complained that apart from a brief period in the late 1990s, before the latest government budgetary cuts, they have not been able to get any grants. In addition, the Taiwanese state policy of focusing on specific niches is not appropriate to the current state of the Taiwanese software industry: it denies many promising software companies access to R&D capital, even while hardly promoting the creation of new companies in the targeted niches. Representatives of software companies that did manage to secure state grants complained that the bureaucratic regulations forced them to spend more money on getting the grant than the grant itself provided. Those that did get the grants in the late 1990s, though, told us that as other sources of financing were lacking, these grants were critical in helping them finish their first R&D projects.

In sum, even today government policies define a strict division of labor in R&D between state and industry. The state assumes control of research-and-development activities, from screening the technological development path to creating prototypes of specific products. Furthermore, the state focuses on specific technologies up to the level of particular product specification. Our theoretical approach suggests that the likely influence of such policies is that private companies have little incentive or scope to develop innovative R&D capabilities. The end result is the continuation of the same capability-development trajectory that the Taiwanese IT developed so far: focusing on second-generation innovation, integrated design, and process-and-manufacturing innovation.

Financial Constraints

The manner by which the Taiwanese state regulated and interacted with the financial markets also strengthened the tendency of the Taiwanese IT industry to focus on the development of a narrower set of innovational capabilities. There are two main financial constraints on IT companies that wish to develop new innovation-based products in Taiwan, one in the beginning of a firm's life, and one toward the end of its development stage. The first constraint is the almost utter lack of finance in the beginning stages of firms' development process for technologically cutting-edge R&D. The second constraint derives from the fact that the Taiwanese stock-option system gives enormous advantages to companies that have already gone public, not only granting them stronger financial capabilities but also giving them an almost total stranglehold on hiring the best engineering graduates.

The special advantages enjoyed by public companies to acquire human and financial capital may be due in part to Taiwan's stock-option regulations. These prohibit companies, both public and private, from giving stock options to employees (one of the main attractions that a cash-starved start-up can offer to entice new employees in the United States, Israel, and Ireland). However, the same regulations allow companies that have already gone public to give actual stocks (not merely options) to their employees at a sharply discounted rate under the profit-sharing system. Moreover, these stock bonuses are taxable only at the time of sale and only on the nominal par value (set by law at NT$10 per share no matter what the market price is), which amounts to an enormous tax-free bonus. According to TSMC's annual reports, the average profit per TSMC employee through stock per year was more than NT$1.5 million in 1996 and reached more than NT$2.5 million in 1998; engineers with master's degrees earned much more than the average. A CFO of a leading IC design house calculated that after four years an engineer with a master's degree would get an annual bonus worth about $300,000 USD; a good annual salary for the same employee stands today at $18,000 USD (IPC interview with IC company's CFO, November 5, 2003). Hence a graduate of a good university with an advanced degree who wants to become well off need only join a public company to be virtually assured of reaching that goal in a few years. Not surprisingly, new private companies find it very difficult to recruit graduates of the top engineering schools.

Consequently, the regulations regarding Taiwanese employees' stock options motivate new companies to seek the shortest and surest route to an IPO. In order to go public on the main exchange, a company needs to display five years of disclosure statements showing constant profits.[36] Hence most Taiwanese IT companies use a business model that assures quick revenues, in contrast to one employed by innovative product–based firms that involve incurring a few years of heavy losses during their R&D phase before sales. In addition, significant state restrictions dissuade companies from having an IPO on a foreign stock exchange.

The lack of available funds for early-stage financing is due to the way the Taiwanese venture capital industry was conceived and developed. The VC industry was created as part of an initiative of K. T. Li, who viewed VCs mainly as a missing pool of finance, not as a distinct industry.[37] Moreover, Li's and subsequent governmental initiatives have taken great care to make sure that the Taiwanese VC industry stays Taiwanese, devoting all their attention to motivating local investor participation. The main mechanism by which the state spurs the creation of the VC industry and maintains its existence is the tax credit. In the beginning the industry was heavily regulated, and many of the main VC funds had ties to various KMT investment vehicles, such as Kung-Kwang and Century. By 2004, according to the Taiwanese VC association, foreign capital still amounted to less than 7 percent.[38]

Looking at private VCs, we found that, unlike their Israeli counterparts, and even more than their Irish counterparts, most of them prefer to invest only in the later stages of development, and only after firms have already proven their success by becoming profitable. There are several institutional reasons for the conservative behavior of VCs. First, by law VCs in Taiwan must be registered companies, not limited partnerships.[39] This limits their ability to invest in young companies in two ways: (*a*) as a registered company a VC is not allowed to invest in a venture that is not already registered, ruling out true seed funding, and (*b*) as a registered company the VC—that is, the individual who acts as a venture capitalist, who in the United States and Europe is called the general partner—must submit all his or her investment decisions to the board of the VC firm.

Taiwanese VCs also are more reticent because of the sources of their capital and the education of the VCs themselves. Most VC funds have strong ties to one individual or company and operate in accordance with the sponsor's investment strategy, which is usually more risk averse and tends to select firms with established business models that the sponsors can easily understand. This is especially evident in software, in which most Taiwanese VC companies do not invest at all.[40] The VCs themselves are drawn mostly from the financial industry or the traditional industries. Hence they do not have intimate knowledge of IT, and prefer less risky endeavors.

Last, but at least as important, we must remember that VCs' main aim is to make profit on their investment in a limited amount of time. The structure and listing regulations of the Taiwanese Stock Exchange, where most of the exits take place, favor companies that already have been profitable for a few years.[41] This, in turn, motivates the VCs to invest in companies with a business model that is focused on achieving large sales figures without a long loss-incurring R&D phase. Even when Taiwanese VCs do invest in young Taiwanese companies, they usually prefer companies that follow the well-trodden path of producing products based on second-generation technologies with the prospect of near-term revenues.

Weaknesses and Strengths of the Taiwanese
IT Industry

The Taiwanese industrial institutional system and the opportunity structure it gives companies was heavily influenced, on the hardware side, by the explicit S&T industrial policies designed to develop an industry supplying critical components and design and manufacturing services to MNCs. The current innovation system of the IT industry motivates new companies to pursue known business strategies, and limits the ability of companies that try to truly innovate.

On the positive side the Taiwanese system, with the existence of world leading OEM-ODMs and pureplay foundries, supplies virtually infinite opportunities for small new companies that follow either the second-generation innovation or OEM-ODM models. Furthermore, the economic and management skills that are needed in order to profitably run those kinds of operations are abundant. The Taiwanese industrial system is richly endowed in the "specific economic competencies" needed to succeed in second-generation innovation-based design and OEM-ODM operations (Carlsson 1995, Carlsson and Eliason 1994).

The whole Taiwanese system of innovation is primed to give private companies constant access to new technologies from abroad. In the past few years this kind of technology channeling has become one of ITRI's main roles. ITRI, especially its Computer and Communication Lab (CCL), changed from being the leader and initiator of the industry, especially in semiconductors, into being a supporting actor in the 1990s, particularly as the main provider of R&D services in the industrial system, as well as an important channel for foreign technology. For example, every IC design company executive interviewed, when asked whether any company conducts technological cutting-edge R&D, replied that the only organization in Taiwan involved in these activities is ITRI and its CCL lab. Top officials of CCL attest that the lab is only too aware of the effect its technology-transfer programs and this division of labor have on the incentives of private industry to develop original product–innovation capabilities.

On the other hand, a company that wants to innovate faces significant obstacles, from the lack of finance, the difficulty in recruiting highly skilled personnel, and the relative scarcity of business and management skills to run a Silicon Valley–like operation. All of these problems are augmented by the fact that if geographical proximity to customers and suppliers helps companies to sell to or become an OEM-ODM company, the distance, both physical and cultural, from their main market for innovative products, the United States, makes their operation more complex and more expensive.

In software the unsuccessful approach of III and the industry's stagnated growth have strengthened our hypothesis that unlike the preaching of the old development school, a too heavy–handed intervention by the state without a dialogue with private industry will not lead to industrial growth. The Taiwanese software sector shows that in the case of RIB industries, attempts by the state not only to lead the industry but to be the industry are doomed. III is a clear case not only of wrong positioning of the developmental agency but of a failure of the developmental agency to manage the co-evolution processes and the unavoidable diminishing of its own power with the growth of private industry. The divergent paths of the software industry and III on the one hand and the hardware industry and ITRI on the other strengthen our argument that structure and timing alone are not the explanation: the sectoral politics of co-evolution are.

However, while III has played an inhibiting role in the development of the software industry, other reasons exist for the particular development path taken by this sector. First, one of Taiwan's main industries has been PC manufacturing; each of those companies was also busily producing software for its own machines and hence preventing the development of a large standardized market that could support independent product-oriented software firms. Second, until the early nineties, partly due to internal competition within the state apparatus and III failure, there were no standards for Chinese input-output and internal conversion (Noble 1998). This spurred many companies to produce Chinese programs to simulate popular English packages, all of which were practically wiped out as soon as the Western companies published a Chinese version of their package. Third, both the private hardware industry and the government saw software not as an independent industry but as a service component needed by other industries. This handicapped the industry in two ways: (*a*) software has never been on an equal footing with hardware in the competition for government budget and grants, and (*b*) software companies had difficulties selling pure software solutions for reasonable prices in the market.

In this chapter I have analyzed the development of the IT industry and the co-evolution of state-industry relations in Taiwan. Following the theoretical framework developed in the first chapter, we can see that the Taiwanese have been very active and that the development of the local industry has used a fundamentally different strategy from that of Israel or Ireland.

In Taiwan the state devised specific solutions to the industrial R&D market failure and the questions of the skills-and-knowledge acquisition by establishing the loci of R&D firmly within the state structure and opting for an active developmental strategy where the state tries to manage and control as much as it can of the industry's technological development path.

Accordingly Taiwan formulated its policies quite differently from Israel, establishing two public research institutes, ITRI and III, to lead its foray into the IT industry. Nevertheless, Taiwan has also supplied funds for industrial R&D, and the state encouraged, even if within its structure, R&D activities on a wide spectrum of technologies. However, in contrast to the development of the hardware industry—for which ITRI saw as its ultimate goal the creation of a thriving private industry and has successfully managed its own diminishing role as the industry grew—the approach to software has been unsuccessful. From its inception, III tried to maximize its control and financial resources, directly competing with private industry. In contrast to ITRI, III has been reluctant to see its power diminish and has continuously competed with the industry. In addition, III focused its strategies and policy initiatives around its own growth, not that of private industry. Thus the Taiwanese software industry presents a case of stage two failure: unwillingness of the state to relinquish its own power over the sectoral industrial system and move from hierarchical to networked governance.

On the local-global front, Taiwan has aimed to help the local industry to excel in supplying components, and manufacturing-and-design services, to the IT industry's production networks. Until recently Taiwan had steered a middle course with regard to the activities of foreign companies in Taiwan. Taiwan encouraged foreign companies to establish manufacturing facilities in the country. But unlike Ireland, Taiwan then pushed these companies to acquire more and more components locally and to transfer the necessary skills and know-how to local suppliers. In addition, Taiwan has been encouraging local companies to be publicly listed on the Taiwan Stock Exchange and not on foreign stock exchanges. It has been targeting almost solely the local financial community as the source for the IT industry's venture capital.

Of our three cases Taiwan's bureaucracy has been an almost ideal-type Asian Weberian-Technocrat model. Recruitment is styled on the Japanese model, where exams screen the candidates into different management and career patterns (Kim et al. 1995). However, unlike in both Israel and Ireland, almost all of the top personnel of the development agencies and ministries have Ph.D.s in various engineering disciplines. In addition, all the ministers responsible for industrial development, telecommunications, and science-and-technology policies have had doctoral degrees in engineering, before and after democratization. Furthermore the state, already relatively well equipped with scientific experts in its decision-making apparatus, opted to acquire the necessary skills and knowledge for IT industrial development by encompassing the industrial technology–creating agents within its bureaucratic structure. These features of the civil service, coupled with its control over both knowledge and finance for many years, led to a particular mode of embeddedness and state-industry co-evolution process, which is significantly different from Israel's and Ireland's.

Taiwan's IT industry developed to become an enormously successful hardware industry in which the first leading firms have focused on supplying components and OEM manufacturing services to foreign companies. This gave rise to an industrial system, which focuses on second-generation, process, and manufacturing innovation, with a division of labor between the state and private firms. The state conducts most of the early technology screening and R&D, and the private companies focus more on final product development. Most of the firms are supplying components and design and manufacturing services to the IT industry's global production networks.

However, the weaknesses of such a system are rooted in the same features that led to its success: in Taiwan both the scope and the resources granted to private firms to conduct R&D are limited. There are no incentives for private companies to develop their own sophisticated R&D, technological screening, or product-innovation capabilities. Companies in the Taiwanese IT industrial system are by and large motivated to specialize in final product development and integrated design. The state grants little scope for private companies to participate and develop capabilities in applicative, not to mention generic or basic, research.[42] As a result the private industry in Taiwan developed limited R&D and technological screening skills, with almost no attempt to develop new product–innovation capabilities.

Chapter 4 A Misunderstood
"Miracle": The State and
the Growth of the IT
Industry in Ireland

Trying to induce private entrepreneurship in Ireland during the 1980s made me feel like I was part of the old lobster joke: A young man goes to the beach, he sees an old fisherman with two untied lobsters in a very low bucket. He comes to the fisherman and tells him, "Sir, your lobsters are not tied and the bucket is very low; you have to tie them or they will run away." And the fisherman answers, "Dear lad, do not worry, these are Irish lobsters! As soon as one of them almost makes it to freedom the other jumps and drags him back down."

—*A former executive of the IDA's Enterprise Development Plan*

If one nation's economic performance in the 1990s has inspired a revolution in international perception, that nation is Ireland. As late as 1995 the common perception of Ireland's economic performance was one of a continuous failure, which doomed Ireland to be the perpetual basketcase of Europe (Guiomard 1995).[1] Less than four years later, sick Ireland seemed to have become the roaring Celtic Tiger (Breathnach 1998, MacSharry and White 2001, O'Hearn 1998, Sweeny 1999). Such Irish software companies as Iona in middleware, Smartforce and Riverdeep in education, or Trintech and Baltimore in data security not only achieved global success but also made their founders and many of their employees rich when they publicly listed on NASDAQ. This success made software the first industry in Irish history to create such a virtuous cycle of entrepreneurship, and helped to transform even the Irish people's perception of themselves.

Indeed, Ireland has become the most invigorated economy of western Europe, a model for the EU's new entrants, with one of the world's most successful IT industries. This achievement has been attributed largely to the Irish developmental agencies that, so it is argued, promoted this accelerated growth by utilizing a series of industrial and S&T policy initiatives. Moreover, this impressive feat has been achieved while both politicians and bureaucrats have strongly adhered to a neoliberal interventionist ideology, an ideology significantly different from Israel's or Taiwan's.

However, even a brief analysis of the Irish IT industry reveals dissonance between the operations of the foreign multinational corporations (MNCs) and those of the indigenous industry. On one hand, the MNCs, a cornerstone of Irish industrial policy since the 1950s, are thriving and delivering great economic growth. Dell, an American MNC, has just surpassed Microsoft, another American MNC, and become the biggest Irish exporter, singlehandedly responsible for 5.8 percent of Irish GDP in 2003.[2] This is an impressive statistic, and shows that even with rising costs, Ireland is still central to the global strategy of leading IT MNCs. However, neither Dell nor Microsoft, together accounting for about 10 percent of Irish GDP, has significant high–added-value activities, such as R&D and product design, in Ireland. This leads many commentators to suspect that behind the impressive Irish GDP and trade figures lies even more impressive showmanship in the form of transfer pricing accounting, utilizing Ireland's low corporate tax regime and the availability of a well-educated labor force.[3]

On the other hand, in the indigenous sector, it is the software industry that has reached global prominence, not the hardware and electronic-manufacturing sector favored by the Irish FDI-based policy. Furthermore, while the state claims great credit in sponsoring the growth of the software sector, it has started to sponsor it systematically only after a few Irish-owned companies achieved global success. Moreover, these state programs appeared to suffer from a slight misconception in regard to their goals and methods, especially in the past four years.[4] The result is that the industry's growth has been brought to almost a complete halt since 2001, with almost no new companies managing to shore up annual revenues of more than $2 million.

Nonetheless, Ireland's state-led transformation from a country that in the

1950s had the least-educated workforce in western Europe to one of the world's top IT producers at the end of the 1990s is nothing but miraculous. Hence we have to suspect that this picture of dissonance is evidence of a misunderstanding—a misunderstanding of what exactly happens in the Irish miracle, and a misunderstanding of what was, and what should be, the role of the state in the development of the indigenous industry.

Utilizing our theoretical framework and comparing Ireland to Israel and Taiwan, in this chapter I offer an interpretation of this dual misconception. What are the causes behind this transformation? What enabled Ireland, the laggard of western Europe, to become the EU's IT industry "shining light" in the time span of one generation? And what are the weaknesses, strengths, and generalizability of the Irish experience?

Throughout this analysis I make the following arguments: first, both the IT industry and the Irish S&T industrial policies evolved within a political system in which the state has had one overarching goal—job creation—a significantly different circumstance than in Israel and Taiwan. In both Taiwan and Israel the primary goal of their respectively very different S&T policies was the creation of new industries. Job creation was only one of the derivative aims of state efforts. This intrinsic difference in policy aims led Ireland to a specific process of state-industry co-evolution with markedly different outcomes in terms of the IT industry's capabilities, structure, and position within the global production networks from those of Taiwan and Israel.

The focus on job creation led the Irish state, following an ideology of "neoliberal interventionalism," to develop an FDI-based industrialization policy. The Irish neoliberal interventionalist ideology is based on two conflicting principles around which the Irish state has been formulating its economic and industrial policies since 1958. On one side, the state, in the levels of both government and the developmental agencies, possesses a strong free-market ideology. On the other side, it also sees a large role for government in enhancing the competitiveness of Ireland and strategically managing its growth. This ideology is radically different from those of Israel and Taiwan, where the state's ideology, until very recently, was a variant of market socialism.

The state, led, from the late 1950s until the early 1990s by the autonomous governmental agency created specifically for the purpose—the Industrial Development Authority (IDA)—was focusing its attention on bringing MNCs to open manufacturing plants in Ireland and on upgrading the physical and educational infrastructure. Throughout this period the Irish state paid relatively little attention to the development of industrial R&D activities in general and indigenous IT industry in particular.[5] Moreover, the state, true to its neoliberal ideology, did not apply pressure on the MNCs to embed with the local industry.[6] This lack of interest in the particular needs of rapid innovation–based industry, coupled with only minimal attempts of the IDA to nurture, embed itself, and network with Irish-owned industry, hurt the early development of the Irish IT industry, in particular the hardware sector.

Even in the 1980s and 1990s, after the IDA and its successors, Forfas, IDA Ireland, and Forbairt/Enterprise Ireland, started their active involvement in the creation of the indigenous IT industry, they were neither technologically savvy nor deeply embedded within the IT industry, nor, for many years, did they view indigenous IT industry development as a task of creating rapid innovation–based industry. Industrial policy has been planned as a derivative of the goal to enhance employment through the creation and growth of enterprises broadly defined. Only in 1991, when industry pressure and the availability of EU funds led to the creation of a new specific subunit within the IDA—the National Software Directorate, whose employees were recruited directly from industry—did the state start to pay continuous attention to the particular needs of R&D-based IT industry. Yet still the policy focused almost solely on software.[7]

Accordingly, my second argument is that the case of the indigenous IT hardware industry in Ireland has been a clear case of stage one failure—the inability or unwillingness of the state to facilitate and participate in the growth of the indigenous hardware sector and its networks.

Interestingly, software was the recipient of focused state policy specifically because it was defined as a tradable service and not as an industry. During the 1980s, with Ireland once again in severe economic crisis, the IDA changed its policies in a few critical domains. One of the changes was to step up the indigenous industry–oriented activity with the creation of the Enterprise Development Program (EDP). The second change was to create a new focus on tradable services on both the indigenous and FDI-based sides of its operations, with software quickly becoming the prominent sector of this new policy.[8] Seen as a service, however, these policies did not take into full account the particular needs of the software sector as an R&D-intensive industry. S&T industrial policies were enacted only after the industry achieved worldwide success. Therefore my interpretation of the role of the Irish state is much less sanguine than that of some writers, such as Sean O'Riain, MacSharry, and others, while at the same time unlike O'Hearn, I still view the state as the critical, and positive, actor in the Irish economic miracle (MacSharry and White 2001, O'Hearn 1998, O'Riain 2004, Sweeny 1999).

HISTORICAL BACKGROUND AND THE
BEGINNING OF THE IT INDUSTRY

After gaining independence, the Republic of Ireland passed through two almost complete U-turns in its industrial policy, and a subtler, but arguably at least as important, transformation since the beginning of the 1990s. Starting with its independence in 1921 and for the first decade of its existence, after conceding to England most of the industrial base, which was concentrated in the northern counties around Belfast, the Irish republic was almost solely an agriculture-based economy. Led by William T. Cosgrave of the Cumann Na nGaedheal party, the newly established republic followed an economic policy focusing solely on the agriculture sector, and was fiercely free trade in its economic ideology. Patrick Hogan, the then minister for agriculture, is famous for describing this policy as "helping the farmer who helped himself and letting all the rest go to the devil" (Haughton 2000). The main elements of this policy were free trade, parity of the Irish currency with the English pound sterling, low taxes, and low and modest government spending and intervention. This policy gave the Irish an almost unbeatable claim to the title of the most conservative revolutionaries in history.[9]

In 1932, in the midst of the global depression, staging a major political transformation in Ireland, Fianna Fáil—the republican or nationalist party— won the elections.[10] Fianna Fáil, led by Eamon de Valera, with Sean Lemass serving by his side as minister for industry and commerce, made the first complete reconstruction of Ireland's economic policy and devised a highly nationalistic policy based on the ideal of an autarkic market. Free trade was abolished, high tariffs were put in place, and a proxy economic war was waged for a very high economic price against England over land annuities. While some debate still exists on whether these economic policies were truly damaging to Ireland or only slightly so, one fact remains clear. The economic gap between Ireland and the United Kingdom grew, and so did the gap between the North of Ireland and the Irish Republic. Moreover, net emigration continued at an alarming pace and an overall pessimism about the future of the republic as an independent state was deeply felt.[11] At that time, at the request of Sean Lemass—who became prime minister (taoiseach) after de Valera—Ken Whitaker, Ireland's most prominent civil servant and the general secretary of the Ministry of Finance, published in 1958 Ireland's first comprehensive economic policy document, the celebrated *Economic Policy* (SO 1958a).

In this report, Whitaker devises the main points that continue to shape Irish economic policy to this day: export-oriented industrial policy tied with free trade and conceptualization of Ireland's main economic threat as severe unemployment leading to alarming large net emigration.[12] It is important to put Irish unemployment in context in order to understand the severity of the Irish situation, and the long-established national preoccupation with jobs. For example, even throughout the 1980s and until 1997 Irish national unemployment rates were higher than 10 percent, reaching 15 percent throughout most of the period, with unemployment outside the Dublin metropolitan area significantly higher. Moreover, these high rates continued even with exceptionally high rates of emigration throughout the same period. By 1991, for example, 20 percent of the Irish male aged 15–19 in 1986 had left the country, and in 1989 alone 1.1 percent of the Irish population emigrated in search of jobs (Walsh 1999).

The publication of Whitaker's *Economic Policy* also marks the crystallization of the Irish neoliberal interventionist ideology. The main goal of the first economic program and of all those that followed has been job creation. Since 1958 there have been three basic elements in Irish economic policy: provision of economic incentives and low corporate tax rates to induce industrial development and investment, transition to free trade, and—the cornerstone of Irish industrial policy until the mid-1990s—attraction of MNCs (mostly American) to locate export-oriented manufacturing activities in Ireland. The most important vehicle for institutionalizing this policy was the strengthening of the Industrial Development Authority, as an autonomous agency responsible for job creation through industrialization. The IDA mandate was to create more jobs with the aim of decreasing the cost per job created through time.

While not focusing on the MNCs sector in its inception, the IDA quickly adopted FDI-based industrialization as the main focus of Irish industrial policy. Using the yardstick of job creation, one can understand the lure of bringing large corporations that could promise the almost instantaneous creation of substantial and quantifiable numbers of jobs, a situation in which employment creation–tied grants make sense to both parties.[13] The IDA rapidly grew in its importance and influence throughout the years and transformed itself into a full "one-stop shop" for attracting and locating MNCs.

In doing so the IDA utilized a double strategy. On one side targeting and approaching MNCs, employing a wide array of techniques to befriend their senior executives, the IDA operated as a marketing agency that sold "Ireland" to MNCs, especially in the United States. The IDA quickly established a network of foreign offices whose job was to create long-term relationships with companies (many times when these companies were still in their early growth phase) that would eventually result in these companies' opening their European facilities in Ireland. The IDA quickly moved to target sectors and internally employed a set of targets based on the number of jobs created and companies moved in each sector.

On the second front, the IDA was busily orchestrating the construction of the infrastructural and financial benefits Ireland could offer to the incoming MNCs. Ireland, like Taiwan, claims to have been the first state to open a duty-free export processing zone, around Shannon International Airport in 1958. Moreover, soon thereafter many of these tax incentives were applied to the whole republic. In 1958 the Export Profit Tax Relief provided 100 percent tax relief on export profit growth—that is, a full tax relief for new export-oriented facilities. In the beginning these policies were similar to Taiwan's. However, in 1964 the neoliberal interventionist ideology of Ireland sharply moved Ireland down a different path. All restrictions on foreign ownership and reparation of profits were eliminated, no pressures were put on MNCs to source locally, and the idea of demanding, or even asking, MNCs to transfer knowledge to local component suppliers was not even floated.

As part of making itself into a one-stop shop for MNCs, the IDA became the biggest industrial land developer and owner in Ireland, and took it upon itself to cater to the needs of the MNCs even after they had already moved to the country, representing their interests within the Irish state. Unlike local enterprises, MNCs coming to Ireland have been offered land, complete factories, and one centralized agency that represents the MNCs in all their dealings with other state and local agencies.

The IDA reached the zenith of its power in the 1980s. Not only was the IDA formally semi-independent (defined as a public agency, it was not part of the civil service), which allowed it to act as a bridge between other governmental ministries and departments, but its policy domain also included everything that related to industrial development broadly defined. Its strong political connection to MNCs and responsibility over local industry gave it an immense political clout. This was especially true in the period until the early 1990s, when the IDA was seen as effective in job creation—the national mission at the time.

The fact that the IDA was responsible for the recruitment of MNCs as well as one of the largest landowners in Ireland was especially important. In the context of the Irish electoral system—a single-transferable-vote system in which Ireland is divided into districts, each electing three to five members of the Dáil—the IDA was perceived to have significant influence on MNCs' ultimate location decision within Ireland. Thus in terms of bringing the "pork" back home to specific constituencies, IDA's decisions carried a lot of weight on the economic future of specific localities, and accordingly on the future of their elected officials. To further enhance its political muscle, the IDA was actively organizing the local managers of the MNCs into a coherent lobbying group around its policy initiatives (O'Riain 1999). The IDA also benefited by having internal cohesion and extremely high-skilled personnel. The agency recruited the top high school graduates into a long career pattern within it, in which they were also given opportunities to acquire higher education. Hence it was stuffed with highly skilled, very motivated, and extremely loyal personnel who were able to use the IDA's semi-independence to make the agency into a crucial policy entrepreneur by utilizing the structural holes of the Irish bureaucracy to attain its own goals by connecting different organizations with weak social ties (Burt 1992, Granovetter 1973).

This policy turnaround, coupled with the MNC-focused industrial policy, followed by membership in the European Community since 1973 and entry into the European Monetary System in 1979, led to relative economic growth until the 1980s. However, while manufacturing output growth was quite stable throughout the years, employment growth stayed slow and even took a dip in the 1980s. Moreover, the macro-level figures hide a negative facet of Irish economic performance until the 1990s: the huge jobs turnaround, as a large number of jobs were lost, especially in Irish-owned firms.[14] That is, at the same time many jobs were created a very high number of jobs were destroyed. Consequently, for many Irish the prospects of stable job tenure, and with it secure economic prosperity, remained low.

Building the Human Infrastructure: The Buildup of the Irish Education System

At the same time, Ireland was passing through a much more subtle transformation, a change arguably at least as important as any for the future growth of the IT industry. Within two generations Ireland went from being the western

European country possessing the least-educated workforce to a nation with one of the most highly educated young workforces in the world.

Until 1966 less than 50 percent of the Irish population enjoyed education above the sixth grade. However, that situation quickly changed after the minister of education, Donogh O'Malley, following a heated debate started by a 1965 OECD sponsored survey, *Investment in Education,* decreed that second-level education was to be given free to all Irish children. While publicly Lemass conveyed utter surprise at the move, some argue that O'Malley had the blessing of Lemass, who hoped to circumvent a public debate in which the Ministry of Finance might delay or prevent this change from taking place. In an interview, Ken Whitaker, then the general secretary of the Ministry of Finance, strengthened this assumption, stating that he felt a need to protest only to find that Lemass not only was approving of O'Malley's "surprise" decree but was quite prepared for it.[15]

The OECD influence was also critical in the early 1960s in the establishment of the regional technical colleges, which have been recently upgraded to institutes of technologies (OECD 1965, 1969). This was the first in a series of changes that overhauled the Irish higher education system, first in the 1960s and continuing in more vigorous fashion in the 1980s after the IDA included education policy in its overall view of the supply side of Irish industrial policy.[16] In the 1950s only 33 percent of Irish school leavers finished secondary education, and only 10 percent had any experience of third-level education.[17] By the mid-1990s these levels had grown to 80 percent and 50 percent, respectively, and the percentage of under-twenty-eight-year-olds attending college in Ireland is one of the highest among OECD countries (Breathnach 1998).

The role of the IDA in this transformation was immense. In the 1980s, when its FDI-attracting focus changed from manufacturing activities to more technologically advanced activities in general and the IT industry in particular, the IDA realized that Ireland needed a much more technologically skilled workforce in order to attract the MNCs it targeted. Using its influence, the IDA first managed to bridge the gap between the universities and the government that had delayed the improvement of the higher education system, especially research, for more than a decade. This feud between, on the one hand, UCD and Trinity, the two prominent Dublin-based colleges, and, on the other, the Irish government, began in the 1960s. The government tried to force the merger of the two institutions and to establish a firmer control over the merged entity. The plan was quickly abandoned, but animosity between the political elite and the two leading Irish universities remained until the

1980s. In retrospect, this bungled move by the government was one of the most important to the creation of the Irish software industry. Immediately after the government announced the plan, under which Trinity's engineering faculty was to disband and move to UCD, Trinity moved to counter it by creating and rapidly expanding a new engineering department of computer science in 1969. UCD followed suit by expanding its own computer science program located in the sciences. These two departments became crucial to the development of the Irish IT industry in later years.

Second, the IDA managed to accelerate changes that upgraded the whole education system. Within a decade and a half the regional technical colleges became full-fledged academic establishments, the National University of Ireland system was expanded, and a few more higher education institutions became full-fledged universities (White 2001).[18]

There were major differences between the Irish education system and policies and those of Israel and Taiwan. Education in Ireland was seen as an economic supply-side issue, and consequently the system's main aim was to create highly skilled labor that could work for the incoming MNCs.[19] Indeed, even today, if a regional college wishes to open a new degree course, it has to show that the industries around it not only want these skills but also approve the specific curricula offered. Many of the managers of the large MNCs whom I interviewed, such as those of Intel, Digital, or Ericsson, talked at length about the involvement of their corporation in the development of the nearby colleges' course of studies.[20]

In one important respect, quality and quantity of academic research, Ireland is still far behind Israel, Taiwan, or most OECD countries, though very recently a small positive change appears to have occurred.[21] In the 1970s the state supplied very minimal resources for academic R&D, about £27 million (IEP), and during the financial crisis in the 1980s even that amount dipped sharply to almost nothing. EU grants became the main source of capital. Only in the mid-1990s, with the looming future expansion of the EU, did policy makers and politicians realize that Ireland must upgrade its R&D capabilities if it was to compete with the eastern European countries for MNCs.

These developments triggered the establishment of Science Foundation Ireland (SFI) and the Programme for Research in Third-Level Institutions (PRTLI) in 1998.[22] SFI has been built on a similar basis to the American NSF. Indeed its first director general, William Harris, an American of Irish origin, was formerly a director of one of the NSF divisions. SFI was envisioned as a five-year targeted effort to create high-quality research in the areas of biotechnology and ICT, but this focus was somewhat expanded. The SFI also continues another recurring theme of Irish economic policies: there is an intentional bias to award grants for teams that are led by foreign-based internationally renowned researchers. The argument behind this partiality has been that Ireland needs to attract high-quality researchers if it wants to conduct top-level research. While Ireland has the advantage over Israel and Taiwan of being a highly developed English-speaking country with a high quality of living that can attract foreign talent, others argue that this move symbolizes the inability of the Irish state to trust its own citizens. As of 2006, SFI's budget for its first period of operation, 2000–2006, was €646 million (SFI 2006).

PRTLI is the twin effort of SFI, and its main aim is to enable the building of the necessary research infrastructure within the university system. PRTLI allocates its funds on a competitive basis. As of 2004 the PRTLI had three multiyear funding cycles. It was envisioned as a state-industry initiative. As of 2006, not including private contributions, €605 million had been allocated in three investment cycles starting in 1999 (HEA 2006).

By establishing these two programs in 1998 the Irish state indicated its seriousness about transforming the academic research infrastructure. However, there are still many caveats as to the continuous state support for SFI and its medium- and long-term influence. Moreover, even when finally moving to upgrade the Irish research apparatus, the Irish state still employs an FDI orientation—for example, in its insistence on the participation of foreign-based scientists. Hence questions remain as to whether the goal of the SFI is a genuine attempt to change the Irish economy capabilities toward rapid innovation–based industrialization or just the last stage of supply-side policies to create MNC-attracting human capital.

Thus, although the development of the Irish education system is unprecedented in Irish history and has greatly helped to propel Ireland along the track of high-skills IT industrial development, it appears that the strategic view behind these developments treated the education mainly as a way to produce high-skilled labor, not innovation and research. Only in the past five years have policies with a vision of making the Irish higher education system more research oriented been implemented.

Seeds of the IT Industry: From the 1960s to the Early 1980s

Throughout the same period the seeds of the future IT industry in Ireland were planted. In both the public and the private sectors, computerization activities were taking place that would eventually give birth to the Irish-owned IT industry. The official beginning of computerization in Ireland was in 1958. In that year Suicra—the state-owned Irish Sugar Company—decided to computerize its operations and brought the first computer to Ireland.[23] Throughout the 1960s and early 1970s, big public and private companies and organizations were the main loci of professional IT training and knowledge diffusion, especially as formal third-level education was beyond the means of most young high school graduates at the time, and most universities didn't offer computer-science degrees.[24] Barry Murphy, the first director of the National Software Directorate and before and after CEO of a few leading Irish-owned software companies, such as Insight, Openet Telecom, and Netsure, echoed the claims of many that these institutions are the unsung heroes of the industry: "Those big companies were the only institutions that were actually training people at the time; these companies were the likes of the banks and insurance companies. They gave superb training to cohorts of young people, which they all lost in five to seven years' time. These companies made an immense contribution to the Irish software industry" (interview, November 6, 2000).

The early Irish IT companies were established in the 1960s and 1970s. Most, due to the high cost of computers at the time and the capital constraints in Ireland, concentrated either on consulting and services or on outsourcing of IT services' business models.[25] The first Irish software company was System Dynamics, founded in 1968 by a team of former IBM Ireland employees and focused on software consultancy services. System Dynamics was also important for three other reasons: first, it spawned a few of the biggest Irish software consultancies, such as Chaco and Delphi, which in turn spawned others, such as Enovation.[26] Second, System Dynamics' founder Tom McGovern was a key actor in raising the profile of the Irish software industry and creating its identity as a distinct sociopolitical group within the Irish industrial landscape. Third, McGovern, in a way similar to other successful early IT entrepreneurs, such as Michael Peirce of Mentec, played a crucial role in the early financing of other, more product-oriented, companies. As other sources of finance did not exist, and as the Irish banks were not even willing to extend overdraft facilities to many software companies until the early 1990s, such a role must not be underestimated.[27]

The Irish IT companies in that period, unlike the MNCs, had to surmount extensive difficulties in order to commence and maintain operations. Not only was there no source of funding, nor entrepreneurial financiers such as the Israeli Tolkowsky and Discount Investment, but banks were not even willing to extend loans or simple credit facilities to indigenous IT companies. The result has been that those few individuals still daring to be entrepreneurs typically needed to mortgage their own houses to secure working capital. As a result of these constraints, most of these early IT companies stayed financially fragile and collapsed at the slightest change to their monthly cash flow. Moreover, unlike the MNCs, local new technology–based firms (NTBFs) were not offered land and offices in the IDA's industrial estates, and many property owners turned out to be as conservative as the banks, unwilling to rent space for software companies.[28]

Slowly but surely, the first Irish companies moved on the backs of their customers to product development. Timing and the movement of the MNCs into Ireland were important catalysts in this development. In the 1970s the MNCs led the progress in Ireland away from the mainframe platform into minicomputers. The opening of the new and smaller Irish MNC subsidiaries coincided with the rise of minicomputer technology; as a result, Ireland became one of the world's heaviest per capita users of minicomputers.

Because minicomputers were a new platform, they did not have an established base of software—and were incompatible with software employed at the MNCs' foreign headquarters. As a result, many local companies managed to get development projects that could easily be packaged (a new concept at the time) into software products. The more successful of these packages quickly secured a few more sales in Ireland and the United Kingdom. However, a second and much more important transformation of the local software industry happened when the computer manufacturers, such as Digital, IBM, and ICL, invited some Irish companies to market their products together as bundled solutions.

Kindle, one of the first Irish software companies to reach successful constant overseas sales, is an example of this model of organizational development. Kindle, founded in 1981 as Triple A Systems, first developed banking systems on the ICL platform.[29] ICL sold its computers around the world, especially in former British colonies, and did not have many banking packages that ran on its platform. It added Kindle to its official list of ICL software vendors as a banking package specialist. Soon thereafter, Kindle got orders from all of the former British colonies. In the second part of the 1980s, Kindle converted its products to other platforms. Kindle is now owned by a British company and is a five hundred–person software house with a global sales and support network. However, its main locus of activity and R&D is no longer in Ireland.

The early 1980s brought an overall maturation of the Irish software industry. This process coincided with the beginning of the changes in the IDA view of the indigenous IT industry and the tradable services industries. With the establishment of the Enterprise Development Program by the IDA, the agency started to become more proactive in assisting local IT NTBFs, though on a very low scale and with relatively small amounts compared to the aid given to MNCs. Furthermore, the IDA and many leading politicians developed a relationship of mutual distrust with the indigenous IT industry, a state of affairs that continued to the mid-1990s.

Apart from Kindle, two other software companies whose rise and fall changed the way the IDA and subsequently Enterprise Ireland managed their R&D grant schemes were Insight Software and Real-Time Software (RTS). The two companies, in particular RTS, were different from earlier Irish-owned companies in being product based from their inception. They were also representative of the particular profile of the Irish software industry at the time: the products of both were based around Maapics. Maapics was the main software suite for manufacturing facilities offered by IBM as part of its own foray into the minicomputer arena.[30] Both companies grew out of the relative strengths of the Irish industrial base in the early 1980s—manufacturing facilities that were world leaders in utilizing the new minicomputer technologies.

Insight was originally the name of a package for financial reporting and analysis built to work on top of the Maapics package by Vector Software, a product-oriented venture of AMS. Insight was sold by AMS, which also financed all the development efforts from its IT consulting revenues. AMS started to directly sell the Insight packages around the world in 1980 and changed its own name to Insight Software in 1983. The company reached record product sales for an Irish company in the early 1980s, and by 1988 was poised to sell its more advanced software package for the IBM AS/400. However, the company started to suffer severe cash flow problems. These were caused by a series of factors: (*a*) the need to financially rely solely on its own revenues, (*b*) its use of a business model that necessitated a costly international direct sales operations, (*c*) the fact that Insight, with Vector acting as its R&D center, still maintained both the product line and the consultancy business, and (*d*) the added difficulties in moving into the higher priced software package on a newly launched platform. In the end the founders were glad to sell Insight to the Hoskyns Group, a publicly listed British software house, in 1988.[31]

Real-Time Software was given more attention by the IDA, mainly because it was perceived to be the first technology-based spin-off to form from a subsidiary of foreign MNCs, and as such was celebrated as a political success story.

The company was founded to develop software packages and tools around the Maapics software. Its seed finance came from it cofounders, one of whom then proceeded to sell his services as a consultant to finance the initial product R&D. Starting by offering multicurrency modules, RTS developed a whole suite of financial packages. By 1985 the company had revenues of a few million dollars and a chain of foreign offices. However, it still did not manage to secure investment anywhere in Ireland, and even though RTS managed to raise a relatively small amount of capital in the United States and the United Kingdom by the end of 1985, it was clear that its better-funded American rivals were winning market share. In 1986 the company suffered heavy losses that brought its founders to sell it to the American company MSA. Soon thereafter MSA itself faced difficulties, closing down its Dublin operations in 1988.

In the same period, many politicians as well as other parts of the IDA aired concerns that the EDP was investing too heavily in risky indigenous software businesses without generating enough employment. In the three years between 1986 and 1989 these concerns were strengthened when many of the leading software companies went bankrupt. In addition, as the result of the foreign merger and acquisition of RTS, Insight, and CBT, some of their founders made what was considered in Ireland at the time a small fortune. That these entrepreneurs made this fortune by selling their companies—perceived to entail the destruction of jobs instead of the creation of jobs—triggered severe resentment. Both the public and the politicians, only too willing to spend millions on MNCs, saw the newfound riches of the software entrepreneurs who benefited from relatively minuscule IDA grants not as a sign of success but as socially unfair gains. Moreover, the growing number of bankruptcies created a wariness about the chances that a local industry would ever be able to achieve continuous and sustained growth.[32] In the end a decision was made that state aid should be constructed to share the upturn of businesses it invested in and not just their risks. Direct pressure from the then new minister of finance, Albert Reynolds, brought the IDA to introduce a small, later to be proved critical, change to the conditions of its grants: starting in 1988 the Irish state started to take equity stakes in return for financial aid.

The tales of these three companies also show the most significant difference between the Irish and the Israeli software industry. The Israeli software industry grew within an innovation system already focused on R&D. As a result, many of the products of its software companies were software development tools. The Irish software industry followed a different track, developing software applications for particular business domains, such as finance, insurance, or manufacturing control. Only with the rise of university research in the early 1990s would Ireland manage to grow successful software companies with a focus on developing software technology itself. However, when one such company, Iona, was listed on NASDAQ, it epitomized the new international success of the industry and completely changed its perception in Ireland.

An almost forgotten fact about these early years of the Irish IT industry is that the first IT companies that truly reached sustained global success were hardware, not software, firms. In the mid- to late 1980s the Irish IT hardware industry briefly enjoyed unprecedented success. The two prominent companies of that period were Lake Electronics and Mentec, and their development stories also explain why there were only a few Irish hardware companies until the mid-1990s.

Harry Lynam set up Lake Electronics in the end of 1976. Lynam, a physicist, worked for many years in the engineering part of the Post and Telecommunication Ministry, where Jim Mountjoy, another important entrepreneur, also gained his first experience. In 1976 Lynam become fascinated by microprocessors and decided to sell his house and move with his family to his inlaws to secure the seed finance for Lake Electronics. Luckily for Lake, in the same period the IDA established the EDP, and Lake became one of its first clients. An early employee of Lake described the effect of this state help as critical:

> More than anything else at that period in Ireland [the IDA's backing the company produced a positive] psychological effect. We were frowned on, seven adults with families leaving good secure jobs to start some adventure in a technological area nobody understood. The fact that the esteemed and all-powerful IDA thought that we were making something useful gave us the mental strength to continue. (interview, July 9, 2001)

That injection of capital from the IDA also transformed the way in which the banks treated the company, and together with a first project for Lynam's former employer, the Ministry of Post and Telecommunication, Lake managed to develop its first product: a private-branch exchange (PBX).[33] Lake secured a critical alliance with British Telecom (then a state-owned enterprise) in 1979. Building on its first major international sale, Lake soon expanded worldwide and by 1983 grew to become a two hundred–person–strong company with revenues of £10 million. However, the company suffered from lack of management skills and encountered recurring cash flow problems. The result of these unstable times was the sale of the company in 1988 to Landis and Gyr, a Swiss engineering MNC.[34]

Thus 1988, the year in which the remains of RTS's Dublin operation closed down and Insight Software and CBT's first incarnation were bought by Hoskyns, became the year in which the first generation of international successful Irish IT companies suffered heavy setbacks and the image of the indigenous sector was tarnished.[35]

Mentec's creation story has many similarities to Lake's. Mike Peirce, who was a lecturer on Trinity's engineering faculty at the time, founded Mentec in 1978. Peirce's expertise was in the use of computers in manufacturing. In 1978, together with one of his graduate students, he went on a study trip in Japan to see the use of robots in manufacturing. The trip proved to be a needed catalyst, and Peirce and his student-turned-partner mortgaged their assets to secure seed financing in the form of a bank loan. Fortunately for them the IDA's EDP agreed not only to match their funds but also to guarantee 50 percent of a £100,000 bank loan. The fact that the IDA agreed to assist the company at the time was critical, according to an interviewee working for Mentec at the time:

> We could absolutely not get started without the IDA; the banks were unwilling to talk with us before the IDA chipped in. As a matter of fact, we probably would not have even tried. When we floated the idea of opening a company, almost all the people we knew told us that we are crazy and that to leave secure respectable careers at Trinity is madness. Many reminded us that we have families and children to think of. (interview, June 10, 2003)

With the IDA's backing, Mentec approached the banks. However, the banks insisted that Mentec buy "real assets" worth £50,000 to secure the 50 percent of the loan not covered by the IDA. Hence, Mentec's first activity was the building of its own offices. The banks were pleased, but Mentec was left with no working capital and no way to finance R&D activities.

At the time the biggest IT MNC in Ireland was Digital Equipment of Massachusetts, which had large facilities around Galway. Mentec first focused on projects to develop custom hardware solutions around Data General's computers, but switched allegiance to Digital in 1979. Digital, unlike the other MNCs at the time, had an active and developed OEM partnership program and was looking for suppliers to develop bundled solutions for its PDP computer line. In order to help its smaller suppliers, it gave them complete and open documentation of its systems. Mentec soon became Digital's most important OEM supplier in Ireland. Focusing on product development, Mentec created its core product in 1982, a single-board computer-controller based around Digital's J-11 CPU, to be used in manufacturing control systems. This basis led to many other developments around Digital's and Mentec's own chips that were fabricated by Texas Instruments. In its prime, Mentec had revenues of £10 million and employed more than two hundred people in Dublin and a few score more in the United States and England. At one point, sixty-five of Mentec's employees worked on R&D, a unique feature in the Irish IT industry of those days. Mentec also benefited from becoming an official partner of Ireland's foremost MNC, and the IDA gave it more than a few R&D grants throughout the years.[36]

The stories of Mentec and Lake Electronics exemplify the difficulties that Irish hardware companies had over and above the significant obstacles that software companies were facing. Not only is hardware product development a much costlier endeavor than software, but the opportunities for consulting projects, especially those that can ultimately lead to product development, were scarce. In addition, at that time both software and hardware companies had to face a hostile social environment that either saw technological entrepreneurs as risk takers when they failed, or resented them when they succeeded. Thus, whereas in Israel and Taiwan the pioneers of the IT industry were seen to advance the national dream—soldiers in the war for national growth and glory—in Ireland, under the political context of job creation, the same pioneers were seen as unstable and untrustworthy gamblers.[37] Banks and other financial institutions not only were unwilling to invest in the industry but also refused to extend even the minimal necessary financial services to IT companies. Only those founders willing to risk everything they had by mortgaging their own property managed to secure enough capital to open their businesses. Accordingly, the financial backing of the IDA, even if limited, was absolutely critical.

Even in the relatively simple issue of finding office space, indigenous Irish IT companies have been facing severe difficulties and discrimination compared with the MNCs and traditional businesses. Regulation and tradition in regard to commercial space in Ireland have led to a system in which private property owners prefer to lease almost solely for multiyear terms. Furthermore, almost none of them were willing to lease their offices to NTBFs, which they perceived as too risky. Thus, if on the one side the IDA was busily developing purpose-built industrial estates for its MNC clients (hence, probably lowering the profitability of developing industrial commercial spaces for private property developers), on the other side the indigenous companies faced immense difficulties in securing even a small office space. Many of my interviewees as late as 2002 still argued that finding office space was one of their most difficult obstacles, even for well-funded companies.

The experiences from the creation of the IT industry in Galway after the closure of Digital's facilities in the early 1990s are representative. The founders of both Storm and Toucan, two of the most successful companies to be created by former employees of Digital after it closed, quickly found out that even with state and regional agencies backing their efforts, and even at a time when their success was deemed crucial for the economic future of their communities, no one was willing to rent them office space. In the end the only way in which they managed to secure space was by the IDA's allowing both companies to build their own premises in one of its industrial estates, a solution that forced both firms to spend a large percentage of their limited resources. Last but not least, while throughout this period MNCs were offered a wide array of tax incentives, the indigenous IT companies, like all Irish businesses, had to pay the full, high, corporate taxes rates.

State Policies and the Discovery of IT and
Tradable Services: The Evolution of State
Policies in the 1980s and Early 1990s

On the IDA's side, the late 1970s were the years in which the agency started to appreciate the potential of the IT industry. If in the 1950s and 1960s the IDA was recruiting MNCs from a broad array, it became much more focused in the late 1970s, especially with the "growth without jobs" socioeconomic crisis of the 1980s. The IDA's biggest coup in the 1970s was attracting Digital Equipment. Digital, then and throughout the 1980s one of the world's top IT companies, opened its facilities in Galway in 1971 and soon became the biggest MNC in Ireland. Together with Ericsson, which has large facilities in Athlone, Digital has also been one of the first MNCs to move more advanced R&D operations to Ireland.

By the late 1970s the IDA started to focus on the tradable-services industries and on high-technology electronics. This process was soon accelerated when it became clear in the 1980s that manufacturing MNC subsidiaries preferred to increase their investment in capital equipment, not in expanding their headcount. Thus, while overall production grew, the number of jobs did not.

In 1975 the IDA established the International Services Program (ISP), which, through political lobbying, extended to the service sectors the incentives formerly given only to the manufacturing sectors. In the beginning software was not considered to be the main target, but by 1981 it became one of the ten designated sectors of internationally traded services to which tax incentives were fully extended. The IDA pushed for and succeeded in getting incentives, approval, and recognition for a rainbow of tradable-services industries, from English-language schools to software, finance, and film. These incentives and the actions of the IDA to both bring MNCs and create local enterprises in these areas developed the institutional framework in which the perception of service industry firms gained in reputation and legitimization.

In 1978 the IDA institutionalized its support to indigenous companies by creating the Enterprise Development Program (EDP). The main goals behind the creation of the EDP were to (*a*) increase employment, (*b*) lower Ireland's reliance on FDI by growing indigenous companies, (*c*) create a set of suppliers to attract more MNCs, and (*d*) change the attitude against entrepreneurship and local enterprises in Ireland. The focus was on all sectors, both traditional and technological.

The same officials who were running the MNC-focused International Services Program were also given the responsibility over the EDP. Thus, unlike the case of the indigenous hardware industry, which was continuously treated as an extension of the already established MNC-oriented policies, the birth of indigenous software industry coincided with changes within the developmental agencies that institutionalized their interest and focus around the industry.[38]

The two programs, ISP and EDP, were not focused on the IT sector in particular or on NTBF promotion in general, but on promoting any kind of entrepreneurial activity in Ireland.[39] However, processes related both to state activities and to the activities of private entrepreneurs, coupled with changes in global demand for IT, propelled the software sector as the first in which indigenous companies achieved worldwide success. This success, in turn, refocused most of the attention of the newly created state agencies on the IT sector, specifically enhancing the software industry and aiding its continuous growth since the mid-1990s. Indeed, an executive of the EDP program strongly insisted:

> There was no aim to create science-based industry at the time; the program [EDP] evolved in a case-by-case process. Slowly it became clear that services are the main beneficiary, and that in reality we were mainly dealing with software. This is why we quickly added software to the list of sectors to get the full tax benefits and why later policy was constructed around software. But we had no idea of creating a technological industry in Ireland at the time. We just aimed to create more enterprises and jobs. (interview, March 14, 2001)

A similar response was given by all other former executives of the EDP who were interviewed. The EDP became crucial not only in the funding of companies but also in actively convincing potential entrepreneurs to start their business. At least as important, the EDP's actions granted some legitimacy to technological entrepreneurship and risk taking. The latter might have been the most important accomplishment of the EDP, considering Ireland's ultra-conservative business and financial landscape at the time. In addition, on the FDI-oriented policy side, the new policies and the actions taken by the ISP culminated in major software companies' opening subsidiaries in Ireland. A consensus evolved that the future of Irish industry did not rely solely on the manufacturing sector.

The first major software MNC that arrived in Ireland, transforming it into the world capital for software localization, was Lotus in 1985.[40] In contrast to the indifferent reaction of the political establishment to the activities of local companies, the political and social elite attended the opening ceremony of Lotus's Irish operation, and the company gained the goodwill of both the Irish developmental agencies and leading politicians. John Sterne argues that the main reason why Lotus was greeted with such esteem is specifically because it did not conduct any R&D activities in Ireland but concentrated on localization, packaging, and logistics. Therefore Lotus was seen as a real manufacturing company with sensible well-understood operations (Sterne 2004, pp. 101–108).[41] Following Lotus almost all of the top software MNCs, such as Oracle, Symantec, Corel, Novell, and Microsoft, opened localization, packaging, and logistics operations in Ireland during the 1990s. Microsoft soon became Ireland's top exporter, and the sales attributed to its Irish subsidiary alone would make Ireland the world's biggest software exporter.

In the 1980s the commitment of the state expressly to the software industry was further strengthened with the establishment of the National Software Center (NSC). The NSC was the first failed attempt to create within the IDA a subunit stuffed with industry experts to promote the growth of the software industry. In 1983 two competing proposals for a National Software Center were put forward. One, by a coalition of the Science and Technology Board, the Higher Education Authority, and representatives of the indigenous industry, envisioned a nonprofit center providing the industry with a wide range of services. The second proposal, of the IDA, was focused on the MNCs sector and envisioned the NSC as a self-financed operation giving services to the industry for a fee. Unlike the Science and Technology Board and the Higher Education Authority, the IDA did not bother to consult with the indigenous industry (O'Riain 1999, 2004, Sterne 2004).

In another example of the IDA's power at the time, although the local industry supported the competing plan, the NSC was created on the basis of the

IDA's proposal.[42] Brian Dugan was recruited from a position of vice president in Standard and Poor's in New York to become the NSC's first director. The NSC's first board of directors also consisted solely of MNC representatives. However, the NSC quickly focused more on the indigenous industry. By 1987–1988 the NSC had become one of the main institutions in which the state and the indigenous software industry were collaborating. Nevertheless, the NSC's need to become self-financed ultimately led to conflicts as well as perceived and real competition with industry. In addition, its focus on the indigenous sector cost it its IDA support. By June 1988 the NSC had closed.

Before it closed the NSC managed to complete the first survey of the industry. The result of this survey shows how different from the Israeli, and how similar to the Taiwanese, the Irish software industry was in the 1980s. If in Israel the leading companies at the time were focusing on solutions to R&D and software programming processes, in Ireland most of the companies either imitated already established packages of foreign companies on new platforms or focused on industry-specific applications, with little in terms of R&D or innovation. For example, in 1984 there were twenty-four companies selling packages for insurance agents, eighteen with software for lawyers' offices, and twelve selling applications for television rental stores (Sterne 2004, p. 17).

By 1988 the political landscape in Ireland had changed, and the further development of the indigenous software industry was very much on the agenda. As soon as the NSC was closed, two proposals for centers to replace it were put forward. The first, focusing on skill development, resulted in the ultimately ill-fated PAT university-industry linkage centers established with EU funds. The second, developed together by the Ministry of Industry and Commerce and the indigenous industry, resulted in the creation of the National Software Directorate within the IDA in 1991.

In a symbolic move, very different from the IDA's choice of an American to be the NSC's first director in 1984, an Irishman, Barry Murphy, was chosen to become the NSD's first director. Murphy, Insight Software's CEO and a member of the board of the ISA's predecessor, the Irish Computer Services Association (ICSA), has been one of the most vocal and prominent leaders of the indigenous industry.

The NSD became crucial on three fronts. It was the first organization to chart the size and scope of the software industry in Ireland on a comprehensive and regular basis, finding it, in the words of Murphy, "to have more companies than anyone thought at the time" (interview with Barry Murphy, November 6, 2000). Following that initiative, the NSD became the main center

devoted to collecting, processing, and publishing data on the software industry. Second, the NSD became the main promoter of the movement toward the
product-development business model and away from the consulting-business
model. Last but not least, using EU financing, the NSD became one of the
main initiators of the high tech–oriented venture capital industry in Ireland.

At least as important, however, was the effect of the NSD within the Irish
developmental agencies. Unlike any other sector, software companies now had
a direct line and a voice within the Irish developmental agencies, first the IDA
and then Forbairt and EI. With the NSD pushing for more resources to be
channeled toward the indigenous software sector, and with its people sitting
on the grant-giving committees of the EI, software soon became the pilot sector around which Ireland's science-and-technology industrial policies, focusing on the indigenous industry, were planned and implanted.

THE RESTRUCTURING OF THE
DEVELOPMENTAL AGENCIES

Even with the IDA's new programs and focus in the 1980s, the "growth without jobs" crisis, coupled with the failure of fiscal expansion policies, left Ireland in a dire situation. Emigration reached new heights, with 1.1 percent of
the population leaving Ireland in 1989 alone, many of those from the young
and highly educated segment of the population. This turn of events, together
with a growing public resentment of the IDA's focus on MNCs, started subtle but important changes in Ireland's industrial policy, which, in the end, refocused it around the high-technology sectors in the 1980s and 1990s.

The latest restructuring of Irish industrial policies around the high-
technology industries started during the latest Irish economic crisis. In the
early 1980s, major policy and social upheavals started the realignment process
of Ireland's institutional system along the path of NTBFs-oriented industrial
development. In the sociopolitical arena resentment toward what was seen as
the excessive focus of IDA on MNCs with much smaller amounts of resources channeled into the indigenous industry, coupled with the severe crisis
of Irish industry, culminated in the Telesis report.

The report, commissioned by the National Economic and Social Council
(NESC), hence with substantial political support behind it, argued for an almost complete renovation of Irish industrial policy. The report concluded that
Ireland's economic growth should have a "double engine" of FDI and Irish-
owned companies. The report also argued for the building of national cham-

pions, and contended that the level of organizational and management capabilities of Irish firms was too low for them to succeed without a hands-on industrial policy. Thus the report called for a break with the traditional neoliberal interventionalist industrial policy. Nevertheless, the report itself did not give any conditions whatsoever as to how national champions and winners should be selected, or to how the state should employ direct intervention to strengthen the management and organizational capabilities of Irish-owned firms.

The Telesis report was published in February 1982, and a heated debate about industrial policy followed. However, in the 1984 White Paper on Industrial Policy, the Telesis report recommendations were mostly ignored (O'Sullivan 2000b). Nevertheless, the report's long-term impact was larger than it seemed at the time. It both started and lent legitimacy to a long process of refocusing industrial policy around the indigenous industry. This process culminated in another committee report, the 1992 Culliton report.

The Culliton report's most important recommendation was that the state should direct its assistance into fixing general financial market failures—that is, into helping companies, in all sectors of the economy, that were deemed too risky by the existing conservative financial institutions to be granted finance.[43] Moreover, the Culliton report envisioned a restructuring of the development agencies' organization.

As a result of the Culliton report, two waves of bureaucratic reshuffling occurred. In the first, under the Industrial Development Act of 1993, the IDA was restructured into two main agencies: Forbairt took charge of the indigenous industry development and the Irish Science and Technology Board (Eolas); the IDA, still influential but with reduced power, was renamed as the Industrial Development Agency Ireland and given the mandate over the MNCs and FDI-related activities. In addition, a strategic, coordination and advisory agency—Forfas—was created. In 1998 the reshuffling was completed as Forbairt merged with the Irish Trade Board and parts of FAS (the training agency) into one agency with capabilities and responsibilities for promoting Irish-owned industry in both Ireland and abroad. The merged agency was renamed Enterprise Ireland.

This period also strengthened Ireland's particular neoliberal interventionist ideology. These bureaucratic reconstruction efforts progressed side by side with the establishment of a neocorporatist regime by the new right-center government. In 1987, in a stark contrast to both the United States and the United Kingdom, when a new center-right government gained power in Ireland from a center-left one, it opted not only not to crush the labor unions but also to enhance their power by structuring an Irish-style neocorporatist frame-work—the social partnership agreements. This framework led to a series of ever more comprehensive three-year agreements, which are an integral part of the Irish industrial and economic policy to this day (Hardiman 2000, 2002).

Thus Ireland, led by an ideologically center-right government, possessing an industrial base consisting mainly of American MNCs, and under strong pressure from the IMF and the World Bank, decided on and successfully im-plemented a neocorporatist framework. Moreover, the Fianna Fáil govern-ment accomplished this feat at exactly the same time that their ideological contemporaries and partners, Thatcher in the United Kingdom and Reagan in the United States, were busily dismantling union power. Thus the end of the 1980s and the beginning of the 1990s brought major policy changes to Ireland. These policy changes, taken together as part of a major restructuring of the Irish industrial policies, have been very different from those taken in Taiwan and Israel in the same period.

THE RISE OF THE SOFTWARE SECTOR AND THE
CONTINUED STAGNATION OF THE HARDWARE
SECTOR: DEVELOPMENT AND STATE-INDUSTRY
CO-EVOLUTION IN THE 1990s

By the latter half of the 1980s, the success of the Irish product-oriented soft-ware houses, together with the PC revolution, started to change the Irish IT industry's landscape, and a growing number of software companies were founded around specific product ideas. Nevertheless, as the stories of the first few years of even the most successful Irish companies like Iona, Aldiscon (now Logica-Aldiscon), and Smartforce (formerly CBT and now part of Skillsoft) attested, the industry's main problem remained the acute lack of capital.

An example of the difficulties of the indigenous companies in these years is the story of Glockenspiel. Glockenspiel is also important to the development of the Irish software industry for three reasons: first, it was the first globally successful Irish company that utilized the path common to the Israeli software industry—development and sales of software tools to developers. Moreover, Glockenspiel pioneered in Ireland a particular strategy for doing so: the quick implantation of the latest international standards of a particular software de-velopment technology, with the company becoming the first to the market of-fering a workable product based on these standards. This is the exact strategy executed later by Iona, Ireland software industry's flagship company, and since then imitated by many of Iona's spin-offs. Second, Glockenspiel became famed for operating a high-technology firm in one of the roughest neighborhoods in Dublin's inner city. This, while irritating some, also gave the indigenous software industry in general, and Glockenspiel in particular, some political goodwill. The strategy later became an integral goal of the Irish state IT development schemes.[44] Third, the story of the rise and fall of Glockenspiel portrays the ambivalent way in which the IDA was treating the indigenous industry. The IDA's treatment of the company when it faced crisis became a focal point for the growing resentment of the agency by the software industry.

John Carolan, an Irish software programmer with extensive knowledge and networks with research institutions and developers outside Ireland, founded Glockenspiel in 1984. At that time, Carolan became involved with the new technologies of object-oriented programming and the new C++ language standard. Glockenspiel utilized his knowledge of the C++ standard and became the first software company worldwide to develop a C++ compiler for the PC platform. In its first years Glockenspiel financed its product development mainly from C++ consulting.[45]

In 1988, the same year in which many major Irish IT companies succumbed to financial difficulties, Glockenspiel reached a point at which most of its revenues came from export sales of its products. Very quickly Glockenspiel taught the Irish software industry the lesson already well learned by the Israeli one: software development tools which are sold directly to engineers and developers need no localization and can be sold all over the world without costly modifications. Moreover, the customers for these products, being engineers and programmers, are more sophisticated than the average consumer; hence products that are too complex and crude in their user interface to be sold to the consumer market can still be sold to these highly skilled customers. Building on its C++ expertise, Glockenspiel started to offer a wider range of RAD tools for C++ development. The company's deep technical knowledge enabled it to develop award-winning products, and both IBM and Microsoft promoted their sales.

However, in Ireland, this technology development–oriented business model was so different from any other Irish company ever to exist that it led both the IDA and the financial institutions to treat the company with suspicion and mistrust. In 1991 Glockenspiel achieved record sales and was the second top indigenous software exporter after CBT. In 1992, however, its American distributor went bankrupt. Almost immediately its bank in Ireland informed the company that it had to pay its overdraft facility in full, and the IDA declined to extend any aid. Shortly thereafter Computer Associated bought Glockenspiel out of receivership, and the IDA, in a move that instilled further distrust within the indigenous industry—and that directly contradicts the logic of solving market failures by risk sharing—demanded that every grant the company ever received should be paid back in full (O'Riain 1999, Sterne 2004).

By the early 1990s the software industry had notably grown, and a number of product-oriented companies had attained global success. For the first time, Irish software companies managed to successfully cross the Atlantic and thrive in the American market. Furthermore, the Irish software industry became much more technologically savvy. One of the most important factors in enabling this development had nothing to do with the Irish state but a lot to do with the Irish university sector and the EU.

Starting at the end of the 1980s, and with growing importance in the 1990s, the Irish colleges and universities, in particular Trinity, started to participate in EU research framework schemes. In a short period of time, Trinity's computer science department became one of the largest recipients in Europe of ESPRIT grants for computer science. These grants not only enabled Trinity to expand its computer science research activities but allowed several research groups to form and then spin out as already established companies with working products and strong IP.[46]

The most important software company to rise out of these particular institutional settings was Iona. Iona had its origins when Trinity received approval to offer the first undergraduate computer science degree course in 1979. Trinity needed to expand its faculty quickly and enrolled as lecturers many of its graduate students, among them both Chris Horn and Sean Baker. At the time there was little money for research in Ireland. However, in 1980, one of the senior lecturers in the department, Neville Harris, came back from a sabbatical at Stanford, bringing with him in his baggage four Sun Microsystems processors and a 3mb-per-second Ethernet card to establish the Distributed System Group (DSG). In 1983 the coming of the ESPRIT program suddenly changed the research landscape in the department. ESPRIT allowed for research groups to apply for funding on a multiple-year basis. In 1984 the DSG group, then consisting of four lecturers, managed to get its first multiyear project. This allowed the group to expand, and joined by Chris Horn, who came back from Brussels after being part of the EU team forming the ESPRIT program, the group quickly managed to get enough funding to make it the biggest and richest computer science research group in Ireland. By 1985 the DSG group grew to encompass six lecturers and about forty graduate students. At that time the group was already run almost as an independent financial entity, a unique and novel experience in the Irish higher education system.

In 1991 a group within the DSG led by Chris Horn, Sean Baker, and Annari O'Toole decided to open Iona, a campus company based around their knowledge of distributed systems.[47] By that time, Horn and Baker were already active in a new international standard group, the Object Management Group (OMG). The founders saw a window of opportunity utilizing a strategy similar to Glockenspiel: being the first company to offer products that implant OMG's new middleware standard.[48] However, in 1991, no one in Ireland was willing to invest in a company with such extensive R&D-based business plans. From 1991 to 1993 the company was financed from consulting revenues, including the fees the founders earned for teaching C++ and system analysis, from two ESPRIT projects, and from some savings. This financial situation allowed Iona to start product development only in June 1992. By that time Iona had also managed to get an IDA employment grant of £150,000, for which the IDA took a 7 percent stake of the company.[49]

By June 1993 Iona had become one of the first companies to offer a product implanting the new CORBA middleware standard with C++ compatibility. This raised the interest of Sun Microsystems. In December, Sun offered to invest $600,000 (USD) for 25 percent of the company. This offer from a leading MNC completely changed the reputation of Iona in Ireland, transforming it from an untrustworthy R&D-based IT operation into a legitimate and promising company. It was here that the development agencies' misconception of the software industry again proved to be a hurdle. The inward-looking development agency, by then restructured as Forbairt, as well as Trinity, refused to let its stake in Iona be diluted by Sun's investment. Only when the founders threatened to close down the company did the two institutions back down and the IDA agree to match Sun's funding to keep its stake from being diluted.[50]

Quickly the new relationship with Sun, much as its alliance with the Israeli Checkpoint or as Amdoc's alliance with SBC had done, opened the doors of the U.S. industry for Iona. By 1995 both Boeing and Motorola were using Iona's products, and in February 1997 Iona became the second Irish company, after CBT, to go through an IPO on NASDAQ. Since by that time Sun had decided to sell its entire 25 percent stake in Iona, the IPO became the fifth-largest software IPO on NASDAQ up to that point.[51] The sums involved and the extensive publicity helped to transform the perception of the indigenous software industry both within and outside Ireland.[52] Software had become the jewel in the crown of S&T industrial policies in Ireland. This was especially true as EI's growing portfolio of Irish IT companies' stocks soon made it the most profitable Irish venture capital organization. Nevertheless, as we shall see, the growing fixation of EI on profitable investments has by now become an obstacle to the industry's continuous growth.

The DSG group and Iona also offered a development paradigm for the evolution of other research groups, many of them turned into commercial spin-offs in Trinity's computer science department. Some examples of these have been Wilde Technologies, another spin-off of the DSG group focusing on software design; Prediction Dynamics, which develops financial modeling software and was founded by Padraig Cunningham and John Carney, based on Carney's Ph.D.; and Havok, which is the commercial reincarnation of the Graphic Users Group. In addition, EU programs and the incentives they supplied to organize the research into semi-independent applicative technology research groups gave rise to some of the relatively few successful Irish hardware companies in the late 1990s, such as Haptica and MV Technologies. As Trinity, even under the constraints of minuscule research budgets, has spun off many other companies both before and after, including another two of the only six Irish software firms ever to go public on NASDAQ, Baltimore and Trintech, one wonders why in Ireland the universities' research efforts are seen to have failed to positively affect the growth of the industry. This is especially remarkable in that other universities, including University College Dublin, Dublin City University, and University College Cork, were also breeding grounds for many software companies throughout the years, if not to the same degree as Trinity.

Iona itself was also critical for the development of the industry in another way. Iona has become the educator of experienced managers and entrepreneurs in a whole cohort of computer science students. These students joined the company before its IPO and passed through its rapid growth phase. Many of them left the company after 1999 to establish their own companies. There are now more than a dozen direct Iona spin-offs. In the case of one of these, Cape Clear, not only did Iona invest, but two of Iona's founders, Colin Newman and Annari O'Toole, left Iona to join and manage the spin-off.[53]

Accordingly, by 1994–1995, the time of the restructuring of the development agencies and the NSD initiative to develop a high tech–oriented VC industry, the landscape of the indigenous software industry was already transformed. Smartforce/CBT had become the first Irish software company to become public on NASDAQ, Iona had secured major partnerships with Sun, Motorola, and Boeing, and by 1995 Aldiscon was the market leader in the new mobile phone technology of short text messaging (SMS).[54] In short, by the time the industrial policy restructuring process had begun in 1994, the indigenous software industry was already established as the leading and most successful export-oriented sector in Ireland.[55]

Many product-oriented firms had to support their R&D efforts by offering services and consulting, a fact that not only slowed their R&D efforts but limited their ability to develop large-scale, complex, R&D-based products. This situation started to change only after the reconstruction of Irish industrial policy and the refocusing of a more significant portion of that policy on the indigenous industry. The formal creation of Forbairt, the forerunner of Enterprise Ireland, in 1994 increased state support for Irish-owned software companies.

In the hardware sector, however, there was no significant improvement. The two prominent hardware companies that became major exporters in the 1990s were Silicon and Software Systems (S3) and Parthus, both IC design houses. The circumstances involving their establishment were unique, making them the exception rather than the rule. S3 was founded in 1986, and it has been managed since as an independent company by Maurice Whelan, a professor at Trinity. However, S3 was established as part of efforts by Whelan, a former researcher for Philips Electronics, and by the IDA to persuade Philips to open a subsidiary in Ireland. These efforts culminated in Philips's agreeing to open S3 as a joint venture with Whelan, with Philips owning 90 percent of its shares.

Parthus was established as Silicon Systems in 1993 when Brian Long, then the chief design engineer of Digital in Ireland, decided not to move with Digital to Scotland after Digital's operation in Galway closed. Instead, Long, with the help of the IDA, which also matched him with Peter McManamon, Parthus's financial cofounder, co-established Parthus. The IDA's help in the launch of Parthus was part of the agency's effort to reconstruct the IT industry in Galway after the closure of Digital, by far the biggest employer in the region. However, what allowed the company to start operations and grow was a combination of financial backing and aid from Michael Peirce of Mentec;

seed financing and a stream of orders from STMicroelectronics, obtained through Long's industry contacts; and Long's and McManamon's savings. Only after securing these financial resources did Parthus obtain a matching grant from the then newly established EI. Parthus was started as a service IC design house, mainly for STMicroelectronics, which supplied Parthus with more than 65 percent of revenues in its first three years. However, luckily for Parthus, the contract with STMicroelectronics stated that the IP developed was to be owned by Parthus.

In 1998, building on the already established reputation of the Irish software industry, Parthus changed its business model to an IP licensing, utilizing what has been one of the biggest investments by Goldman Sachs in an Irish IT company, $16 million. In 2000 Parthus became the first and only Irish hardware company to be publicly listed on NASDAQ when it double listed on the London Stock Exchange and NASDAQ. In 2002 Parthus was bought by an Israeli company, DSP group, and was merged with DSP's own IP licensing division to be refloated as Parthus-Ceva; in 2003 the name was changed to Ceva.

Thus the stories of S3 and Philips, Parthus and STMicroelectronics, as well as the earlier relationship of Mentec and Digital, show that in the context of the Irish innovation system, with its dearth of both capital and a semiconductor industrial ecosystem, such as Taiwan's, only with a rare combination of long-term support of an MNC and of the development agencies could a successful hardware NTBF grow. With the development agencies focused as they were on the indigenous software sector, treating the indigenous hardware sector only as a derivative of the MNC-focused policy, it is not surprising that stories of successful Irish hardware companies are few and far between.

The Creation and Limitations of the Local VC Industry

The venture financing situation improved significantly after 1995. NSD, by then a part of EI, led an initiative to distribute EU-backed finance in an attempt to spur the establishment of high technology–oriented venture capital funds. This effort, coupled with the proof for profits by the publicly listed companies and some high-profile M&As after 1995, culminated in a small but vibrant local VC industry. By 1999, for the first time in the history of the industry, local software entrepreneurs could reasonably expect to find enough investment capital to start up a product-oriented company.[56]

The first government initiative to create a VC industry in Ireland was not at all aimed at the high-tech sector. In 1994 the government, realizing that financial institutions in Ireland were overly conservative and unwilling to grant working and growing capital to new enterprises in any industry, used a policy of veiled threats to persuade the big pension funds to make available up to £100 million to venture capital very broadly defined.[57] Using this finance, three VC funds were established: Delta, Act, and ICC. The three invested most of the funds in later-stage development of businesses, mostly in traditional companies, and not in IT.

In 1995 the NSD initiated the first attempt to spur a high technology–oriented VC industry. The NSD VC initiative, using EU money from the Operational Program for Industrial Development, 1994–1999, distributed €43.9 million to establish sixteen funds under a scheme in which half of each fund's finance was granted by the state and the other half was raised in the private market.[58] The state position in all these funds was that of a regular general partner. This created the ironic situation whereby in Ireland—where, unlike in Taiwan and Israel, the state specifically chose policy vehicles with the aim of limiting its direct intervention in the market—representatives of EI, often the same people, sit on the boards of the VC funds, the boards of companies in which EI invest, and EI investment committees that choose companies in which to invest.

The Irish state, much like the Taiwanese, saw VC as a missing pool of finance and not as a separate industry with specific capabilities to be developed. Hence, while one of the declared aims of the policy, as for Israel's, was to enlarge not only the pool of finance but also the pool of financiers, the state opted to cooperate with local investors, who lacked specialized high-technology VC knowledge and background, and not with foreign VC-skilled institutions.[59] The first fund to be established was the ICC software fund I. ICC fund I started operation in 1996, and Maurice McHenry, an old NSD and EDP hand, relocated from the NSD to become the fund's manager. Aside from one large and recent VC fund (Cross Atlantic) and a few semi-institutionalized funds of successful entrepreneurs (Mentor, Oyster, and Island are the prominent ones), all the VC funds operating in Ireland were created as part of the NSD initiative.

In 2002 Enterprise Ireland announced another VC initiative, this time more regionally and sectorally oriented and fully funded by the Irish government. Under this new initiative the Irish government distributes €95 million to ten funds, most of which are the new funds of the same management companies of the first initiative, with the hope of stimulating the commitment of a total of €500 million to these funds' management.[60] It is the ironic result of the inherent conflicts of Ireland's neoliberal interventionalist ideology that the state's attempts not to interfere with the market's price-setting mechanisms ended with the only nation of our three cases to fully subscribe to free-market principles, Ireland, becoming the one case where the state is not only the biggest VC in itself, owning shares in all of Ireland's promising IT companies, but also the biggest investor in the VC industry. Accordingly, the state also has a claim to a large stake of the VC industry's investments and a significant role in shaping its decision making.

The VC initiatives of the Irish government through Enterprise Ireland and the NSD bore some fruit. However, as can be seen in figure 4.1, by the end of 2006, especially in comparison with Israel, the Irish VC industry is smaller, less professional, and still intimately linked to established Irish financial institutions. Whereas in Israel many of the VCs are former technological entrepreneurs, in Ireland most of the VCs are former accountants and management consultants. Moreover, the Irish VC industry is less internationally connected than the Israeli one, with the sources of its financing and its connections concentrated in Ireland and Europe. Thus, especially in the software industry, where the United States is the main market, the VC industry in Ireland is still lacking.

On the other hand, it might be that some of these features, principally the close connection with local institutional investors and the fact that Ireland possesses very developed institutional pension funds, made it attractive to Irish firms to double list on both the NASDAQ and the Dublin (or another European) stock exchanges. This double-listing option is one that all the Irish IT companies listed on NASDAQ followed, and it probably diminishes the need to transfer more and more activities to the United States.[61] The greatest concerns regarding the Irish VC industry today are (*a*) its ultraconservatism and lack of will to invest in seed-stage companies and (*b*) its continuous reliance on the state for both its investment decision making and financing.

FROM THE LATE 1990s TO THE CURRENT STATE
OF AFFAIRS: THE STRENGTHS AND
WEAKNESSES OF IRELAND

In the late 1990s the Irish software industry enjoyed its greatest success so far. Six software companies—CBT/Smartforce, Iona, Trintech, Baltimore, Datalex, and Riverdeep—listed on NASDAQ. Together with a few large-scale M&As, these high-profile success stories helped to change the perception of

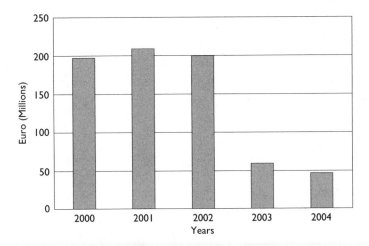

Figure 4.1. Capital Raised by Irish VCs, 2000–2004. *Sources:* PwC 2000, 2005, 2006). *Note:* There is no distinction between Private Equity and VC in Ireland, hence only an estimated average of 70 percent of the figures above has been allocated to technology-based investment.

the industry both within and outside Ireland. In 1998–2001, the new generation of NTBFs also enjoyed the advent of the VC industry and could raise enough financing to utilize product R&D–focused business models. In addition, many established companies, such as SoftCo and Fineos, transformed their business model into a product-based one, often using VC financing to accomplish it.

However, as can be seen from figure 4.2, the average sales per employee in the Irish indigenous sector, while vastly improving from a low of $45,000 in 1991, is still only 40 percent of the average of the Israeli IT industry. This seems to imply two points: (*a*) from an optimistic perspective, there is still a lot of room for improvement, but (*b*) a larger percentage of the Irish industry is still focused on the less profitable activities of service, consulting, and bespoke development.

Furthermore, as can be seen from table 4.1, the composition of the Irish indigenous software industry deteriorated after the late 1990s. By comparison, the Israeli industry was hit hard, but its companies managed to regain high levels of growth and, in tandem with the U.S. industry, has since 2004 successfully gone back to IPOs on NASDAQ. However, in 2007 only three Irish companies are still listed on NASDAQ, and a new generation of NASDAQ high flyers is not in sight.

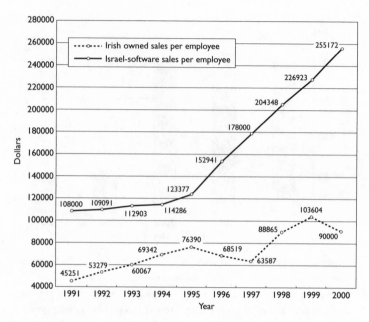

Figure 4.2. Software Sales per Employee, Ireland and Israel. *Sources:* IASH 2003, NID 2006.

Table 4.1. Irish-Owned Software Sector: Employment, Revenues, and Exports

Year	Employment	Sales (€ millions)	Exports (€ millions)
1991	3,801	191	78
1993	4,495	300	147
1995	5,773	490	287
1997	9,200	650	455
1998	9,250	913	566
1999	11,100	1,278	792
2000	14,000	1,400	875
2001	15,000	1,508	1,228
2002	12,600	1,537	1,313
2003	10,710	1,365	1,102
2004	11,250	1,369	946

Source: NID 2006.

Table 4.2. EI Support and Profits, All Sectors,
1998–2004 (€ millions)

Year	Capability Building	Equity and VC Funds	Funds Gained by EI from Equity
1998	58	14	14.3
1999	68	33	12
2000	65	38	49.56
2001	51	72	101.58
2002	31	38	34.3
2003	26	38	14.6

Notes: Capability building is defined as an investment in R&D, training, and new market development; thus it includes, but does not solely consist of, R&D grants. Equity and VC funds are financing channeled to the private VC industry. Unlike in Israel, funds gained by EI are delivered to the exchequer and *are not* channeled back into the industry.
Source: EI various years.

Enterprise Ireland has also been intensifying its own grant-giving mechanism, as can be seen in table 4.2. Between 1994 and 2003 Enterprise Ireland directly gave companies an annual average of £16 million.

However, the grant-giving mechanisms of Enterprise Ireland highlight the different underlying objectives of the Israeli and Irish industrial policies, and exacerbate the main obstacle that still exists for many Irish entrepreneurs: the acute lack of very early– and early-stage financing for NTBFs. EI financial aid packages for new companies consist of both a hodgepodge of grants—some of which are the remnants of older grant schemes mixed with some new ones—and equity-based investment. In order for companies to get special tax benefits and qualify for R&D grants, EI needs to approve them as "fast-growing start-ups," a classification devised by the NSD in the early 1990s. Fast-growing start-ups are companies that are seen as capable of reaching sales of €2 million within a few years. Only a limited number of companies can be approved, however, and only limited resources are given to the NSD and EI to conduct the necessary analyses. Hence a bottleneck develops specifically in this critical development stage, at which the firms are in their most dire need for state aid.

This situation is further complicated by the equity base of the EI grant-giving mechanisms. EI, in one of the most paradoxical twists of the Irish neoliberal interventionist ideology, claims on the one hand that the state can and should take large stakes in private companies. However, adhering to neoliberal principles on the other hand, EI wishes to avoid a situation in which a government agency determines the market capitalization evaluation of a private company. This creates a situation in which the firms seeking EI aid must find private-market investors that would resolve the evaluation process. Only then would EI join the investment round on the same valuation basis. Many investors, though, agree to invest only in companies that have already received EI's seal of approval. This seeming Catch-22 situation is even more complex when we realize that EI is itself the single largest financier of the Irish VC industry. Hence, in many cases, EI actions make the Irish VC industry even more conservative in its investment decisions than it already is.

This process, in effect, makes it impossible for most early-stage IT start-ups to get sufficient financial aid from the state. As early-stage investment is riskiest and the uncertainty highest, EI investments do almost nothing to solve the most intense market failure inherent in new technology development. In addition, it can be argued that EI financial aid packages, as they are organized now, help more in lowering the risk for the VCs than they help NTBFs to secure larger amounts of capital than they could without this venue.[62] These shortcomings are readily admitted by EI. Accordingly, EI's then-CEO Dan Flinters mused: "I agree with some of what you say, especially with the fact that we are still lacking a good mechanism to finance seed and early-stage companies, on which we are working, but considering our goals and resources, I think we have the best-working scheme" (interview, February 5, 2002).

Indeed, considering that the goal of EI is not to generate the maximum amount of R&D but to maximize the number of successful indigenous businesses that supply the highest number of jobs for the lowest cost to the taxpayer, EI mechanisms are sufficiently well suited. Nevertheless, the continuous crisis of the industry since 2001, coupled with the fact that there have been almost no seed investments by Irish VC companies since then, raises the question of whether EI policies and grants answer the needs of the indigenous industry, or whether they have in fact become an obstacle to its growth. This sentiment was voiced not only by many companies but also by former EI executives. One can indeed defend the Irish record by arguing that since 2001 there has been a global crisis of the IT industry in general and VC financing in particular. Nevertheless, this does not explain why Ireland fared so much worse than either Israel or Taiwan, especially when Ireland has just culminated a major policy effort, including VC creation, whose main aim was specifically to set in motion more NTBF formation, not less.

A founder of a successful company in the 1980s reflects on EI's changing policies: "When we opened our first company, EI, then the IDA, was crucial. They also proved very, very helpful throughout the years and early 1990s. Now they just [have] become too conservative. They are no longer that helpful, especially to new young firms" (interview, April 18, 2001).

A few founders of younger start-ups concurred:

In the past EI were very helpful to young companies. Now, after they suddenly made money, the only thing they do is to play "king of the lake" games. Meaning that if you are already very successful, EI will come and grant you both money and help. When you actually need them, though, they just ignore you.

The part of EI that deals with helping you to set offices and meetings abroad is superb; not so within Ireland. In the beginning we were desperately looking to get grants from them, and they turned us down. Now after our success and after getting some VC money, they [EI] are running after us trying to convince us to take their money. They think they missed our boat and that they could have made money on us. . . . I really wonder if EI is at all capable of making decisions to invest in truly innovative, hence risky, new IT companies.

For two months I was trying to get money from EI, and then I finally understand that this is a waste of money and time to go to EI. To get good money [large grants] from EI you must already have a good VC deal in your packet.

The funny thing is that I found out that EI is much more aggressive than the VCs themselves asking for a big chunk out of companies. This, and they are so utterly slow and bureaucratic. I truly do not understand why they do it, because on the other hand they are the nicest and friendliest people I ever met. I think that the real problem is that they become omnipotent: you now must have EI approval in order to get anything in Ireland and they are talking with you under so many hats that sometimes I wonder if the person in front of me knew which role he is supposed to be playing now. (interviews with company founders, January 7, March 13, March 20, and April 20, 2001).

Indeed, the situation has become so severe that one former IDA executive who took part in planning the equity-based grant-giving mechanisms argued for a radical change of EU grant-giving mechanisms:

At the time it was a good idea, we had two problems we needed to deal with. First, there was political pressure after politicians became concerned when, on one hand, many software companies who got grants went bankrupt, and, on the other hand, a few were sold to MNCs, with the founders making a large profit. The second was the need of technology companies that do R&D to get a large quantity of capital up front, which we could not do with employment grants, especially as new software start-ups just do not create that many jobs. Thus equity-based grants seemed like an ideal solution for both and could be worked within existing regulations. I also must say that in the beginning, when we did not make any profit, it worked like a charm. The problems started when EI holdings in a few companies were suddenly worth millions. The more EI turned into the most successful VC organization in Ireland, the more profits became a yardstick, with the result that investment decisions are becoming more and more conservative and profit-oriented. EI is now so obsessed about making money and does not care enough about the overarching goal that the state should have—the development and growth of the industry. (interview, March 10, 2001)

However, the most telling example of the acute lack of true seed capital might be the political battle the ISA led to prevent the cancellation of the Business Expansion Scheme (BES) and the Seed Capital Scheme (SCS). BES and SCS are tax schemes under which a group of private investors pool capital of up to €250,000 to invest in exchange for stocks in a specific enterprise under special tax discount procedures. The two, in particular the older BES, have provided a crucial source of capital for all newly established enterprises, especially IT NTBFs. Almost all of the Irish IT companies have used the BES as their main, and sometime sole, source of seed financing.

The two schemes were supposed to phase out in the end of 2003. The Ministry of Finance argued that with Irish technology-oriented VC industry having the largest-ever amount of capital under management, along with EI help, the two schemes, which need a special approval from the EU competition commission, should be scrapped. However, with the Irish VC industry and EI in effect reaching a deadlock over seed investment, the importance of the two schemes to the industry rose instead of declining after 2000. After extensive lobbying by the ISA, the two schemes were prolonged until 2006 and their maximum award was raised to €1 million. It is symbolic of the current missteps and misunderstandings of the Irish state-industry co-evolution processes that in a newspaper interview the then-chairman of the ISA, Cathal Friel, who has also been a top manager in the Irish VC and corporate finance industry, described the schemes as the only source of funding available for start-ups in the software sector, apart from EI aid (O'Halloran 2003, Smyth 2004a, Taylor 2003).

Hence it seems that even with all the new initiatives and the greater amount of finance designated for investment in the IT sector, the actual situation of the Irish IT industry in 2004 is not much different from that of the Irish IT industry in the beginning of the 1990s. This, again, hurts the IT hardware industry more than it hurt the software industry. The main reason for this disadvantage is that the hardware product R&D phase is both longer and more expensive; therefore the risk associated with hardware R&D is higher. The reactions of two leading VCs and hardware entrepreneurs to questions about the lack of investment in the hardware sector are revealing:

> It is obvious why there are almost no new hardware companies. The risks are a lot higher than in the software sector, so we prefer not to invest in them.

> There are no hardware followers to us because there is no money; you need a lot more money in hardware than in software, and when there is almost no money, period, then software companies, which can also generate revenues through consultancy and bespoke development, will be the only ones that survive.

> Hardware investment is just too risky for Irish VCs: the development phase is long with no revenues, the costs are an order of magnitude higher than software; this is just too risky. Even in software we dislike investing in companies with no source of revenues. You want to know what was the best VC investment of the year in my opinion? It was this lovely company, three ex-Iona founders, they already generated €3 million in consultancy fees, and now they talk about a product. They do not really know what the product is going to be, just that it is going to be in middleware in the mobile domain. You see? Three trusted veterans, a constant stream of revenue, and low risk that they will go belly-up. These are the kind of investments we like to take part in, not some haphazard idea for some hardware product development. (interviews June 10, 2003; February 5, 2004; February 4, 2002)

This crisis in new company formation coincides directly with the culmination of the most extensive initiative to expand the Irish technology VC industry. Moreover, it coincides with the most extensive efforts ever to create significant academic R&D activities, with the aim of fostering the continuous growth of the IT industry in Ireland. In sum, it seems as if the co-evolutionary process of state-industry relations in Ireland is now out of step. With EI's centrality in each and every point of the system and with its new zeal for profit-generating investment, one must wonder whether the future development of the indigenous software industry in Ireland is now in danger of suffering from a stage two failure—the inability of the state to relinquish its own power over the sectoral industrial system.[63]

The crisis in the formation of new firms is not the only one the Irish indigenous software industry is facing. Internal reports by the ISA strategic vision group in late 2003 showed that only twenty-four of the total of seven hundred Irish software companies reached the very low barrier of €2 million in annual sales. These findings suggest that even established software firms find it very difficult to expand their activities under the current conditions. Moreover, fewer than 30 percent of surveyed companies in 2004 were even willing to look for VC funding; this is a sharp decrease and another indicator of the growing mistrust between industry, investors, and the state agencies (ISA 2003, 2004, McManus 2002).

The one sector of the Irish IT industry to which this crisis is irrelevant is the MNC sector. As can be seen in table 4.3, MNCs not only extended their R&D activities in Ireland by buying Irish IT firms for their technologies but also, in the past five years, moved to open their own in-house R&D operations. Both Intel and IBM announced the opening of new R&D facilities, and the MNCs' participation in the new Science Foundation Ireland schemes is growing, compared with the almost insignificant participation of the local software industry.

Accordingly, it seems as if without some changes in policy the end result of the new S&T industrial policy initiatives, aimed at least partly to diminish Ireland's overreliance on the MNC sector, might end up increasing it (ISA 2004, IT 2003a, 2003b, Lillington 2003a, 2003b, Smyth 2004b).

In this chapter I have analyzed the development of the IT industry and the co-evolution of state-industry relations in Ireland. In particular, I have inquired into the different ways in which the state acquired its technological and scientific skills, the industry's evolution, and the interdependencies between state policies and the industrial development. Unlike Israel or Taiwan, the Irish state's almost sole development focus for many years was job creation. The state has also been following a much less active strategy with regard to the indigenous IT industry. While vastly improving the educational, physical, and communication infrastructures, Ireland's industrial policy focused mainly on bringing foreign companies to open manufacturing facilities within its borders. Some thought was given to the ultimate goal of embedding these firms within the Irish industrial system, but there have not been, until very re-

Table 4.3. Top IT MNCs R&D by Expenditures,
Republic of Ireland, 2003

Rank	Name	USD (millions)
1	Analog Devices	80
2	Ericsson	79
3	Nortel	24
4	CMG Telecommunications	13
5	Loctite	13
6	Lucent	10
7	HP	10
8	Bausch & Lomb	9
9	Mednova	7
10	SUN Microsystems	6
11	Intel	6
12	Schering-Plough	5
13	PMC Sierra	5
14	M/A Com	5
15	Motorola	5

Source: IDA 2006.
Note: Due to the Irish tax regulation and the practice of price transfer-ring, these figures should be treated solely as estimates and not as di-rect representation of the scope and intensity of the R&D activities themselves.

cently, coherent attempts to do so. As a result, many of these companies even-tually left Ireland.

In contrast to Israel and Taiwan there were limited resources devoted to R&D in Ireland. Even when the IDA established a program to promote local industry in the late 1980s, its focus was on job creation and not R&D. This especially hurt the hardware sector. Furthermore, during the 1980s the hardware industry had to compete fiercely for the limited pool of skilled engineers against MNCs who were recruiting for both their Irish and global facilities. With meager financial re-sources and unable to offer secure long-term employment, the Irish hardware in-dustry was at a severe disadvantage. This failure of the state to engage with the specific needs of the Irish hardware industry and to embed itself within it—even when the first successes of the indigenous industry, Mentec and Lake Electronics, were both hardware companies—is a case of stage one failure.

This failure, and the particular way in which state and industry finally did embed more successfully around the software industry, had much to do with the way in which the Irish bureaucracy is structured, specifically in the way knowledge in gathered and employed. For many years the Irish bureaucracy development agencies followed the ideal-type Weberian structure, with internal recruiting, training, and career development procedures. However, it has an English flavor, including a strong distinction between the social science–humanities–law "general educated" employees, who are being groomed to management, and the technical-engineering "expert educated" personnel, whose careers do not lead them to high management positions (Rose 1981, 1986). Since the 1960s there has been only one secretary general of a ministry who joined the civil service technical personnel career track with an engineering background.[64] Accordingly, Ireland opted to follow the third strategy of acquiring technology- and industry-specific skills—creating domain-specific subunits stuffed with industry insiders—when these skills were deemed necessary.

For these reasons the Irish state, focused as much as it was on FDI, was unable to allocate enough resources and attention to devise specific policy initiatives and embed itself within the industry to spur its growth. It was only a decade later, after a few software companies achieved some commercial success in foreign markets, with the software industry using all its political muscle, and with the IDA already changing its focus of attention, that Ireland developed a coherent IT industry–focused industrial policy. Even then, the industrial policy was geared toward the indigenous software and not hardware sector.

Only in the late 1990s did Ireland start to pay close attention to the assistance its local companies might need abroad, and even then the state limited its role to that of a promoter of companies in various foreign markets and did not attempt to structure specific relationships between local and foreign firms. With regard to foreign financial markets, the state, while happy that some IT firms publicly listed on foreign stock exchanges, has also encouraged them to list locally. In addition, while employing and channeling EU grants, the state focused on local financial institutions as the main loci for its various initiatives to create a local venture capital industry.

Toward the end of the 1990s, with the efforts of EI and the establishment of SFI and PRTLI, coupled with the successful state actions to create and grow a local, and locally financed and managed, technologically oriented VC industry, it seems as if the Irish IT industrial innovation system has been finally transformed. However, the particular way in which this system evolved and the devotion of the Irish developmental agencies to the two contradictory ideals of the neoliberal interventionalist ideology still prevent the indigenous industry from enjoying most, if not all, of these newfound riches. With their resources and knowledge and their new interest in moving more R&D activities to Ireland, the MNCs are much better poised to utilize the growing academic R&D infrastructure in Ireland. Already American MNCs are by far the largest patent issuers in Ireland, and the inability of the indigenous industry to successfully grow firms leaves it extremely vulnerable vis-à-vis the MNCs in two fronts. Hence, without extensive changes in the indigenous-focused science-and-technology industrial policy, the new move of Ireland into high-level R&D, hailed as a way for Ireland to become less dependent on FDI, would end up making the Irish economy even more dominated by MNCs than before.

Conclusion: Comparing Choices and Consequences in Rapid Innovation–Based Industrialization

Choice: the act of choosing: SELECTION; power of choosing: OPTION
Consequence: something produced by a cause or necessarily following from a set of conditions

—Merriam-Webster's Collegiate Dictionary, *eleventh edition*

This book has been motivated by two puzzles. First, what is the role of the state in the development of rapid innovation–based industries in less-developed economies, under the conditions of intensified globalization and fragmented production? Second, does the IT industry's very different development paths—in particular in Israel, Ireland, and Taiwan—suggest that multiple developmental choices are available to emerging economies?

The study shows that emerging economies do have the ability to craft and select different paths in nurturing the growth of successful rapid innovation–based industries. Thus the argument of this book: that real choices for economic development exist. In the empirical chapters I elaborated on how diverse S&T industrial policies distinctly shaped the development of each IT industry. In so doing, I have dispelled theories that solely attribute the explanatory power either to the timing of industrialization or to specific states' structures. The stories of Israel, Ireland, and Taiwan suggest that four factors are crucial in order for a state to spur RIB industrial development.

First, the state needs to actively engage with industry to solve the fundamental market failure in industrial R&D. Otherwise, the inherent characteristics of industrial R&D—its indivisibility, inappropriability, and high uncertainties, all of which are accentuated in the case of emerging economies with their lack of technological capabilities and finance—would lead private investors to allocate suboptimal amounts of resources to research.

Second, state action is also of crucial importance because the innovation process itself is an inherently collective endeavor. As such, innovation is iterative and cooperative in nature; therefore, there is a significant role for public actors in facilitating, enhancing, and maintaining innovative activities.

Third, the state must actively link the local industry with global markets, both production networks and financial markets.

Lastly, in each specific industrial sector, the state and industry need to be able to manage constant change. State actions and policies that prove successful in early stages of the industry's development might prove harmful in later stages. Specifically, the development agencies need to be able to manage the political reality of their own diminishing importance as the industry grows.

The theoretical framework presented in the first chapter offers a specific understanding of the different consequences and final outcomes of the diverse choices taken by Israel, Ireland, and Taiwan. First, our theory argues that specific industrial R&D, dynamic economic capabilities, and business models are more suitable for certain stages of the production process. Secondly, the analysis of the dynamics of production-stage specialization and economies of scale and scope indicates that industrial systems specializing in specific stages of production tend, if successful, with time and effort, to become ever more competitive and innovative in these specific stages. Consequently, to understand the different evolutionary processes of rapid innovation–based industrial growth we must (*a*) comprehend how industrial R&D and dynamic economic capabilities are created, improved, and maintained in each of our cases, (*b*) follow the growing utilization of certain business models in each of our cases, and (*c*) understand the development of specific relationships that the local industry has with the global industrial and financial markets.

In short, our framework has motivated us to a specific analysis of how different behavior and structure of the state influences the development of the IT industry's R&D capabilities in each of our cases, by looking at a few critical domains:

- Domain one: state decisions on necessary R&D skill acquirement.
- Domain two: state decisions on the degree of control it attempts to have on the technological development path of the industry, including decisions of how, and whom, to finance. These decisions affect both the R&D resources available to the industry and the scope of R&D activities.
- Domain three: state efforts to build the early local leading companies, and state decisions concerning the involvement of foreign firms and investors within its national borders, as well as decisions concerning whether to enhance specific relationships between local and foreign companies outside the state's national borders. These decisions shape the resources, and the particular feedback and information the industry gets from its main customers, as well as the diffusion and development of specific innovative capabilities.

Accordingly, private firms in the high-technology industry of emerging economies would have more limited R&D capabilities if the state tried to control the industrial R&D development path, encompassed the R&D conducting agents within its structure, supplied only limited resources, refrained from urging foreign companies to conduct R&D activities within its borders, and limited the involvement of foreigners as financiers. Throughout the three empirical chapters, this framework proved to be effective in enabling us to comprehend how the particular choices of the three states led to the specific industrial outcomes in each case. Moreover, unlike other theoretical frameworks, our framework proved helpful in understanding not only successes and failures but also the specific strengths and weaknesses of each industry. In short, the theory helps not only in explaining results at the aggregate level but also in comprehending the true nuances and consequences of the choices made and the actions taken. Consequently, by showing the plurality of actions and choices that emerging economies have in order to develop their RIB industries, and by analyzing their particular consequences, both positive and negative, I have in this study emphasized the importance of politics—the process of crafting, debating, deciding, and acting on different alternatives.

In this concluding chapter I take a more comparative approach to this last point and show how political debates, on both the national and sectoral levels, influenced key decisions about the critical variables of our framework. I present detailed comparisons on three issues: MNCs, R&D market failures, and venture financing. Together, these examples strengthen our arguments not only on how we should reformulate our thinking on rapid innovation–based industrial development but on the role of politics at both the national and sectoral levels in defining the very diverse economic growth paths emerging economies can, and should, follow.

DEALING WITH THE "KING KONGS": THE
POLITICS OF MNC-FOCUSED POLICIES

One of the critical factors in understanding the diverse development paths of the IT industries in Israel, Ireland, and Taiwan is the different ways in which the state has linked the local industry with the global industry. Nowhere are these differences more apparent than in the diverse policies that the three countries employed with regard to MNCs. This is also a crucial political choice as decisions with regard to MNCs (*a*) are about the nationality of the ownership of local production, and hence about the level of dependency on the international system and markets that the local economy is willing to sustain, and (*b*) intimately attest to the national perception of the local industry's current and potential capabilities as well as status. Therefore various policies followed by the three countries reflect the diversity of their national identities as well as their perception of the world system.

Looking at the political context in which these policies developed, we find that in 1950 Ireland was a country brought to the brink of poverty by two decades of extreme nationalistic-autarkic industrial and economic policy, aimed at severing its dependence on the United Kingdom. In this political situation, job creation became the national mission, and a significant social backlash spread against the ideals of national economic independence and industrial isolation. Consequently, local industry was thoroughly discredited and its capabilities and motives were suspect. The fact that the IDA's MNC-focused policies were quickly perceived as effective in large-scale job creation, even as local industry continued its downward spiral, strengthened this political atmosphere. Only by understanding the sociopolitical context in which Ireland's first industrial policies evolved can we understand why, until very recently, the main aim of Irish S&T and industrial policies was to maximize inward FDI and bring more MNCs to open labor-intensive manufacturing facilities in Ireland, and why the local industry, specifically the IT industry, was treated indifferently and its leaders regarded with doubt.

On the other hand, we have Taiwan, a state that, while much more willing to create dependencies on international markets than its neighbors in north Asia, Japan and South Korea, was much keener than Ireland to see the nationality of the ownership of a significant percentage of the Taiwanese industry stay Taiwanese (Fuller 2002). Taiwan, in the context of its growing political isolation, was actively trying to link its local industry as a strategic supplier and partner to the world's leading MNCs. However, to accomplish this vision, Taiwan still needed to create a critical mass of local industry, specifically locally owned, in the context of a political system distrusting the concentration of power in big multidivisional conglomerates, and within a financial system designed to prevent the use of large-scale long-term debt. Only by taking account of these political constraints and wishes can we understand why the Taiwanese state at the same time tried to lure MNCs into Taiwan, employing tactics similar to Ireland's, and pressure these MNCs to source a significant percentage of their components locally, as well as to transfer to Taiwanese companies the necessary know-how to manufacture them.

Lastly, Israel conceptualized its economic future in terms not of job creation but of the creation of a science-based industry. Hence the policy goal was to maximize a certain set of activities and to build an industry whose main activities in Israel would be the creation and development of new products and technologies. Moreover, in the political context in which Israel has operated since 1967, under the Arab embargo, cooperation with MNCs was perceived as a significant international achievement, especially when these MNCs could be persuaded to locate activities of strategic importance in Israel. This is especially true since the vision of a science-based industry, unlike the Taiwanese industrial vision, does not inherently necessitate national ownership of the organization conducting these activities.

Looking at the behavior of American IT MNCs in the three preceding chapters, we saw that these diverse national policies translated into marked differences in the ways in which MNCs linked with the Israeli, Irish, and Taiwanese industries, as well as in the activities the MNCs located in the three countries. In contrast with the way American IT MNCs have been operating in Ireland and Taiwan, in Israel many if not all of the MNCs' first activity was to open R&D centers, or to buy Israeli NTBFs and transform them into R&D centers, moving only later, if at all, to manufacturing activities. These diverse MNC behaviors translated into the different outputs MNCs supplied to the local industrial system, and the different inputs they sourced from it. Accordingly, these differences translated to different incentives for capabilities development, as well as different resources and opportunities available in pursuing them for the local IT industry.

Two examples of the different paths pursued by two leading MNCs, Intel and 3Com, in Israel and Ireland serve as a way to highlight these differences and their impact. In 1974 Dov Frohman, a senior Israeli researcher in Intel's California headquarters, decided to return to Israel and accept a professorship in the School for Applied Physics at the Hebrew University of Jerusalem.[1] As Intel wanted to retain the services of Frohman, the company agreed to open its first design and development center outside the United States in Israel, with five employees.[2] In doing so, Intel pioneered a mode by which many MNCs started operations in Israel.[3] Over the years, the Intel center was highly successful and continuously enlarged its R&D activities. By 2002 it encompassed seven centers. In 1985 Intel Israel also pioneered the first movement of Intel toward silicon chip fabrication activities outside the United States when the first Intel fab in Israel started operations in Jerusalem. In 1999 Intel started the operation of its second fab in Israel. In 2000, following the acquisition by Intel of two companies with major R&D centers in Israel, DSPC and Dialogic Israel, Intel's R&D activities evolved into two more product platforms. Beyond these, the activities in Israel of Intel Capital, Intel's venture capital arm, are the most comprehensive in terms of investment outside the United States. During 2002–2003, Intel Capital was the most active foreign investor in Israel.

Throughout the years, Intel Israel R&D has been responsible for some critical components in Intel's global strategy, including the 8088 (IBM's famous choice as a CPU for its first PC) and the Pentium MMX technology. In 2000 Intel Israel had revenues of $2 billion (USD) and employed four thousand people; as of 2002 Intel Israel was responsible for the development of the next generation's laptop-oriented CPUs, 3G mobile network products, and a few other critical components of Intel's global R&D strategy, such as the development of the latest technologies for optoelectronic chips manufacturing.

In 1989 Intel decided to start manufacturing operations in Ireland. The main reason behind Intel's decision to locate in Ireland was the company's fear of an imminent creation of "Fortress Europe" by the EC (now EU) in 1992. A year after the first box assembly operation began, Intel decided to open a full-scale fab, making Ireland the only other place apart from Israel with an Intel fab at the time. Within a few years, Intel realized that Fortress Europe was not an imminent danger and the box assembly line was closed. However, fabrication activities continued. Moreover, local management, spurred by the shock of the closing and helped by an Israeli who became the fab developer and manager, and using his experience in Israel, started low-profile R&D activities aimed at the creation of a center of excellence in specific technologies in Ireland. Intel Ireland also managed to lobby Intel head-quarters to create a special position for Intel Capital in Ireland, which started operations in 2001 and has already invested in a few local start-ups.[4]

3Com's involvement in Israel enlightens the second and newer route used by MNCs starting operation in Israel. In 1994, 3Com bought NiceCom, an Is-raeli company that developed local area network asynchronous transfer mode (ATM) switches.[5] NiceCom was then transformed into the NiceCom division inside 3Com, responsible for the development of all ATM technology in 3Com, which enlarged its Israeli NiceCom R&D center through a few more M&As and ended with a critical mass of three hundred people in Herzelia. At the end of the 1990s 3Com became a large, complex company and suffered from growing financial difficulties. As a result, 3Com started a process in which it spun off, among others, Palm, its handheld division; its modem divi-sion under the old U.S. Robotics brand (another company with an R&D cen-ter in Israel, which 3Com had acquired); and, in February 2000, Atrica, a new Israeli start-up developing urban optical networks and headed by none other than the old NiceCom executive team. As of 2004 Atrica had inherited all of 3Com's R&D activities in Israel and has been considered one of Israel's most promising start-ups, managing by the beginning of 2005 to secure more than $160 million in investment. Moreover, the former CEO and now chairman of 3Com and CEO and chairman of Palm, Eric Benhamou, serves as Atrica's chairman.

For reasons similar to Intel's Fortress Europe strategy, 3Com started its Irish operation in 1992 by opening a plant in Dublin. Over the years, the Dublin operation became the best in quality and yields, and 3Com opened a small R&D center in Dublin. Even as 3Com was reeling from eighteen months of downsizing in 2002, the Irish R&D center was still operative when all others were closed or spun off, and although 3Com has outsourced all of its manu-facturing activities, mainly to Flextronics, and closed down all of its other plants worldwide, the Irish plant was the last to close. According to 3Com, the reasons behind this decision have been a mix of the high quality and yields for the Dublin plant, the Irish tax regime, the fact that Ireland is part of the EU, the excellent infrastructure for European deliveries around Dublin, and the excellent relationship with the Irish government.[6]

Thus the stories of Intel and 3Com exemplify the very different ways in which their national IT industries are embedded in the MNCs' global pro-duction network. Israel has always been first and foremost a location for high-level R&D activities, while Ireland was mainly deemed a strategic location for manufacturing. These different relationships brought leading American MNCs to locate very different activities in each location, creating very different relationships with, demands from, economic incentives for, and opportunity structures and resource availability for the local IT industry.

FACILITATING INDUSTRIAL R&D: THE POLITICS
OF THE STATE AS A RESEARCHER

A second critical component in understanding the different development paths of the Israeli, Irish, and Taiwanese IT industries involves the ways in which the three states devised different solutions to the problem of industrial R&D market failure. Of particular importance is the question of the location of the R&D-generating agents within the industrial system, public versus private. In all three countries this debate was intimately connected to the national perception of capabilities, status, and identity, as well as to the politics and the bureaucratic structure of knowledge. Taiwan and Israel are the two cases between which a deeper comparison is most revealing.

Looking at Israel in 1968, with a total of 886 R&D workers with academic degrees in the whole civilian industrial sector, one might wonder how the Katchalski Committee came to the conclusion that the growth of science-based industry should be the core of Israel's S&T industrial policy goals. However, even more interesting, and easily forgotten, is the fact that the committee's recommendations, which were transformed to specific policies, viewed state-run public research institutions as the main vehicle for this socioeconomic transformation. Hence, between 1968 and 1973, Israel undertook major steps toward following a development path similar to Taiwan's. Nonetheless, by 1974 the reliance on public research institutions was quickly curtailed, and the system refocused around a policy regime viewing private companies as the main agents for industrial R&D and technological development. Thus two questions arise: why did Israel, unlike Taiwan, choose to change course? And what enabled Israel to do so with such speed and without any significant political backlash?

The answers to these two questions are intimately related to these two countries' different politics of technological knowledge, perceptions of national identity, state-industry relations, and the political-bureaucratic structures of power. First, let us look at the question of each country's political context of state-industry relations and the politics of technological knowledge. In Taiwan the ruling party, the KMT, while viewing the growth of private industry as the ultimate end, at the same time mistrusted private entrepreneurs and their motives and was actively pursuing policies to prevent the growth of competing centers of power (Cheng 1993, Fields 1995, Gold 1986, Hong 1997, Wade 1990, Wu 2001). In Israel, on the other hand, the ruling Labor Party actively tried to grow a strong private industry and was pursuing policies to limit the power of the public and semipublic sectors (Levi-Faur 1998, 2001). Accordingly, if at the starting point in both societies the existing infrastructure of industrial R&D consisted mainly of public research institutions, in the political context of Taiwan such a system would have offered an optimal solution to competing political goals. In Israel, on the other hand, a system focusing on public research institutions not only clashed with the ultimate goal of building private science-based industry, and hence an industry with significant R&D capabilities, but also clashed with the political-economic goal of the ruling Labor Party to strengthen the private sector at the expense of the public sector.

However, at least as important in facilitating the Israeli course change were the different politics of knowledge in the two states. Here the bureaucratic structure of knowledge and power, as well as the perception and structure of the academic system, was of key importance. In Taiwan the decision to create ITRI and later III was the personal undertaking of two prominent KMT leaders, Y. S. Sun and K. T. Li. As a consequence, the two public research institutions were under the direct patronage of two leading politician-bureaucrats who had direct interest in their continuous development. From the mid-1970s onward, K. T. Li devoted his career and considerable power to the development of the Taiwanese IT industry through ITRI and III.

In addition, the high echelons of the Taiwanese bureaucracy consisted of engineers. Therefore, the view of a state deeply involved in charting the technological development of its industry and locating the R&D agents within the state structure was accepted not only as natural but also as politically prudent, and helped to directly enhance the power and status of the two patrons of ITRI and III. Lastly, during that period, the university system in Taiwan was thoroughly controlled by the KMT, with virtually all the professors and administrators nominated by the KMT and members of stature in the party. Academic freedom was not a widely held value, and the goals of academic research were intimately tied to the national aims of improving Taiwan's economic and political power.

In Israel, the situation was almost directly opposite. No leading politician had any direct interest in Israel's public research institutions. The political leaders who decided the fate of Israel's S&T industrial policies did not possess Ph.D. degrees, nor did they personally undertake the development of the IT industry. S&T industrial policy in Israel was always deemed to be a professional domain. Values of academic freedom and "pure" basic research were strong. Until the late 1970s developing the research capability of strictly academic institutions was a high national priority, sometimes even higher than national security and the growth of the defense industry. A case in point is the story of the transfer of a whole department to the Weizmann Institute of Science from RAFAEL, the public research institution for the development of armaments. This was done in order to enhance the national academic research infrastructure, and against the wishes of RAFAEL, which invested significant resources into the development of this department and viewed it as critical to its future R&D plans (Mardor 1981, pp. 113–117).[7]

Consequently, after the 1973 war, when the government of Israel decided to give higher priority to the development of industrial R&D and science-based industry by recruiting a prominent and strong-willed professional, Itzhak Yaakov, to head the OCS, he was given the power to transform it into an active agency, and had authority to formulate and implement policies. Coming from within the military, and possessing strong international connections and education, Yaakov was ideologically opposed to public research institutions. In an interview he concluded:

> My second guiding principle was that a state cannot guide the industry. The state cannot come and say from now on we will develop engines for helicopters; this is a complete dead-end. Successful industrial R&D comes from the people themselves. Therefore the problem of the state is to give the entrepreneurs who think they know what they are doing the ability to do so. The key to understand is that we cannot control the consumers; accordingly good ideas have to come from the market, not from the state. These are the reasons why in my second year I decided to cut the budget of the public research institutes by 70 percent and transfer the finance directly to industry. (interview, September 28, 2000)

The different national political contexts, the ideologies of development and science, political patronage for the public research institutes, and the bureaucratic structure of power were the main reasons why in Israel, once Yaakov decided to dismantle the public research institution-based S&T industrial policy, he could do so in matters of days, while in Taiwan, this option was not even considered.

These decisions have had decisive long-term consequences on the development path of the IT industries in Israel and Taiwan. In Israel, the focus on the enhancement of technological cutting-edge R&D activities of private firms has propelled IT companies to develop capabilities that facilitated novel products innovation based on the latest technologies, the newest technologies themselves, or new applications of these technologies, and has led Israel's IT industry into its position as a supplier of new technologies to the global IT industry's production networks. Nonetheless, the source of the industry's Achilles' heel is also the state's almost exclusive focus on promoting private firms to conduct R&D activities and follow business models based on new innovations. Because the development of management and business skills has lagged, many Israeli companies have difficulties in maintaining enduring success.

In Taiwan the decision to utilize public research institutions–based S&T industrial policy led to the development of an industrial innovation system with strong division of labor between industry and public research institutions. This pattern limits the development of R&D capabilities of private firms by motivating these firms to concentrate more on the development part of the R&D. In this system it is the public research institutions that decide which R&D projects should be pursued, conduct nearly all R&D, and only then diffuse the results to private industry; accordingly, the development of core R&D capabilities is concentrated within the public sector. Thus in Taiwan, specifically because of its institutional system, the industry successfully developed advanced capabilities in second-generation, process, and manufacturing innovation, but not in new-product development. While this system propelled Taiwan to unprecedented success in the IT hardware sector, it is an open question as to whether Taiwan can change this system so that it can move to original, new-product R&D activities in the future.

FINANCING AND RESOURCES: GOING LOCAL
OR GOING GLOBAL?

A third critical variable in the diverse development paths of the IT industries in Israel, Ireland, and Taiwan has been the connection of industry with the global financial markets. In all three countries, key decisions by the state were taken as part of policy initiatives to create local VC industries. These were again decisions that are closely linked to questions about the ownership and the long-term embeddedness of the industry within the national context. On the one hand, a tight relationship with the global investing community and financial markets gives the industry an opening to an immensely rich supply of skills, resources, and capital. On the other hand, this same linking transfers a large portion of the ownership of local industry into foreign hands, and this same dependency on foreign financial markets weakens the industry's national linkages. Moreover, the more connected the industry is to the global financial markets, the more the fruits of the local IT industry's success are redistributed to foreign investors who are not as inclined as local investors to reinvest their gains in the national economy. Lastly, national governments have more power to influence the behavior of local financiers. Hence, while from the point of view of overall industrial development, linking the IT industry with experienced foreign VCs might be preferred, governments might favor working with local institutions and individuals.

In each of our cases, the developmental agencies followed very different VC creation policies. A large percentage of these differences can indeed be explained by the different conceptualizations by policy makers of the VC industry itself. In Chapters 2–4 I showed the distinction between two VC creation policy styles: one that sees VC creation as a problem of a missing pool of capital, and a second that sees VC as a distinct industry with specific skills and capabilities (Avnimelech and Teubal 2003a, 2006a, 2006b). This distinction explains much of the outcome in terms of VC behavior. Nevertheless, this distinction obscures the intense political nature of these policies, specifically since, in the case of emerging economies, a decision to treat VC as a distinct industry strongly suggests a need to tightly connect the local with the global VC industry and financial markets.

In Taiwan the VC industry was, like many other initiatives, the brainchild of the leading technocrat-politician K. T. Li. Impressed by the U.S. VC industry in the early 1980s, Li viewed the VC industry mainly as a supplier of a dedicated pool of capital. In the Taiwanese political context, Li considered it essential that the main investors in the industry would be Taiwanese. In 1983, under his influence, VCs were allowed to register as companies rather than as limited partnerships. The main vehicle to channel capital to these newly formed companies was a tax credit of 20 percent to shareholders in VC firms. This tax incentive remained in place until 2000 and was the main reason behind the extensive amount of finance channeled specifically to VCs. It is not surprising that in this political context many of the early VCs were financial subsidiaries of different KMT investment vehicles. For the most part, the VC industry in Taiwan remains captive to various investors, both financial and industrial. The VCs themselves lack extensive industry experience and are

mainly recruited from those with financial background. Taiwan's VC industry, operating under the regulations that force VCs to be registered as companies, also continued to be extremely local. As of 2004, according to the Taiwanese VC association, foreign capital still amounted to less than 7 percent.[8]

In Israel the political and industrial contexts were almost the opposite. By
the beginning of the 1990s, not only was the IT industry already relatively
well embedded in the American financial markets, with a cumulative number
of about a dozen companies already listed on NASDAQ, but the first private
VCs also appeared, and foreign financiers were their main investors. The OCS
took the lead after a first failed attempt, Inbal, which was headed by the Ministry of Finance, to spur a local VC industry with an organizational form similar to Taiwan's: VCs as publicly listed holding companies on the Tel Aviv
Stock Exchange. Unlike Taiwan or Ireland, the OCS linked VC policy and
made it an integral part of its overall reconfiguration program for the high-
technology industrial environment in the early 1990s. In this political context,
we can understand why Yozma, as the VC creation initiative was known, was
conceptualized the way it was.

In the early 1990s the OCS used the political window of opportunity created by the massive waves of immigration from the former Soviet Union to
launch a series of policy initiatives. Each of these three initiatives was part of
an overall program to fix what the OCS analyzed as areas of persistent weakness with Israel's RIB industries: extremely early seed investment, skills and finance in the more mature market-penetration stage of firms' development,
and advanced generic R&D capabilities. Thus the creation of the VC industry was conceptualized not solely as a problem of financing but as part of a
systemic weakness of missing capabilities. It is in this context, with the already
deep embeddedness of the Israeli industry within the American financial markets, and only after the failure of the Inbal program to create a locally financed VC industry, that we can understand the advancement of the Yozma
program. In particular, it conceptualized VC as an industry with skills that
were lacking in Israel, and it made a deliberate political attempt to increase
both the field of investors and their clients, as well as to tie the Israeli IT industry more fully with the global financial markets.

In Ireland, the one rarely talked about but quite striking political constraint,
in the period when the IT-focused VC initiative materialized in the second
half of the 1990s, was the recent reorganization of the developmental agencies
and the sharp division of labor between their two domains and clientele. On
one side of the divide was IDA Ireland, whose domain comprised MNCs and

all FDI inflows into Ireland. On the other side was the newly structured Enterprise Ireland, out to prove itself with a domain comprising local industry and all local enterprise and investment. VC policy, under other political circumstances a bridge with which to connect FDI inflows with local enterprise development, fell within the domain of EI and was led by the NSD.

Hence, even with the declared aim of the NSD VC initiative to embed the Irish IT industry more intimately with the global markets and to aid Irish companies in their pursuit of foreign success, and even with the acknowledged political goal of increasing the circle of financiers in Ireland, which was deemed too narrow, the political institutional constraints limited the NSD to seek established local financial institutions as partners for its VC program. Accordingly, the NSD, utilizing EU funds, opted on the one side to enforce the organizational form of limited partnerships, similar to Israel and in imitation of the United States, but on the other side specifically chose only Irish institutions as its partners.[9] The institutional division between the IDA and EI is also becoming an artificial obstacle with the growing interest of the MNCs in the Irish IT industry. Consequently, many managers of MNCs and their VC arms find that their "natural" political interlocutors are located within the IDA. However, the proper interlocutors for issues of Irish IT industrial development are all situated in EI.

All the very different VC creation policy initiatives of Ireland, Israel, and Taiwan have been exceptionally successful. However, all three have had very different outcomes in terms of the VC industries created, and in terms of the tremendously different relationships between the local IT industry and foreign markets they nurtured.

In Taiwan the creation and rapid growth of this VC industry has helped the Taiwanese IT industry, in particular the hardware industry, to evolve as it did. Taiwanese VCs are both much more conservative than their U.S. counterparts and also much less capable of giving added value in running a true R&D-based young venture. The VC industry in Taiwan prefers to invest in companies with the more established business models of second-generation innovation or OEM-ODM. Moreover, as virtually all of its financings are Taiwanese, and as the VCs are registered Taiwanese companies, the Taiwanese VCs are under no pressure to seek financial exits in foreign financial markets. Hence, not only does the Taiwanese VC industry strengthen the linkage of the Taiwanese IT industry within Taiwan, but it also defuses some of the need it otherwise might have had to embed itself more tightly into the global financial markets. Thus it seems as if the political goal of keeping the Taiwanese industry Taiwanese has been achieved, though only at the price of a less sophisticated and much more conservative VC industry.

In Israel, on the other hand, the VC industry that rapidly grew in the late 1990s is better seen as an extension of the American financial markets and VC community than as a purely Israeli industry. Almost all of the financing of the industry is foreign, with the share of local investors actually diminishing after the dot-com crash on NASDAQ. Most of the biggest funds not only have offices in the United States and Europe but also have general partners who are experienced American and European VCs. Most of the VCs have industry experience and operate very similarly to Silicon Valley VCs. Even more important, with the finance and the organizational modes coming from the United States, Israeli VCs are seeking foreign financial exits. Thus the linkage of the IT industry with the rest of the Israeli economy is severely weakened, while its embeddedness in the global financial markets is growing. In addition, the need to seek foreign exits and the diffusion of the Silicon Valley VC model limit the Israeli IT industry to employ, almost exclusively, novel R&D-based models. Lastly, with the investors of the VC industry mostly being foreign institutions, most of their profits are transferred back to the investors, and hence, out of the Israeli economy, with, relative to Taiwan, only a small fraction of the capital staying within Israel. The existence of such a VC industry is thus both positive and negative. For example, only with such intimate connections to foreign capital markets could Atrica, the spin-off of 3Com's Israeli R&D center, raise more than $160 million to support novel R&D activities, a sum that is alone larger than the combined capital managed by the biggest Irish VC companies. However, Atrica's CEO is no longer Israeli, the HQ is no longer in Israel, and the financial gains of Atrica's success, if and when they arrive, will be mostly enjoyed by foreigners.

In Ireland the VC industry seems to be stuck in the middle. On the one hand the industry tries to imitate the American model and employ a hands-on value-added investment-and-management policy. On the other hand, most of its finance, and hence its connections, are with Irish financial institutions, and the VCs' background is mainly in the financial and management-consulting industry. Therefore the Irish VCs' ability to add value and to link their companies to foreign financial markets is limited. Indeed, with the Irish government being the single biggest source of funds, the VC industry is keener to be seen as helping the growth of the Irish IT industry. However, apart from a short period in the end of the 1990s, the VCs' apparent influence vis-à-vis the sums under the industry's management has actually declined. Nonetheless, the creation of a growing VC industry in Ireland has changed the rules of the game. Unlike in the past, a pure R&D business model is no longer seen as a taboo. Moreover, the strong connection of the VC industry to Ireland, in a very similar way to the case of Taiwan, aids in defusing some of the pressure of Irish IT firms to embed themselves more strongly in foreign markets at the expense of their "Irishness." With a VC industry flush with capital it is also plausible to expect that once the global IT industry shows signs of substantial improvement, Irish IT NTBFs can hope to raise significant amounts of finance for R&D. Nonetheless, as of 2006, not only had the rapid growth of the Irish VC industry not transformed the shape and size of the Irish IT industry, but the existence of the VC industry and the attention it had gained from the state might actually have hurt the ability of NTBFs to commence operations in the short run.

The premise of this book is that—with the extensive and rapid changes of industries, the international system, and the nature of industrial production itself—there is a need to establish a framework to analyze the role of the state in rapid innovation–based industrial development. Since the early days of the late-development theory, research on industrial production, innovation, and economic growth has diverged. Hence we no longer have a coherent body of literature capable of answering the questions that motivate this study. Accordingly, in the first chapter I developed a new theoretical framework by debating and building upon the work of three schools of thought—late development, systems of innovation, and globalization, particularly the globalization of production networks. I then used this framework to analyze the role of the state in the development of the IT industry in Israel, Ireland, and Taiwan. This inquiry was conducted in order to answer three questions: first, what are the roles of the state in RIB industrial development in emerging economies? Second, do states and societies have choices in their economic development strategies? And third, how does globalization, especially the radical transformation of production, influence the development opportunities of peripheral economies?

Our analysis of the development of the IT industries in Israel, Ireland, and Taiwan yielded the following answers.

First, there is a significant role for the state in creating and sustaining rapid innovation–based industrial development. This role, however, is not fixed. Emerging economies have many different choices in their efforts to develop RIB industries. Each of these choices has major consequences for the developmental path of each industry. This is particularly true with regard to industrial and innovational capabilities, and the ways in which each of these national industries is embedded into the global product networks and financial markets. For this reason, while globalization might limit the scope of state capabilities to develop their national industries in the strong development state method used by South Korea or Japan, globalization, especially the growing fragmentation of production, opens numerous new entry points for rapid innovation–based industries in emerging economies.

As a consequence, the role of the state in RIB industrial development has significantly changed. First, the state needs to actively engage in the fostering of industrial R&D and innovation. In so doing, the state is devising different solutions to (*a*) the inherent industrial R&D market failure, which is heightened in the case of emerging economies, and (*b*) the need to start a collective—that is to say, a community—effort to foster innovation, which stems from the fact that innovation by its very nature is an iterative and social endeavor. However, precisely because of this, and because long-term strategic planning is less feasible in rapid innovation–based industries where technology itself or its latest application are the products, the state cannot assume a position of central planning and command. Rather, the state role is more limited to that of creating capabilities, spurring specific activities, and motivating private enterprises for sustained efforts in RIB industries.

A second finding is that the proper level of analysis of states' rapid innovation–based industrial development efforts should be in the specific industrial sector level and at the level of particular state agencies, not solely in the national level. States can both fail and succeed in their RIB industrialization efforts in different sectors. Furthermore, many times sectoral, not national, policies have more direct influence on industrial development. This is especially true as, in contrast with the traditional Weberian ideals, our view of the state bureaucracy is of a fragmented and flexible civil service deeply embedded in various industrial sectors. For this reason, we should no longer view the state as a monolithic whole. Thus a crucial factor in understanding industrial success is to comprehend the political processes of state-industry co-evolution at both the national and sectoral levels.

Another crucial role of the state is to link its local burgeoning rapid innovation–based industry with global markets, to both production networks and financial markets, and both inside and outside its national borders. Our theory allowed us to explain why in the case of Taiwan a hardware industry developed that excels in second-generation innovation and high-level design-

and-manufacturing services, as well as in the supplying of components. This occurred because in Taiwan the state (*a*) located the R&D-conducting agents mostly within its own structure, (*b*) is intimately involved in decisions about the technological development path of the industry, (*c*) has been aiming specifically at developing companies that excel as ODM-OEMs, as well as actively trying to foster OEM-ODM relationships between local companies and MNCs, and (*d*) has been striving to limit the relationship of Taiwanese NTBFs to Taiwanese financial institutions.

In the case of Israel an IT industry developed that excels in novel product innovation and new technology creation, specifically because the state (*a*) focused on motivating private firms to innovate and refrained from targeting specific technological development paths, instead focusing on fostering a specific set of activities, R&D, (*b*) has been actively helping in the creation of particular relationships between local companies and MNCs where Israeli firms focus on new-product R&D, (*c*) has had an FDI-focused industrial policy whose sole goal was to motivate MNCs to open R&D subsidiaries in Israel, and (*d*) has been vigorously trying to tie the local companies as closely as it can with foreign financial institutions. Nevertheless, the Israeli IT industry lacks several managerial skills and is not highly tied to Israel and the rest of the Israeli economy.

In Ireland an IT industry developed that excels in developing software products of mid-level sophistication, usually offering applications of novel technologies in new markets and industries, rarely developing the new technologies itself. This happen because the state (*a*) focused on job creation for many years, attempting to bring MNCs to open large-scale manufacturing facilities in Ireland and paying much less attention to the creation of the local IT industry, (*b*) was not actively trying to embed these MNCs with the local industry, (*c*) was for a long time not channeling many resources for industrial R&D activities, and since then has been concentrating on the software industry, taking less notice of the hardware industry, and (*d*) while not specifically dissuading local industry from deeply interacting with the global financial institutions, was, nevertheless, growing an Irish-owned vastly state-dependent VC industry.

The most important conclusion of this book is that states and societies still have real choices with regard to developing their own rapid innovation–based industries. Moreover, each set of choices has particular consequences that can be at least partly foreseen. These lessons, however, should be divided in two.

On the political economy side, there are a few important points to remember. First, in all three cases the financial investments by the state have been minuscule, especially in comparison to what the same government invested in other more traditional industries, or what other governments, many times less successfully, invested in their IT industries. The second point to remember is that the development of RIB industries is not a one-time effort. In Israel, Ireland, and Taiwan, sustained efforts by the state continued for a couple of decades before a true economic transformation occurred. Consequently, the third point to remember is that what allowed Israel, Ireland, and Taiwan to sustain their efforts has been the institutionalization of their S&T and innovation policies. Hence one lesson to be learned by emerging economies is that long sustained efforts with relatively minor financial investment are probably more transformative than short-term costly efforts done with a big political fanfare. Nonetheless, this lesson only heightens one of our main arguments: it is critical to manage the political process of industry-state co-evolution, especially the changing, and usually diminishing, role of the state.

The second set of lessons to be learned is directly related to our theoretical framework. Looking at their international and internal socioeconomic-political situation and defining their particular economic goals, emerging economies, while they can never know exactly what products and technologies their industries will develop, can use this framework to map what kind of capabilities, business models, and relationships with the global production networks their industry will have. By deciding how and where to locate the main R&D conducting agents, nurturing particular relationships with leading MNCs both inside and outside their borders, and influencing the role of foreign financiers and financial markets, emerging economies can partly shape the development path of their rapid innovation industries. Specifically, state actions influence two key domains: (*a*) what kind, and to what degree, private industry develops original R&D capabilities, and (*b*) what entry points, and hence what kind of inputs and relationships, their industry has with global production networks. Furthermore, each one of these choices also affects the economic distribution of success and its sustainability. For example, while many might see Israel, with its wide array of innovational capabilities and the success of its companies on NASDAQ, as the optimum of success, it is sobering to remember that whereas Taiwan and Ireland have managed to a great degree to achieve economic growth and equality, in Israel inequality has been growing rapidly, and it is not clear whether a large percentage of the Israeli society has ever enjoyed any of the fruits of the IT industry's impressive success.

The final message of this study is a positive one: less-developed states and societies still have extensive opportunities to improve their economic well-being and spur rapid innovation–based industrial development. Moreover, there is more than one model to follow in order to achieve success. Israel, Ireland, and Taiwan have demonstrated that there are at least three, and probably more, development paths that other countries can follow. Moreover, our theoretical framework has shown the feasibility of developing models that would help us to predict the industrial outcomes in both capabilities development and the social distribution of success of different choice sets. For that reason this book constitutes a step in a research continuum that will grant us greater understanding of the politics and outcomes of rapid innovation–based industrial development.

Notes

1. PLURALITY, CHOICE, AND THE POLITICS OF INDUSTRIAL INNOVATION

1. For the purpose of this book, success in rapid innovation–based industrial growth is defined as the development of an industry based around NTBFs, which contribute a significant amount of growth in gross domestic product (GDP), exports, and employment, making the industry a critical sector of the national economy. I use the common definition of NTBF from the literature: a company whose products are new technologies or are based on their own and others' R&D effort to commercialize applications of new technology, or a company whose main revenue stream is based on R&D efforts to develop new technologies. I further elaborate on the definition by treating an IT NTBF as a company whose main product or products are either a new technology or a new application of new technology whose main function is the gathering, transferring, processing, or presenting of information, and where the company is conducting the R&D that leads to the product itself, either with or without cooperation with other organizations.

2. For two recent examples of such research, one from the varieties of capitalism perspective and one from the development-paths perspective, see Guillen 2001, Hall and Soskice 2001.

3. On Japan's and South Korea's conglomerate-based industrial development, see, for example, Amsden 1989, Anchordoguy 1989, Calder 1993, Evans 1995, Fields 1995, Johnson 1982, Okimoto 1987.

4. For a collection of theoretical and empirical articles elaborating more on the argument

that small states will have significant and unique problems in developing innovative high-technology industries, see Freeman and Lundvall 1988.

5. In Israel annual overall sales in the high-tech electronic industry, excluding software, more than septupled from 1986 to 2004, from $2.003 billion to more than $15 billion. Exports rose even faster, from $1.135 billion to $13 billion. Software sales had the highest growth rates, rising from overall sales of $380 million in 1989 to more than $4 billion in 2004. Software exports grew from $5 million in 1984 to more than $3 billion in 2004.

Ireland, a country that lost 1.1 percent of its total population in 1989 due to economic emigration, has seen its IT industry achieve remarkable growth. Software was the main sector where indigenous companies, and not only Irish subsidiaries of MNCs, achieved worldwide success. The number of indigenous software companies in Ireland rose from 291 in 1991 to 630 in 1998, while the total number of firms rose from 365 to 760. Revenues in 2004 reached a total of €16.9 billion, out of which exports were around €16 billion. The total sales of Irish-owned companies in 2004 were €1.369 billion, a marked improvement from 1991, when total revenues were €2.198 billion, out of which only €191 million came from the Irish-owned sector.

In Taiwan, a country in which the first IC chip was fabricated in a demonstration fabrication facility of a public research institution only in 1977, its IT companies manufactured, in 2001, 70 percent of global production of motherboards, 55 percent of laptops, 56 percent of LCD monitors, 51 percent of color-display-tube monitors, and 36 percent of digital still cameras. In addition, with 225 companies and NT$147.8 billion in sales, Taiwan's IC design subsector is the second largest in the world after the United States'. In 2002 the total sales of the Taiwanese electrical and electronics industry reached almost $88 billion USD, and on top of that the semiconductor industry added another $21.4 billion.

Sources: Israel, CBS 2001, 2004a, IAEI 2006, IASH 2003, MOTI 1998; Ireland, IDA 2000, NID 2006; Taiwan, ITRI 2003, MoEA various years. As the SEC filing of the leading Israeli software firms were higher than the reported sale figures of the Israeli Association of Software Houses, there is reason to believe that the figures above are underestimated.

6. Of the 482 interviews (not counting repeats), 137 were conducted in Ireland or with Irish companies and officials in the United States, 110 were conducted in Israel or with Israeli companies and officials in the United States, and 235 were conducted in Taiwan or with Taiwanese companies and officials in the United States. Unless otherwise stated, data on company profiles and information were gathered through interviews, SEC filings, the Hoover online database, and companies' Web sites. Because many interviewees from private companies have requested anonymity not only for themselves but for their firms, I decided that when possible I would not specify which of the companies described in this book were interviewed.

7. While the interviews were open ended, an interview theme was adhered to consisting of forty questions organized around eight subthemes, with all questions touched upon during the one- to two-hour-long interview. The interviews' transcripts were then uploaded onto a server running custom-made software that allows access to the extended database through a Web portal with enhanced search engine capabilities.

8. Together with Rostow, Gerschenkron gave a paradigmatic all-powerful stature in economic development studies to the notion that economic development should be seen almost as an organic process that must pass through certain specific stages before achieving full blossom, with the ability to innovate on the scientific edge being the last capability to develop (Rostow 1960). A more recent proponent of the linear model in regard to innovation and the IT industry in Asia was Linsu Kim, with his influential model of innovational catch-up progression (Kim 1997). For an argument that changes in the 1990s made this linear model of sequential innovational progression less compelling in Asia, see Ernst 2005b.

9. See, for example, O'Riain 2004, pp. 6–8, or Amsden, proposing the same theoretical argument in her recent works (2001, p. 2).

10. Johnson's pilot agency argument has a long history of being reinvented and elaborated under different names in the literature; for two recent examples, see Chibber 2002, Weiss 1998.

11. Among Japanese specialists a disagreement with Johnson's assessment of the state's extreme power and importance evolved. For examples of studies that strongly disagree with Johnson, see Calder 1993, Freeman 1987, Okimoto 1987, Samuels 1988, 1994; for examples of studies that only slightly disagree with Johnson, or even agree with him, see Anchordoguy 1989, Chinworth 1992. Nonetheless, all these studies agree with the basic Gerschenkronian model of industrial growth, and all agree that the state was highly important in the development of the industry in Japan.

12. Parts of this version of this economic-growth theory have been sanctified by the World Bank (WB 1993).

13. There are some differences among the neo-developmental-state theorists, in particular between those who argue that the state should continue to advance national champions, and those who argue for a strategy based around SMEs. It is unclear whether these differences arise because of the different context of location, timing, and industries that the different writers researched. However, in the critical part of theorizing about the optimal role and behavior of the state in its attempt to spur the growth of high-technology industries and in their treatment of the state for all practical purposes as a unitary actor, the authors are similar enough to be treated as advancing one model.

14. The reason why I argue that this point is implicit and not explicit in the neo-developmental-state theories is that while some writers—for example, Peter Evans—present a typology of the different roles of the state, none of the neodevelopment statists pays enough attention to the political process of the state initiating the creation of the industry and then managing its own retreat from a commanding and planning position to a more supporting and less controlling role. Nonetheless, these exact political processes determine both whether sustained success is achieved, and how different models of industrial systems are shaped.

15. As such the neo-developmental-state theorists are different from the earlier critics of the strong developmental-state argument, such as Samuels's model of the politics of reciprocal consent. These earlier critics' main aim was to reinquire into the exact roles of the state and the nature of state-business relations in the development of industries that are not based on rapid innovation, at a period before the advent of globalized

fragmented production, not to propose a new model of the developmental state suitable for rapid innovation–based industries (Samuels 1988).

16. Just using the simple Evans-Ruach measurement of "Weberianism" in the structure of the bureaucracy in regard to meritocratic recruitment and career patterns reveals some surprises. While Taiwan and Ireland score very high (12 and 12.5 respectively on a 14-point scale), Israel's score is a relatively low 7 (Evans and Rauch 1999, O'Riain 2004, pp. 145–146). Israel's score equals that of Morocco and Turkey and is below that of Mexico, Brazil, Sri Lanka, and Egypt. (Ireland's score was evaluated by a different study using the Evans-Ruach measurement, an evaluation which is strengthened by my own analysis; see Chapter 4.) This result suggests that the strong coherent Weberian bureaucracy hypothesis does not hold a lot of generalizable explanatory power over the three cases. This is before we even note that bureaucracies are very different in their traditions and social roles, as well as in the social origins, educational backgrounds, and influence on the political decision making process of their members.

17. For example, Sean O'Riain, a neodevelopmental statist who specifically looks at the growth of SMEs in the software industry of Ireland, still argues for one specific model of development and state behavior that he terms either as Flexible Developmental State or as Developmental Networked State, which is different from the old developmental-state model that he terms Bureaucratic Developmental State (O'Riain 2000, 2004).

18. For papers outlining the different terminology used in the literature, see Henderson et al. 2002, Sturgeon 2001.

19. In effect this process takes Adam Smith's argument about the division of labor, specialization, efficiency, and the size of the market one step further (Smith 1937, in particular book 1, chapters 1 and 3).

20. Market failure is defined as a case where due to lack, or asymmetries, of information and/or the specific characteristics of the industry or activity, we should expect a free market to allocate resources in suboptimal fashion.

21. For an excellent example of a theoretical model for the importance of the creation of a users-innovators community to the successful implementation and continuous improvement of new technology, see Teubal et al. 1991.

22. Systems-of-innovation theories usually do not pertain to the important national difference between the regulation of venture capital and stock exchanges. Thus while they argue for a more general observation, claiming that VC financing leads to the rapid diffusion and use of American-like start-up businesses models, I prefer to refine their argument. Thus I claim that only VC funds whose source of finance is the global capital markets and that are linked to the leading global stock exchanges would affect the business development in such a way.

23. Since 2003 the ministry is called the Ministry of Trade Industry and Employment.

24. In 2003 the National Software Directorate was renamed the National Informatics Directorate.

25. That is not to say that the state was not important in the early development of the industry in Ireland; indeed, the Industrial Development Agency (IDA)—then focused mainly on foreign direct investment (FDI)—was critical in the industry's development

in the 1980s through its Enterprise Development Plan. However, as the name suggests, the aim of that policy initiative was to develop business in all sectors of the economy, without regard to R&D, and its main goal remained job creation.

26. In 2001 the Taiwanese Department of Industrial Technology (DOIT) embarked on an initiative specifically to lure MNCs to open R&D centers in Taiwan. This initiative has been quite successful, with thirteen MNCs opening facilities in Taiwan within two years and ten more MNCs on the waiting list. Indeed, if this new trend is sustained, and these MNCs consistently conduct high-level R&D activities in Taiwan, a very interesting future research project would be to gauge their influence on the Taiwanese IT industry after a decade or so of operations.

2. THE DEVELOPMENT OF THE IT INDUSTRY IN ISRAEL

1. The total number of workers with academic education involved in R&D activities in all branches of the civilian industry was 886; in addition, there were 671 R&D workers with some technical education (Bar 1990, p. 41).

2. It might be telling that there is no direct translation in Hebrew to the verb *sustain* or to the adjective *sustained*.

3. As the main positive effect attributed to IT is growing productivity, the fact that productivity in the business sector was decreasing in the 1996–2000 period, the same years that the IT industry achieved its greatest success, is especially worrisome (BOI 2004).

4. This is not to say that this bureaucratic structure does not pose its own problems, such as governance and the low status of the civil service.

5. The Ministry of Trade and Industry changed its name a few times during this period, from Commerce and Industry, to Trade and Industry, and in 2003 to the Ministry of Trade, Industry, and Employment. The Ministry of Development was dismantled.

6. According to the developmental-state theories, stable long-term relationships between industry and state are key for the creation of specific patterns of development and the ability of the state to influence industrial development. For example, see Samuels 1988, p. 2.

7. The alliance with the United States did not commence until after the 1973 war, and even today the United States does not allow Israel access to a number of crucial technologies (Vekstein 1999).

8. Not only was France the main source of Israel's advanced weapon systems, but the two states also had many co-development research projects. France and Israel were also crucial for each other's nuclear programs, with France licensing the technology developed at the Weizmann Institute for the production of heavy water, helping Israel in return to build its nuclear reactors. Indeed, one commentator from the defense sector has portrayed that co-development defense-industry relationship as being closer and more satisfactory for Israel then the later one with the United States (Amit 1988).

9. It should be noted, however, that the Golems were highly advanced worldwide. The first electronic computer in the United States was finished in 1952; the first Golem, which was built on a similar scale to the first U.S. computer, was finished in 1954; see also Ariav and Goodman 1994.

10. Some might find it ironic that Raphael is the biblical angel responsible for healing (Rapha is the verb for heal, while Al stands for god).

11. The story behind the formation of RAFAEL is also of interest as it illuminates the significant influence and importance that prominent scientists had on public policy in the decades before and after Israel's independence. The initiative to create a special "science corps" was presented by two professors, Aharon Katchalski (the brother of Ephraim, head of the 1968 Katchalski committee) and Yuchanan Rutner, to David Ben-Gurion, the leader of the biggest Zionist organization in preindependence Israel and its first prime minister, before the 1948 Independence War. In 1958 the science corps were separated from the Israeli Defense Forces and another prominent biochemist from the Weizmann Institute, Aharon Bergman, stayed on as its first head (with Munya Mardor as its first managing director).

12. It is important to remember that the head of RAFAEL, even after it was separated from the IDF, was a member of the chief of staff forum (Forum MATCAL), the leading discussion and decision body in the Israeli security apparatus, a telling indication of the importance given to indigenous R&D throughout the history of the Israeli state.

13. For example, RAFAEL pioneered the use of such operations-research and project-management techniques as P.E.R.T. in Israel.

14. Some of the data regarding these decisions are still classified; however, large parts have been published. For more details see the memoirs of Munya Mardor, RAFAEL's first CEO (Mardor 1981), and Efrati 1999, Rehav 1998.

15. Elbit's first product was a minicomputer that competed head-to-head with Digital's. Elbit later moved toward more defense-oriented markets and is now Israel's largest defense high-technology company. In 1971 the American multinational CDC bought the Ministry of Defense's 50 percent share in Elbit. In 1983 Elbit was first listed on NASDAQ, and as of 2002 three of Elbit's companies—Elbit Medical Imaging, Elbit Ltd., and Elbit Vision System—were listed.

16. Interesting and, in retrospect, highly amusing were the conclusions of the 1960 Ministry of Finance committee for the assessment of computer usage in the Israeli national economy. Headed by Professor Dostrovsky from the Weizmann Institute, the committee concluded that two Philco computers should be enough for the needs of the whole national economy in the years to come. These conclusions were sponsored by the Ministry of Defense with the hope that someone would buy a second Philco to be used as a backup to the one in MAMRAM. Fortunately, no one paid any attention to these conclusions, not least the committee's own secretary, Emmanuel Sharon, who at the same time was organizing the computerization of the Ministry of Finance.

17. See Sharon and Naamen 1961.

18. It is at this critical point—the birth of the Israeli high-technology industry—that we see again the importance of Israel's academic infrastructure, Galil started his forays into the private market from the Technion, the Israeli Institute of Technology in Haifa, and recruited Suhami, the cofounder of Elscient (the combination of Elron and Science), while Suhami was still a Ph.D. student. Indeed, Elscient's first medical imaging products, on the basis of which Elscient became the first Israeli company on NASDAQ, were related to Suhami's work in the Technion.

19. Aharon Dovrat, Argentinean born, later left the civil service to become the CEO of Clal, an investment vehicle created by Sapir to channel and manage the investments to Israel of Jews from Latin America. Under his management Clal became one of Israel's prominent holding companies, and Dovrat, who left Clal in 1991, became one of Israel's prominent businessmen. In another example of Israel's porous borders between public and private, Dovrat was also the chairman of a committee on the restructuring of Israel's K-12 education system, whose report has been accepted by the government as the basis for a radical and controversial reform, which the government hoped to start implementing in the 2005–2006 school year.

20. To verify this account, interviews were conducted with Dan Tolkowsky (June 7 and August 10, 2000), Uzia Galil (August 9, 2000), and Fred Adler (September 28, 2000); see also Levav 1998 and Autler 2000.

21. Katchalski would later become the president of Israel, the symbolic head of state. At the time science and scholarly activities were so highly regarded in Israel that the first four presidents of Israel were all renowned scientists or scholars.

22. See the letter of appointment to the committee (Katchalski 1968, pp. A-1–A-2).

23. Positions of chief scientists exist today in all the major ministries and act more or less as envisioned by the Katchalski Committee. The OCS has been the only one of these positions to grow into an industrial development agency.

24. Professor J. Gross was the first chief scientist, starting his tenure in 1965. He used to come to the office for one day per week (interview with OCS's chief economist, May 7, 2002).

25. This concentration on R&D was so high that in the first half of the 1980s the cumulative expenditure on defense R&D was higher than the cumulative expenditure of final systems procurement (Halperin 1987, Halperin and Berman 1990, p. 159). Moreover, in 1984, one project alone, the Lavi (fighter jet), employed 10 percent of the overall supply of skilled R&D scientists and engineers in Israel. This demand, emanating mainly from the defense sector, led to the rapid expansion of the universities' educational capacity. The *total number* of scientists and engineers in the industry (defense and civilian) in 1965 was 2,427; by 1985–1989 the *annual rate* of scientists and engineers finishing their studies (both graduate and undergraduate) in IT-related disciplines was 4,785 (CBS 2004b).

26. Yaakov was also a protégé of Katchalski, who was then president of Israel. After leaving the OCS Yaakov served as a special adviser for the World Bank to Taiwan and South Korea at the time of their rapid high-technology industrialization period.

27. While vastly larger than the funds given to the OCS before, the sufficient financial resources proved to be in the first year just more than 15 million Israeli lire (compared with the about 500 million Israeli lire that were channeled into defense R&D annually at that time).

28. *Science-based firm* was defined as "a firm [whose] operation necessitate[s] a high technological level and highly educational workforce, and that the firm conduct R&D activities that are high in relation to its overall activities, and that a high percentage of its production and exports is based on these R&D activities" (OCS 1974). This definition gave the OCS the ability to define as science based all the firms with approved project proposals.

29. While probably critical in securing the construction of the fabs in Israel, the overall economic effects of the capital investment law were probably negative even in the 1990s; see Bregman et al. 1998.

30. In 1998, 78 percent of total R&D expenditures were spent in the optical and communication electronic subsector (Bentur 2002).

31. Dr. Ed Mlavsky was executive vice president of Mobil Tyco Solar Energy Corporation, a joint venture created by Mobil Corporation and Tyco Laboratories Inc. to develop and commercialize a novel photovoltaic technology initiated under Mlavsky's direction at Tyco, a company of which he was a cofounder in 1960. Until 1974 Mlavsky was a member of Tyco's board of directors and its chief technical officer; in 1973, he became president and chief operating officer.

32. As of 2003, with the growth of large Israeli companies, this division of labor was weakened to an assumption on BIRD's Web site (BIRD 2004).

33. BIRD's track record of success has made the foundation the subject of two Ph.D. dissertations in the United States, one at Wharton and one at Northwestern, that tracked the foundation's project success factors (Bizan 2001, Yahalomi 1991). By 1991, thirtynine countries had approached the United States to establish similar programs, and BIRD itself became in 1988 a model of a Department of Commerce program, which was called the International Partnership for the Commercialization of Technology (IMPACT). In addition, many countries have signed similar agreements with Israel, and many more signed agreements with other countries built on the same model (Yahalomi 1991).

34. During the interview with Ed Mlavsky, he insisted that this particular statistic is not of value because practically every Israeli company operating before the early 1990s used BIRD. Without getting into the debate of the exact influence of BIRD on NASDAQ IPO projects, the fact that BIRD assisted almost every Israeli company in this earlier formative period is another testament to BIRD's critical position in the Israeli IT innovation system during these times. In its first ten years of operation, 1979–1989, BIRD funded 156 full- and miniscale projects, of which 44 percent (69 projects) led to successful sales of new products (Yahalomi 1991, p. 124).

35. Inflation in Israel was so high that by the end of the crisis Israel changed its currency twice. Between December 1978 and March 1986 prices rose by a factor of more than one thousand.

36. For more about the causes of the crisis and the stabilization program, see an article written by the chairman of Israel's central bank at the time (Bruno 1989). Also, see Ben-Bassat 2002, Ben-Porath 1986.

37. For more about the history of neocorporatism in Israel, see Shalev 1992, Grinberg 1991.

38. The military enlists and trains a few thousand technologists annually. There are two paths in which the military itself employs and trains R&D personnel. The first is through the "academic reserve": soldiers who are allowed to complete academic studies before starting active duty, serve as professionals, and in exchange sign for longer period of service. Many of them work in the military R&D units. The second path is the military's own training programs. These operate either in conjunction with the universities and aim to train an elite R&D personnel (the most prestigious program being

Talpiot), or through in-house training, the most significant being software programming and computerization training, which is the sole technological area where the military has built its in-house technological school. For more about the military software school, see Breznitz 2005a. The military has several units where IT R&D is being conducted.

39. The transformation was not that apparent at the time, and many commentators thought it had failed (Teubal 1993).

40. Zoran, "silicon" in Hebrew, was established in 1983 by Levy Gerzberg to try out one of his ideas in the semiconductor industry. Today, after passing through a few transformations, Zoran is a fabless company applying DSP technology—digital signal processing, one of the Israeli IT industry's strengths and another indicator of its advanced R&D capabilities—to the image-processing market, specifically DVD and digital cameras. In 2003, with sales of more than $216 million, a rise of almost 50 percent from 2002, Zoran was one of only a few Israeli companies among the world's thirty largest fabless companies in terms of sales, according to the 2004 McClean Report (IC Insights 2004).

41. For more on the early electromedical industry in Israel, see Teubal et al. 1976, Teubal and Spiller 1977. For a history of the semiconductors industry in Israel, see Autler 2000. For a descriptive history of Israeli high-technology industry, see Levav 1998. For three accounts which briefly discuss the software industry and the causes of its success, see Ariav and Goodman 1994, Breznitz 2006, de Fontenay and Carmel 2001.

42. ECI was established in 1961 and operated mainly as a defense contractor in communications. It went public on the NASDAQ in 1982 on the basis of its first internationally successful civilian product, an analog multiplexer, which doubled the transmission capacity of telephone lines. After 1982 ECI quickly grew to become one of Israel's most commercially successful companies until the end of the 1990s. At its commercial zenith, ECI had annual sales of more than $1 billion; today the company is in flux, its annual sales plummeting to $421 million in 2003 before rebounding to $629 million in 2005.

43. Bynet commenced operations as early as 1973. RAD, the manufacturing, R&D, and internationally oriented part of the group, was established in 1981.

44. Hanigal later became a VC, first with Star Seed, and currently is one of the three Israeli partners of Sequoia Capital, a prominent Silicon Valley VC firm with a dedicated branch in Israel.

45. In an interview, one of the Lannet executives remarked that without the OCS's assistance, Lannet would have never been established.

46. Unlike past public offering of Israeli firms, Lannet's IPO valuation of $190 million was considered high even for NASDAQ in that period. Thus Lannet's IPO, together with the IPOs in 1992 of Fourth (New) Dimension, Teledata, Comverse, Lanoptics, and Sapiens, all of which with valuations of over $100 million, was critical in changing the perception of American investors toward Israeli companies as able to supply a profitable exit even for American VCs.

47. As of 2005 the RAD group companies that were listed on NASDAQ as independent companies were Radware, established in 1997 by Yehuda's son Roy; Silicom, esta-

blished in 1987; Radvision, established in 1993; RiT Technologies, established in 1989; Radcom, established in 1991; and Ceragon Networks, established in 1996 as Giganet.

48. National Semiconductor activities were also important, as it was the second MNC to open fabrication facilities in Israel. The fab was opened in 1986, spun off as Tower Semiconductors, Israel's first pureplay foundry, and listed on NASDAQ in 1994. Hence Israel had one of the first pureplay foundries in the world after Taiwan. The existence of Tower's and Intel's fabs helped Israeli firms to access and try new semiconductor technologies; for example, Saifun, which went through an IPO on November 2005 and in which Tower is an investor, develops some of the most advanced technologies to maximize the performance of FLASH memory chips. However, Tower never grew to become a globally leading pureplay foundry, and many Israeli fabless firms prefer to subcontract their chip fabrication to TSMC and UMC.

49. VLSI stands for very large scale integration. To put the Israeli VLSI skills in context: TSMC's spin-off in 1987 was the successful conclusion of ITRI's VLSI project in Taiwan. Ten years earlier, Israeli engineers, in Israel, were already working on cutting-edge innovative design. The skills of the Israeli industry were well enough known that when National Semiconductor decided to start CPU design and manufacturing operations, it chose to open an Israeli subsidiary to manage this new business venture.

50. Comverse's beginning was in 1982. Kobi Alexander, an Israeli, was working as an investment banker for Shearson Loeb Rhodes (now Salomon Smith Barney) in New York, when he met an Israeli engineer, Boaz Misholi. Misholi had an idea for a business venture developing centralized voice and fax-messaging hardware systems to enable big organizations and telecommunication service providers to offer voice and fax mail to their customers. Within a week, the two returned to Israel and established Efrat Future Technology with the aim of applying for OCS grants to finance their R&D. In 1984 the founders came back to New York and established Comverse, which became the parent company of the Israeli Efrat. In 1986, like many Israeli companies in that period, Comverse went public on NASDAQ and used its IPO as a final VC round. During the 1990s Comverse moved to rely more on software than on hardware products and started to grow also by acquiring other companies in Israel and the United States. In 2000 Comverse's revenues were $1.2 billion; in 2002, after spinning off two publicly traded software companies, Verinet and Ulticom, Comverse's revenues were $735 million. While the full details of all the support Comverse has been granted through the various OCS and BIRD programs are not public, Comverse companies were awarded at least sixty-nine R&D grants for different projects through the main OCS program between 1990 and 2000.

Mercury Interactive became Israel's third-largest software company in terms of sales in 2003. It was founded by Aryeh Finegold, an Israeli who was the founder and manager in the 1980s of a once-high-flying Silicon Valley firm, Daisy, and a group of former Daisy executives led by Amnon Landan. The group decided that although they were well connected in Silicon Valley, they would establish Mercury with the help of OCS grants in Israel. At first Mercury, following the well-trodden path for Israeli companies to focus on products assisting in R&D and software development, developed a software-debugging tool. The company listed on NASDAQ in 1993, started to acquire other companies in 1995, and, with the growth in the importance of the Internet, changed its focus from software debugging to testing and analyzing the performance of enterprise and Web-based applications.

51. It was also fortunate for the Israeli IT industry that the same technologies (telecommunication, DSP, and command and control) have also been some of the core technologies developed as part of the defense R&D efforts.

52. For more on the role of the military in the development of the software industry, see Breznitz 2005a.

53. One company, Comet, which offered information management systems on IBM platform, was established in 1969 and had an IPO in 1994 but very quickly thereafter declared bankruptcy.

54. By 1984 the local sales of the Israeli software industry were $365 million (1984 terms), higher than the total sales of the Irish-owned software industry in 1994 (1994 terms); the local market could support the growth of more than a few software companies.

55. For papers focusing on the evolution of the Israeli software industry and the histories of its various firms, see Breznitz 2005d, 2005e.

56. Yossi Holnder, the technological founder of the Fourth Dimension, served as a software technologist in one of the military intelligence units, and had looked into the idea of acquiring the rights to several programs developed inside the military before settling on that specific one.

57. An example of a predicament caused solely by the lack of financial management knowledge was the 1987 crisis of New Dimension, one of Israel's premier software companies to be. The company found itself in acute financial difficulties. It had a couple of million dollars in future orders but not enough working capital. At that time, the founders, all technologists without any business education, started to look around frantically for available venture capital. Fortunately, the wife of one of them worked for Comverse, and Kobi Alexander, Comverse's financial entrepreneur, agreed to meet with them. He was somewhat surprised to learn that they sought investment instead of using the simple financial tool of bridge loans.

58. During the early 1990s more than twenty thousand employees, both skilled and unskilled, were fired from the defense industries (Rehav 1998).

59. For more about the present R&D policy and schemes, see Trajtenberg 2000.

60. For four works that influenced the construction of these programs, see Brodet et al. 1990, JIM 1987, Justman et al. 1993, Teubal et al. 1996.

61. Interview with Yigal Erlich, August 21, 2000.

62. On the importance of discerning between policies that treat VC as a pool of capital and those that treat it as an industry, see Avnimelech and Teubal 2003a, 2006a, 2006b.

63. By the end of 2000, twenty-four incubators were in operation and 883 companies had participated in the program. Of these, 240 were still in the incubation centers and 643 had graduated. Of those that graduated, 53 percent have continued operations and 47 percent have closed. The total private VC financing that the graduating companies managed to secure was more than $525 million. In addition, one company, Compugen, is already publicly listed on NASDAQ, and a few more have been acquired by American MNCs, with the biggest sale being that of X-Technologies (a medical equipment

company) to Guidant in 2003. Compugen is exemplary in showing how deep and multidisciplinary R&D skills are available in Israel even to tiny new companies. Compugen's first product has been a dedicated computing hardware for biological molecular calculation (gene research) that the company started to sell in 1994. The second line of products is software based: algorithms that help in the discovery of new genes, which Compugen both sells and uses in house to find and patent genes. Following that line of business Compugen decided in 1998 that in order to be taken seriously in the gene discovery business, it needed to develop strong "wet" biology skills; it opened a full-scale lab and a third line of business. All of these extremely advanced and multidisciplinary R&D activities were conducted before its IPO on NASADQ in August 2000. After the IPO Compugen also spun off a subsidiary, Evogene, for plant-and-agriculture biotechnology.

64. Interview with Rina Pridor, February 8, 2000, Trajtenberg 2000, and the incubation program Web site http://www.incubators.org.il. There is an obvious mistake in the reporting; we assume that Others should be listed as 20 percent.

65. There are two recent reports on the incubation program. One was conducted independently (Shefer and Frenkel 2002) and the other done under the auspices of the OCS (Economics 2001).

66. The need for government action to expand the pool of financiers was also strongly emphasized in Ireland; see Chapter 4.

67. Erlich interview, August 21, 2000.

68. A three-year study of the Israeli VC industry was recently concluded. For some of the results, see Avnimelech and Teubal 2003a, 2003b, 2004, 2006a, 2006b.

69. Examples include Benjamin Hanigal of Lannet, now a partner of Sequoia Capital in Israel; Moty Ben-Arie, cofounder and manager of Radcom, now a partner of Walden Israel; Orna Berry, cofounder and manager of Ornet before becoming the chief scientist, who joined Gemini in 2000; and Arad Naveh, cofounder and manager of Class Data, an Israeli software company acquired by Cisco, now a partner at Benchmark Israel.

70. In Ireland there has been no attempt by the Irish state to establish any program of research consortia; see Chapter 4.

71. The founder of one medical equipment company, Medinol, on which comprehensive data on the founders have not yet been added, is a new immigrant. However, the story of how Medinol was founded by Kobbi Richter, a successful and experienced Israeli-born entrepreneur, who befriended Medinol's immigrant technological founder on the beach, points to the exceptional circumstances of its founding and to the difficulties that immigrants from the former USSR have has in establishing successful NTBFs in a capitalist economy.

72. Looking at three subcategories of the high-tech labor markets from 1995 to 1999, we find that the total number of new immigrant workers in industry (more routine and maintenance jobs) rose at a higher rate than that of Israelis. In telecommunication there was a slight increase in the number of new immigrants, but the number of Israelis grew faster; 95 percent of the workers were Israelis. However, in the most high-

skilled labor-market category, computerization and R&D (high-level R&D and programming jobs), the total number of new immigrants decreased while the total number of Israelis increased by more than 25 percent.

73. By the end of the 2002 financial year, the OCS had supported more than 4,500 companies since 1968 (OCS 2002, 2003).

74. By 1998, 78 percent of R&D expenditure in Israel went to telecommunication. This is probably an overconcentration of investment from the national point of view, since it is 20 percent more than the equivalent figures for Finland, including the activities of Nokia, and 60 percent more than the OECD average (Bentur 2002).

75. Cisco is one MNC that is rapidly expanding its activities in Israel to rival Intel, IBM, and Motorola for the top position as the MNC with the most R&D activities in Israel. Cisco bought six companies since 1999 and recently finished the development of the world's fastest router in its Israeli R&D center.

76. OEM is a subcontracting manufacturing relationship in which one side manufactures equipment for the other side to be sold under the second side's brand name and in accordance with the second side's detailed specifications. ODM—original-design manufacturing—is a subcontracting relationship in which the manufacturing side is also giving detailed and integrated design services to the brand-name company, which supplies it with only high-level design specifications. Under OBM—own-brand manufacturing—the manufacturer makes products to be sold under its own brand.

77. Adi Shamir of the Weizmann Institute of Science is one of the three developers of the famous RSA algorithm (the S stands for Shamir), which has been the basis for the public-private key data–security infrastructure, and from which RSA corporation took its name.

78. A public key infrastructure. (PKI) allows users of a public unsecured network, such as the Internet, to safely exchange information by using a public and a private cryptographic key pair, obtained from a trusted authority. The public key infrastructure enables a digital certificate identifying individuals or organizations.

79. Graphology is analysis of handwriting for personality testing procedures.

80. During 1991–1993, this strategy worked very well in Europe for the Margalit brothers, but they did not manage to sell in the United States. After the establishment of a U.S. subsidiary, Aladdin Inc., in 1991, Aladdin went public on NASDAQ in 1993. Aladdin continued to grow through 1991–1996 through revenues and acquisitions of Israeli and foreign companies. However, starting in 1998, Aladdin faced difficulties in adapting itself and its products to the new era of the Internet. These difficulties arose because Aladdin needed at the same time to branch out into new market segments and to change its core business—the safeguarding software IPR on users' PCs with embedded software plugs—to network and TCP/IP (transmission control protocol/Internet protocol) environment and customer relations. Nonetheless, in 2004 Aladdin's sales were $69.1 million, an almost 50 percent growth since 2001.

81. At the time a few more antivirus companies were established in Israel, such as Iris, Carmel, and Eliashim, which was later bought by Aladdin.

82. Following this turn of events, BRM quickly signed an OEM agreement with a leading

American software company—Fifth Generation—that renamed the product and sold it worldwide. In addition, as Fifth Generation's R&D capabilities were weak, BRM started to do more and more R&D projects for its American partner. As a result, it started to diversify and tried, not very successfully, to imitate the business model of its antivirus program with other technologies. In 1993, partly because no bank in Israel, before the advent of the VC industry, was willing to secure a working-capital loan for what was deemed to be a small company with no tangible assets, BRM sold its antivirus technology to Fifth Generation (which was later bought by Norton) for what was then considered in Israel to be a significant amount of capital. While still in flux after the sale and without any clear business strategy BRM, stumbled on what turned out to be Israel's most successful data-security company, Checkpoint. Following Checkpoint's success, BRM transformed itself into a technological investment house.

83. This proved to be a boon for BRM, which not only profited from the high share price of Checkpoint when it went public but also got its $300,000 loan back.

84. Reliable longitudinal international comparative studies of elementary and secondary student achievements are notoriously rare. However, the TIMSS study of 1995 and the Repeat-TIMSS of 1999, the biggest international studies conducted to date, might give us a glimpse. In each, the Israeli students scored lower than average in math and science, and their scoring had one of the sharpest decreases from 1995 to 1998 (Beaton et al. 1996, Martin et al. 2000, Mullis et al. 1997, 2000).

85. According to Israel's Central Bureau of Statistics, the level of state support for universities in the 1990s was between 51 percent and 57 percent, while the OECD average for 1997 was 82 percent, leaving a gap of more than 20 percent. In addition, while the OECD average of the state expenditure on third-level education out of total expenditures was 2.7 percent, in Israel the average stood at 2.2 percent (Bentur 2002, CBS 1999a, 1999b, 2000a, 2000b).

3. THE DEVELOPMENT OF THE IT INDUSTRY IN TAIWAN

1. In international patent issuing, one of our most reliable proxies for industrial innovation, Taiwan moved from issuing one patent in 1973 to issuing 3,693 in 1999, reaching as early as 1997 a ratio of international patents per capita higher than any of the G7 countries except Japan and the United States (Hall et al. 2001, Trajtenberg 2001).

2. In addition, Taiwanese companies operating on the mainland manufacture a large percentage of the same products that are made in China.

3. Sources: III various years, ITRI various years, MoEA various years.

4. Local assembly of radios started in the 1940s; however, only in the 1960s did the MNCs start to reorganize their global IT production networks and embed Taiwan within them (Wade 1990).

5. The world's first export-processing duty-free zone was in fact opened in Ireland around Shannon International Airport in 1958.

6. The Taiwanese government also urged MNCs to establish joint ventures with local manufactures in which the MNC transferred some of its manufacturing technology to the local suppliers instead of establishing a fully owned subsidiary. In electronics and

electrical consumer goods, unlike semiconductors, the Japanese have always been a more important source of FDI and technology to Taiwan than has the United States.

7. The total resources dedicated to the first Electronic Research and Service Organization (ERSO) project, which culminated in the creation of the United Microelectronics Corporation (UMC), were less than $15 million USD over five years between 1974 and 1979 as part of the first stage of the Electronic Industry Development Program (EDIP) (Fuller et al. 2003, Hong 1997, Meany 1994).

8. At the time, advancement to higher administrative positions in Taiwanese universities was political; hence S. S. Hsu, the president of Taiwan's leading technical university, wielded considerable political power within the KMT.

9. Some authors argue that in building Hsinchu Park the Taiwanese state was utilizing the same model of the export-processing zones geared, this time, toward the development of a local industrial sector (Hwang 1991).

10. In order for the company to have the legal status of a private company, the government could not own more than 49 percent of the shares.

11. As with many other records and statistical data regarding the IT industry in Taiwan, there seems to be a slight disagreement between different researchers and official statements. For two different cost statements, see Hong 1997, Mathews and Cho 2000.

12. Dynamic random access memory (DRAM) chips quickly became the focal point of first Japanese-American and then Korean-Japanese investment and price wars.

13. Before his return to Taiwan to head ITRI, Morris Chang had been the highest-level Taiwanese executive of an American semiconductor MNC, Texas Instruments. He was persuaded to come back to Taiwan to head ITRI by Li and Bob Evans, one of STAG's most influential American members.

14. It is rare to find a returning immigrant in the founding teams of any of the key companies, apart from Morris Chang, who returned not to establish a company but to head ITRI, from which he moved to head TSMC. This should not surprise us since the returning immigrants usually lack strong local knowledge and social networks, which were necessary in the early phases of the industry to secure finance, customers, and high-quality workforce for newly established companies.

15. Interviews with top TSMC executives, May 31, 2001.

16. Masking is a discrete stage in the production of IC chips. It is estimated that about twenty days in the IC production cycle are saved because Taiwanese companies have local masking services available (Amsden and Chu 2003, p. 108, Lin 1987). Hence the perfection of the masking technology was an important part in ERSO's strategy of building a semiconductor industry whose competitive capabilities are related to its ASIC technologies.

17. On the Israeli state-supported research consortia program, see also Breznitz 2005d, 2005e, 2006.

18. Because the American IP protection laws were revised to include computer codes only in 1980, Apple's was one of the first of such lawsuits worldwide.

19. BIOS was the main, if not the sole, subsystem that IBM uniquely developed for its PC; most of the rest of the PC was built on the open-system basis from standardized components that could be bought in the market.

20. MediaTek, while not being part of ITRI's consortia, did subcontract various of ITRI's labs, after being spun off by UMC, for the co-development of specific R&D (Chang and Tsai 2002).

21. The full extent of CSIST's resources is concealed as a matter of national security; however, just in terms of manpower during the early 1980s, CSIST employed 20,000 researchers compared with ITRI's 4,000. As of 2004 CSIST employed about 14,000 and ITRI 6,000.

22. This section and the next are partly based on Breznitz 2005b, 2005c.

23. Interviews with VIA and FIC executives, March 24, 1999, January 17, 2000).

24. For an article that analyzes the relative technological advantages of the Taiwanese IC industry, coming to a similar conclusion, see Hsu and Chiang 2001. Ernst (2005a), trying to explain the move of the IC design industry to East Asia, also follows the same argument with regard to Taiwan's relative strengths.

25. Interviews with an employee of an ITRI IC graduate company, January 28 and 30, 2003.

26. In addition, it is not clear what percentage of the total sales figures should be attributed to foreign companies, and what part of sales are software and not bundled (hardware and software sold together). Furthermore, the official figures include in the definition of the software industry several activities, such as Internet service provision, that are usually not counted as software.

27. Indeed, a critical part of ITRI's efforts in developing the IC design industry was the development, and subsequent transfer to private IC design companies, of design testing and Electronic Design Automation software tools. The case of ITRI and companies providing Electronic Design Automation software tools shows that it is quite possible for a public research institution to have positive effects on the private industry by developing and diffusing technologies (Chang and Tsai 2002).

28. Again, exact statistics are hard to come by. In 2003 the funding III received from the agency that is responsible for the budgeting of Taiwanese research institutions, the Department of Industrial Technology (DOIT), was NT$760 million. DOIT statistics estimate III's 2003 total budget at NT$3 billion, out of which a third is received from projects with other government departments and a third is received in the private market (DOIT 2003). In comparison, the combined total sales of Cyberlink and Ulead, the two leading Taiwanese software-product companies in 2002, were NT$2 billion, or $65 million USD. (Trend Micro, which is now a Japanese company, had sales of $364 million USD.) In a few interviews in 2001 with III's management team, we were told that half of III's budget originates in sources other then DOIT.

29. The story of Jau Huang, a graduate of UCLA, illustrates a similar dynamic to one commonly encountered in the hardware sector: a growing stream of Taiwanese returning from leading American universities with graduate degrees.

30. VGA stands for video graphics array, which is a graphics display system developed for the PC by IBM in 1987. VGA has since become one of the industry's standards.

31. SoC follows a long tradition of upgrading programs in which various agencies, including the National Science Council (NSC), the Ministry of Education, and ITRI team with universities to develop the capabilities needed to build specific technological fields

in Taiwan. The final aim of all these programs is the creation of a particular industrial subsector and products. The expansion of the universities is planned as a derivative of this industrial objective.

32. By late 2003 tenure-track and career-path positions in the Taiwanese universities had been streamlined on the U.S. model (assistant, associate, and full professor) with publication being the main criterion for advancement. In the period preceding, publication was not given such a strong emphasis, and career patterns were less structured. After the creation of Taiwan as a separate entity under the KMT one-party system, professorships and higher academic administrative roles involved political as well as professional decision-making processes.

33. Once we take this overarching view of the universities as a factor needed in order to establish the Taiwanese "technonational" goals, we can easily understand why the NSC, the agency whose main responsibility has been to fund and develop academic research, has also been chosen as the agency to manage and develop the Science-Based Industrial Parks, Hsinchu being the first.

34. Interview with minister of state and S&T policy, November 7, 2003.

35. The amount that channeled directly to the private industry started in 1998 at about 1 percent of total DOIT budget, or NT$200 million; under the new head of DOIT it has grown steadily both in size and as a percentage of budget, to NT$2.8 billion out of a total budget of NT$17.2 billion in 2003. For more about DOIT activities and programs until 2000 see a paper by Chiung-Wen Hsu and Hsueh-Chiao Chiang, then of ITRI and DOIT, respectively (Hsu and Chiang 2001).

36. In an effort to induce younger IT companies as well as software companies to list, new regulations were established to allow listing in the secondary exchange. Some software companies have indeed opted to use them. However, the young hardware companies and some of the more established software companies whose personnel we interviewed regarded the use of this option as a negative signal to the market, preferring instead to use the old regulation and list in the main market. In addition, even under the new regulations the same laws regarding stock options apply; hence the main effect of the new listing regulation is to let IT companies go public faster.

37. On the importance of this distinction, see Avnimelech and Teubal 2003a, 2006a, and 2006b, and Chapter 2 of this book.

38. Interview with TVCA's secretary general, November 3, 2003.

39. The establishment and the specific laws regulating the VC industry are another brainchild of K. T. Li, who, after being exposed to the American VC industry, decided that a local VC industry was a critical component for the development of Taiwan's IT industry in the early 1980s and masterminded its creation. The industry's official year of birth is 1983.

40. Interview with TVCA's secretary general, November 3, 2003.

41. The regulation involving the fixed nominal par value of a stock applies also to private companies. While this does not prevent investors from investing in companies based on changing valuations as they progress through their business plan, in theory this might increase the transaction costs and the risk associated with VC investment in Taiwan. Our interviewees, however, did not regard this as an obstacle.

42. Remember, though, that overall industrial R&D resources, in contrast with the resources channeled to original product–innovation R&D activities of private firms, are relatively high in Taiwan even if prioritized by governmental decisions. Hence overall resources are much higher, for example, than in Ireland.

4. THE STATE AND THE GROWTH OF THE IT INDUSTRY IN IRELAND

1. As late as 1989 Ireland lost 1.1 percent of its population to emigration. Indeed, even today the Irish population is less than 50 percent of the eight million before the great famine of 1845–1850.
2. At around $8 billion, Dell's 2003 annual revenues alone equaled the combined value of the Irish tourism and agriculture sectors.
3. Transfer pricing refers to the internal trade accounting techniques that MNCs use in order to record most of their profits within units or subsidiaries situated in the most favorable corporate tax regimes.
4. One significant result of such missteps is that in 2001, with the Irish VC industry providing record levels of capital, there were only three seed investments, which together equaled $750,000 USD, in the whole of Ireland. Hence at the same time that state-led efforts increased the amounts of IT-designated funding to their highest levels ever, the formation rate of new IT firms dropped to almost zero.
5. The autonomous IDA, building on its ability to lure MNCs and its domain over what was widely perceived as a key issue—job creation—grew to wield immense power of policy formulation and implementation over all issues of industrial and economic development until the 1990s. Hence, between the 1950s and the early 1990s, the IDA was a true pilot agency with sway over the actions of many other agencies (Chibber 2002, Johnson 1982).
6. As will be discussed later, in the early 1990s the structure of the developmental agencies was changed, and after several reorganizations IDA, or IDA Ireland, is now the acronym of the Industrial Development Agency Ireland and no longer of the Industrial Development Authority. IDA Ireland is an autonomous government agency responsible solely for FDI industrial policy. Hence it is a very different and much less powerful agency from the original IDA in its heyday. Currently the structure of industrial developmental agencies consists of Enterprise Ireland (EI), which is responsible for the indigenous industry, and IDA Ireland, which is responsible for the FDI-based industry. Both agencies are nominally under the auspices of Forfas, which is responsible for strategic planning in regard to industrial development. The three are semiautonomous public agencies under the Ministerial Department of Enterprise, Trade, and Employment.
7. The National Software Directorate was moved into Forbairt and then Enterprise Ireland after the two agencies were created. It is now called the National Informatics Directorate. An ill-fated predecessor, called the National Software Center, operated on a much smaller scale within the IDA from 1984 to 1988.
8. Consequently, as will be described in detail, the indigenous hardware industry, never

the focus of targeted policies, continues to face severe disadvantages vis-à-vis both the indigenous software companies and the hardware MNCs.

9. For more on the Irish economic history see Haughton 2000, Kennedy 1989, O'Gr'ada 1997.

10. Two center-right parties have dominated the Irish political system: Fianna Gael and Fianna Fáil. The main difference between the two has been that Fianna Fáil, the Republican Party, until very recently did not officially accept the political separation of the Irish island. Since 1932 Fianna Fáil has managed to secure its position as the largest party and has been in power for most of the period. This makes Ireland a one-party-dominated political system for most of the period of its early industrialization, similarly to Israel and Taiwan.

11. By 1961 the republic population was only 2.8 million, compared with 3.1 million in 1921 and 8 million before the great famine of 1845–1850.

12. Emigration was so severe that the Irish government organized special committees on the subject, and some observers, most notably John O'Brien in the 1953 edited volume *The Vanishing Irish,* questioned the viability of Ireland as an independent state (O'Brien 1953). In the 1958 economic program which followed Whitaker's report, the government described Ireland's main problem: "Production has not been increasing fast enough to provide employment and acceptable living standards for the growing number of our people; *large-scale emigration* has been accompanied by a high level of unemployment. *Emigration will not be checked* nor will unemployment be permanently reduced until the rate of increase in national output is greatly accelerated" (SO 1958b, italics added).

13. The IDA, and Enterprise Ireland after it, have been using employment grant mechanisms as one of their main vehicles for direct financial aid. The agency and its client corporation agree on the number of jobs to be created, and the agency awards the corporation a specific amount of capital per new job. The almost obsessive attention with which job creation and destruction have been followed in Ireland is evident in reading Irish newspapers. The exact number of jobs created or discontinued still appears in the title of all articles dealing with the fortune of foreign (and many local) companies, even if the main thrust of the article deals with other issues.

14. For an assessment and historical description of Ireland's industrial policy, see O'Sullivan 2000a, 2000b. For a critique of Ireland's FDI-oriented industrial policy now and then, see O'Hearn 1998.

15. Interview with Ken Whitaker, September 3, 2003.

16. For a detailed account of the development of the Irish higher education system, see White 2001.

17. Higher education in Ireland was such a rare opportunity in the 1960s that virtually none of the civil servants in the Ministry of Education dealing with higher education policy had a university degree (White 2001, pp. 41–42).

18. In addition to opening the new facilities and institutions, the state has also been using its control of university slot allocation to steer students toward engineering and technology courses.

19. Exposure as interns to various workplaces is still often an integral part of the education in the RTCs/RITs and other, nonuniversity, parts of the Irish higher education system.
20. For a paper trying to measure the economic effect of the expanding education system, see Durkan et al. 1999.
21. See NSB 2000, figures 6-55–6-61.
22. Interview with Don Thornhill, chairman of the Higher Education Authority, February 4, 2002.
23. For accounts of the development of the Irish software industry, see Arora et al. 2001, O'Riain 1997, 1999, Sands 2005, Sterne 2004. For an account based on cluster theory, see O'Gorman et al. 1997. For an interesting collection of papers on the specific experiences of software industries in a few emerging countries, see Arora and Gambardella 2005.
24. For some years, Cara, the computing subsidiary of the national airline, Aer Lingus, was the biggest software company, data processing center, and exporter in Ireland. With its ticket-ordering system and remote terminals, Cara was the first to introduce distributed software systems into Ireland and later also successfully sold hotel management systems in Europe.
25. Some of the local managers of MNCs' subsidiaries claim that the existence of these IT outsourcing-services companies in Ireland granted the Irish subsidiaries a comparative advantage versus other foreign subsidiaries when competing for more activities in the corporate headquarters (interviews with former managers of the Irish subsidiaries of telecommunication MNCs, July 17, 2001).
26. Michael Purser, an employee of System Dynamics who left to become one of the first computer science faculty members at Trinity, founded Chaco. Chaco was created partly to help Purser's students find employment. The company was considered the most technologically oriented of the Irish software companies in the 1970s before it merged with Baltimore, another company that Purser cofounded, together with Jim Mountjoy. A few more service-based companies that later transformed into product companies appeared in that period. The most notable of these were GC McKeown and AMS.
27. McGovern's two most important investments were made in conjunction with his relationship with Jim Mountjoy, the cofounder of Baltimore in 1984 and Euristix in 1990.
28. Because many of the commercial space problems relate directly to the Irish-British tradition of renting commercial property only on long-term leases (five to twenty-five years), even in the 2000–2003 period many interviewees complained about the unwillingness of landowners to rent their offices to newly established software companies.
29. ICL was a leading British computer company that merged into Fujitsu.
30. The Maapics package was introduced to Ireland together with IBM's System/34. IBM launched System/34 in April 1977 as its own approach to minicomputers. System/34 was a low-cost distributive data processing system modeled on the IBM 5340 system.
31. In 1988 Hoskyns also bought the first incarnation of CBT—Computer Based Training—Systems. With the sale of Hoskyns to CapGemini in 1990 the remaining product-based activities of the former Insight were discontinued. Barry Murphy, then CEO of Insight, left to become the first director of the NSD. CBT was established by

Patrick (Pat) McDonagh in 1983. Its first product was a training kit for money market dealers. The domain knowledge, as well as some of the financial backing, came from Dermot Desmond. Desmond was the first private financier to invest significant amounts of capital in the software industry. (His best-known software investment was the backing of Fran Rooney's transformation of Baltimore into a data security company in the late 1990s.) In 1987 McDonagh sold the company to Hoskyns only to buy it back in September 1991 after CapGemini bought Hoskyns. Under the management of Bill McCabe the new CBT concentrated its effort on the American, and not the European, market. Within three years CBT, selling software user–training products, mainly for Lotus Notes, reached revenues of $18 million before becoming the first Irish software company to list on NASDAQ in 1995. CBT later changed its name to Smartforce before merging with Skillsoft in 2002, and is now trading under the Skillsoft name. Using the money he earned from CBT's public listing, in 1995 Patrick McDonagh financed Riverdeep, another educational company selling multimedia school courses. Riverdeep also publicly listed on NASDAQ in 2000, making McDonagh, a schoolteacher by training, the most successful software entrepreneur in Ireland.

32. As one interviewee from the former IDA remarked, "In that period [1986–1989] we joked that in Ireland the best way to create a small Irish software company was to establish a big one and wait" (interview, March 10, 2001).

33. A PBX is a private telephone network used within a specific organization. Users of the PBX share a number of outside lines for making telephone calls outside the PBX.

34. Lynam also became seriously ill in 1988 and retired from the industry. In 1990 he came back and established, together with his wife and son Henry, Klas, a telecommunication hardware company.

35. Landis and Gyr ran into difficulties in 1991 and closed down its Irish subsidiary. Out of its Irish operations two new Irish-owned IT companies were created by MBOs. The first was Lake Communication, which is still managed by several members of the old management team of Lake Electronics who stayed on with Landis and Gyr. The second was Peregrine Software, a financial data-security company that flourished for a few years before being bought in 2000 by Trintech, one of the three Irish software companies that are still listed on NASDAQ in 2006.

36. Mentec and its founders, especially Mike Peirce, became crucial to the continued development of the Irish IT industry. Peirce invested in and was the chairman of Parthus, an Irish IC design house established after the demise of Digital's facilities in Galway, which became the only Irish hardware company ever to be listed on NASDAQ. Peirce and Mentec not only encouraged a few spin-offs, such as Eurologic and AEP, but also became their key early investors. In addition, in 2001 Peirce, together with Peter McManamon, the former director given to Mentec by the IDA, opened Mentor Capital, a small VC fund.

37. John Sterne, a historian of the Irish software industry, remarked that even as late as 1995 a minister of the state, Pat Rabbitte, decided that it would be politically expedient to use a joint conference of the Irish and Massachusetts software associations to chide the Irish software industry for "paying too much for their employees" (Sterne 2004, pp. 86–87).

38. During the interviews, executives of the EDP all remarked that electronics was always considered manufacturing. As a result it was not firmly on the new agenda of indigenous enterprise building and new tradable-services industries.

39. Interviews with former executives of EDP and ISP, March 10 and July 16, 2001, and with the first CEO of EI, Dan Flinters, February 5, 2002.

40. Many smaller foreign software companies arrived in Ireland before Lotus. However, the move of Lotus, at a time when it was considered one of the premier software MNCs, had the effect of legitimizing Ireland as the "place to be" for American software MNCs. The effect was similar to those of DEC's move to Galway in the 1970s and Intel's in the 1990s.

41. Localization is the programming activity of taking a software working in a specific culture or language and translating it into different cultures or languages.

42. O'Riain, reporting on the view of the indigenous industry of that period, cites its position as reflected in its main publication of the time, *Irish Computer:* "If the interests of the indigenous computer services industry companies are safeguarded and promoted, and if there is a proper structure within which they can influence the new body in the interest of their members, then it [NSC] will have the association's support [ISA, then called ICSA]. If they are not met, in the word of a member of the ICSA executive committee, it will be *'total opposition'*" (O'Riain 1999, p. 214, italics added).

43. Again the contrast with Israel is apparent. In Israel the state focused its energies solely around market failures associated with R&D activities, not on general financial market failures.

44. The latest of which is the project to create an R&D-based multimedia-digital hub in the Liberties (around the old Guinness brewery), which brought MIT's Media-lab as its anchor tenant.

45. A complier is a program that decodes instructions written in a specific programming language, such as C, Pascal, or Basic (so-called higher-order languages) and produces an assembly- or machine-language program that can then be executed by the computer.

46. The continuous importance of ESPRIT and other EU framework programs to the research activities in Ireland is evident when one realizes that as late as 1998 more than one-third of the research budget of Trinity, at the time Ireland's university with the biggest research budget at €20.3, came from these programs (Grimes and Collins 2003).

47. Colin Newman was Iona's fourth founder.

48. The specific standard was ORB, which stands for object request broker. ORB is the component in the heart of the common object request broker architecture (CORBA) middleware standard. Middleware is the general name for software whose main task is to allow programs written and operated on different platforms to exchange information and work together.

49. A former executive in Iona argued, when interviewed, that at that period in order for an indigenous company to be approved for the lower tax regime (automatically given to MNCs) the IDA needed to give its consent. The only way to get the IDA approval was to agree to a grant scheme in which the IDA took 7 percent stake in the company.

50. Financial resources for R&D in Ireland were so constrained even after the IDA approval of its second grant to Iona in 1994 that Iona hired a former graduate student of Horn and Baker's to a full-time position of applying for ESPRIT funding.

51. Sun had two reasons for selling its stake: (*a*) by that time it had decided to abandon the CORBA middleware standard and concentrate its efforts on its own self-developed Java technology, and (*b*) Sun Microsystems preferred as a corporation to avoid the legal risks inherent in holding large stakes and board directorship positions in other public companies.

52. Iona had one other key influence. Led by former lecturers at Trinity, the company was the first Irish company to hire entire cohorts of Irish computer science students to conduct R&D work in Ireland. In this Iona helped to transform the perception of Irish computer science students about what should, and can, be done in Ireland.

53. However, later the relationship between Cape Clear and Iona turned sour; Iona took Cape Clear to court in 2002 over hiring issues (Daly 2002).

54. In 1996 Aldiscon was also the first company to secure major investment from the EI-sponsored ICC software fund. In 1997, in the middle of an IPO process, Aldiscon was sold to Logica for £90 million in cash and is now the division that generates most of the revenues and profits for Logica-Aldiscon.

55. At the time, the software industry was the only successful indigenous sector in Irish history apart from agriculture and tourism.

56. Good statistics are lacking, but using multiple resources we can ascertain that starting in 1999 a major upgrade of the Irish VC funds occurred, with actual VC investment in IT of €62 million in 1999 and €162 million in 2000. Sources: M.O.P 2000, PWC 2000, and the Irish Venture Capital funds' Web sites.

57. Unlike the United States, in Europe almost any capital involved in the growing or the restructuring of a business falls under the rubric of venture capital. In effect, the European use of the term VC is similar to the American definition of the private-equity firm.

58. In the end only fifteen funds actually started operations.

59. On the distinction between the two VC industry creation policy types, see Avnimelech and Teubal 2003a, 2006a, 2006b.

60. Interview with Denis Marnane, March 7, 2002. For more information on the distribution of the first EI VC initiative, see EI 2000.

61. In 2001 Israel had acknowledged that problem and changed some of its regulations to make it easier and more attractive to Israeli firms to double list. However, it remains to be seen how widespread will be the effects of those measures.

62. As EI finance is conditional on VC funds' agreement to invest, and as Irish VC funds usually make their investment conditional on the NTBF securing EI financing, EI packages are in a sense complementary finance, which otherwise the VC fund would need to supplement.

63. One measure of the new passion for profits and EI's self-congratulatory mode, which is in part created by the adherence to the neoliberal interventionalist ideology, is the farewell interview that Dan Flinter, EI's first CEO, gave the *Irish Times* before his departure in September 2003. Flinter was quick to point out that Enterprise Ireland realized about €250 million in 1999–2003 while investing "a sinfully small amount!"

Flinter also forcefully defended the status quo, arguing that EI activities are getting the balance exactly right (O'Keeffe 2003).

64. As with Taiwan, and unlike Israel, the top civil servants in each ministry, including the secretary general, or the general manager, are chosen from within the ranks of the civil service.

CONCLUSION

1. In 1971, shortly after joining Intel in 1969 and after the first 1k-bit DRAM was released, Dov Frohman invented the UVEPROM, an electrically programmable memory that holds the programmed values until erased by intense ultraviolet light. Frohman invented, developed, designed, and fabricated the first UVEPROM.

2. One must note, though, that opening a small SC design center is not as capital-intensive a high-risk decision as is opening a fabrication facility; total investment in the Israeli center was $300,000 (1974 terms).

3. Over the years, Israeli senior R&D managers in other American MNCs have followed this pattern and returned to Israel to open R&D operations for their MNCs. National Semi-Conductors and KLA are two prominent examples.

4. The history of Intel in Ireland and Israel is based on interviews with five executives of Intel and Intel Capital in Israel and Ireland and email communication with Dov Frohman. See also Dror 2002; Tania Hershman, "Tech New Promised Land," *Wired*, January 17, 2000, also available online, http://www.wired.com/news/infostructure/0,1377,33537,00.html; and Intel Israel and Intel Ireland Web sites: http://www.intel.com/il/ and http://www.intel.com/ireland/.

5. Asynchronous transfer mode is an international standard for cell relay in which multiple service types (such as voice, video, and data) are conveyed in fixed-length (fifty-three-byte) cells. This makes ATM a fast data transmission protocol, as fixed-length cells allow cell processing to occur in hardware, thereby reducing transit delays.

6. Interview with Eric Benhamou, former CEO and chairman of 3Com, 1990–2000, and current chairman of 3Com and chairman and CEO of Palm, February 13, 2002.

7. Indeed, the social status of academia in Israel was so high in these early years that RAFAEL viewed it as critical to win a political battle to grant its R&D employees recognition as academic personnel, giving them wage agreements and career patterns less typical of engineers than of university professors (Mardor 1981, pp. 88–92).

8. Interview with Taiwan's VC association secretary general, November 3, 2003.

9. Interview with EI VC program official, March 7, 2002.

References

Abouganem, M., and Feldman, M. 2002. *Development of the High-Tech Industry in Israel, 1995–1999: Labour Force and Wages.* Jerusalem: State of Israel Central Bureau of Statistics (in Hebrew).

AFX. 2001. VIA Sees P4 Chipset Dispute Impact Fully Reflected in Q4. *AFX News Limited—AFX Asia.* December 18.

Akamatsu, K. 1962. A Historical Pattern of Economic Growth in Developing Countries. *Developing Economies,* 2, 3–25.

Amit, I. 1988. *The Defense Industry as a Political and Strategic Factor.* The State of Israel—The Ministry of Defense—Armament Development Authority—Center for Military Research, 88/02.

Amsden, A. 1989. *Asia's Next Giant: South Korea and Late Industrialization.* Oxford: Oxford University Press.

———. 2001. *The Rise of "The Rest": Challenges to the West from Late Industrializing Economies.* Oxford: Oxford University Press.

Amsden, A., and Chu, W.-W. 2003. *Beyond Late Development: Taiwan's Upgrading Policies.* Cambridge: MIT Press.

Anchordoguy, M. 1989. *Computers Inc.: Japan's Challenge to IBM.* Cambridge: Harvard University Press.

Ansell, C. K. 2000. The Networked Polity: Regional Development in Western Europe. *Governance,* 13, 279–291.

Arendt, H. 1958. *The Human Condition.* Chicago: University of Chicago Press.

Ariav, G., and Goodman, S. E. 1994. Israel: Of Swords and Software Plowshares. *Communications of the ACM*, 37, 17–21.

Arndt, S. W., and Kierzkowski, H. 2001a. *Fragmentation: New Production Patterns in the World Economy*. Oxford: Oxford University Press.

Arora, A., and Gambardella, A. 2005. *From Underdogs to Tigers: The Rise and Growth of the Software Industry in Some Emerging Economies*. Oxford: Oxford University Press.

Arora, A., Gambardella, A., and Torrisi, S. 2001. In the Footsteps of Silicon Valley? Indian and Irish Software in the International Division of Labour. SIEPR Discussion Paper.

Arrow, J. K. 1962. Economic Welfare and the Allocation of Resources for Invention. In R. R. Nelson (Ed.), *The Rate and Direction of Inventive Activity: Economic and Social Factors* (pp. 609–625). Princeton: Princeton University Press.

Autler, G. H. 2000. Global Networks in High Technology: The Silicon Valley-Israel Connection. Master's thesis, University of California, Berkeley.

Avnimelech, G. and M. Teubal. 2003a. Evolutionary Venture Capital Policies: Insights from a Product Life Cycle Analysis of Israel's Venture Capital Industry. Science, Technology, and the Economy Program (STE) Working Paper Series. Samuel Neaman Institute for Advanced Studies in Science and Technology, Technion, Israel Institute of Technology. Haifa.

———. 2003b. Israel's Venture Capital Industry: Emergence, Operation and Impact. In D. Cetindamar (Ed.), *The Growth of Venture Capital: A Cross Cultural Comparison* (pp. 207–240). Westport, Conn.: Praeger.

———. 2004. Venture Capital Start-Up Co-Evolution and the Emergence and Development of Israel's New High Technology Cluster. *Economics of Innovation and New Technology*, 13, no. 1, 33–60.

———. 2006a. From Direct Support of Business Sector R&D Innovation to Targeting Venture Capital/Private Equity: A Catching-Up Innovation and Technology Policy Life Cycle Perspective. Forthcoming in *Economics of Innovation and New Technology*, special issue on the governance of technological knowledge.

———. 2006b. Creating Venture Capital (VC) Industries that Co-Evolve with High Tech Clusters: Insights from an Extended Industry Life Cycle Perspective of the Israeli Experience. Forthcoming in Research Policy.

Bar, A. 1990. Industry and Industrial Policy in Israel—Landmarks. In Brodet, Justman, and Teubal 1990 (pp. 22–26).

Bathlet, H., Malmberg, A., and Maskell, P. 2002. Clusters and Knowledge: Local Buzz, Global Pipeline, and the Process of Knowledge Creation. DRUID Working Paper 02-12.

Beaton, A., Martin, M., Mullis, I., Gonzalez, E., Smith, T., and Kelly, D. 1996. Science Achievement in the Middle School Years: IEA's Third International Mathematics and Science Study (TIMSS). Chestnut Hill: Boston College, TIMSS International Study Center.

Ben-Bassat, A. 2002. The Israeli Economy, 1985–1998: From Government Intervention to Market Economics. Cambridge: MIT Press.

Ben-Porath, Y. 1986. The Israeli Economy: Maturing Through Crises. Cambridge: Harvard University Press.

Bentur, A. 2002. Investment in Civilian R&D in Israel: Data as a Basis for Discussion in the Purpose of Developing a National Policy. STE Working Papers Series. Technion—Samuel Neaman Institute.

Berger, S. 2006. *How We Compete: What Companies Around the World Are Doing to Make It in Today's Global Economy.* New York: Doubleday.

BIRD. 2000. BIRD Foundation Procedures Handbook. Tel Aviv: BIRD Foundation.

———. 2004. BIRD Foundation Web site. www.birdf.com.

———. Various years. Annual Reports. Tel Aviv: BIRD Foundation.

Bizan, O. 2001. *Essays on the Economics of Research Alliances (Israel).* Ph.D. diss., Northwestern University.

BOI. 2004. Table B-N-15, Total Factor Productivity by Sector 1961–2000. *Israel's Economy: Annual Tables.* Jerusalem: Bank of Israel.

Bowsher, C. A. 1991. General Management Reviews: Building Government's Capacity to Manage. In A. Friedberg, B. Geist, I. Sharkansky, and N. Mizrahi (Eds.), *Accountability and State Audit* (pp. 360–368). Jerusalem: State Comptroller's Office.

Braczyk, H.-J., Cooke, P., and Heidenreich, M. 1998. *Regional Innovation Systems: The Role of Governances in a Globalized World.* London: UCL Press.

Breathnach, P. 1998. Exploring the "Celtic Tiger" Phenomenon: Causes and Consequences of Ireland's Economic Miracle. *European Urban and Regional Studies,* 5, 305–316.

Bregman, A., Fuss, M., and Regev, H. 1998. The Effects of Capital Subsidization on Israeli Industry. NBER Working Paper Series.

Breschi, S., and Malerba, F. 1997. Sectoral Innovation Systems: Technological Regimes, Schumpeterian Dynamics, and Spatial Boundaries. In Edquist 1997 (pp. 130–156).

Breznitz, D. 2005a. Collaborative Public Space in a National Innovation System: A Case Study of the Israeli Military's Impact on the Software Industry. *Industry and Innovation,* 12, 31–64.

———. 2005b. Development, Flexibility, and R&D Performance in the Taiwanese IT industry: Capability Creation and the Effects of State-Industry Co-Evolution. *Industrial and Corporate Change,* 14, 153–187.

———. 2005c. Innovation and the Limits of State Power: IC Design and Software in Taiwan. In S. Berger and R. Lester (Eds.), *Global Taiwan* (pp. 194–227). New York: M. E. Sharpe.

———. 2005d. An Iron Cage or the Final Stage? Intensive Product R&D and the Evolution of the Israeli Software Industry. *Research Policy,* revised and resubmitted.

———. 2005e. Software Tooling: The Development of the Israeli Software Industry. In A. Arora and A. Gambardella (Eds.), *From Underdogs to Tigers: The Software Industry in Emerging Countries* (pp. 72–98). New York: Oxford University Press.

———. 2006. Innovation-Based Industrial Policy in Emerging Economies? The Case of Israel's IT Industry. *Business and Politics,* 8, no. 3, 1–38.

Brodet, D., Justman, M., and Teubal, M. 1990. *Industrial-Technological Policy for Israel.* Jerusalem: Jerusalem Institute for Israel Studies (in Hebrew).

Bruno, M. 1989. Israel's Crisis and Economic Reform: A Historical Perspective. NBER Working Paper Series.

Burt, S. R. 1992. *Structural Holes: The Social Structure of Competition.* Cambridge: Harvard University Press.

Calder, K. E. 1993. *Strategic Capitalism: Private Business and Public Purpose in Japanese Industrial Finance*. Princeton: Princeton University Press.

Carlsson, B. 1995. *Technological Systems and Economic Performance: The Case of Factory Automation*. London: Kluwer.

Carlsson, B., and Eliason, G. 1994. The Nature and Importance of Economic Competence. *Industrial and Corporate Change*, 3, 687–711.

Carlsson, B., Jacobsson, S., Holmen, M., and Rickne, A. 2002. Innovation System: Analytical and Methodological Issues. *Research Policy*, 31, 233–245.

CBS. 1999a. *National Expenditure of Civilian Research and Development, 1989–1998*. Jerusalem: State of Israel Central Bureau of Statistics.

———. 1999b. *National Expenditure on Education, 1962–1997*. Jerusalem: State of Israel Central Bureau of Statistics.

———. 2000a. *Education in Israel and International Comparison, 1995*. Jerusalem: State of Israel Central Bureau of Statistics.

———. 2000b. *National Expenditure of Civilian Research and Development, 1989–1999*. Jerusalem: State of Israel Central Bureau of Statistics.

———. 2001. *Development of Information Communication Technology in the Last Decade*. Jerusalem: Central Bureau of Statistics—Israel.

———. 2004a. *The Development of the ICT Sector in Israel, 2003*. Jerusalem: State of Israel Central Bureau of Statistics.

———. 2004b. *Israel's Statistical Abstract*. Jerusalem: State of Israel Central Bureau of Statistics.

Chang, P.-L., Hsu, C.-W., and Tsai, C.-T. 1999. A Stage Approach for Industrial Development and Implementation: The Case of Taiwan's Computer Industry. *Technovation*, 19, 233–241.

Chang, P.-L., and Tsai, C.-T. 2002. Finding the Niche Position: Competition Strategy of Taiwan's IC Design Industry. *Technovation*, 22, 101–111.

Cheng, T.-J. 1990. Political Regimes and Developmental Strategies: South Korea and Taiwan. In G. Gereffi and D. Wyman (Eds.), *Manufacturing Miracles* (pp. 139–178). Princeton: Princeton University Press.

———. 1993. Guarding the Commanding Heights: The State as Banker in Taiwan. In S. Haggard, C. H. Lee, and S. Maxfield (Eds.), *The Politics of Financing in Developing Countries* (pp. 55–92). Ithaca: Cornell University Press.

Chibber, V. 2002. Bureaucratic Rationalist and the Developmental State. *American Journal of Sociology*, 107, 951–989.

———. 2003. *Locked in Place: State-building and Late Industrialization in India*. Princeton: Princeton University Press.

Chinworth, M. W. 1992. *Inside Japan's Defense*. Washington, D.C.: Brassey's.

Cohen, W. M., and Levinthal, D. A. 1989. Innovation and Learning: The Two Faces of R&D. *Economic Journal*, 99, 569–596.

———. 1990. Absorptive Capacity: A New Perspective on Learning and Innovation. *Administrative Science Quarterly*, 35, 128–152.

Cooke, P., and Morgan, K. 1998. *The Associational Economy*. New York: Oxford University Press.

Cumings, B. 1984. The Origins and Development of Northeast Asian Political Economy: Industrial Sectors, Product Cycles, and Political Consequences. *International Organization,* 38, 1–40.

Daly, G. 2002. "Iona Offspring Surprised by CapeClear Row." *Sunday Business Post.* May 5.

Dedrick, J., and Kraemer, L. K. 1998. Asia's Computer Challenge: Threat or Opportunity for the United States and the World. New York: Oxford University Press.

de Fontenay, C., and Carmel, E. 2001. Israel's Silicon Wadi: The Forces Behind Cluster Formation. *SIEPR Discussion Paper.*

Deri, D. 1993. Political Appointments in Israel: Between Statism and Political Party-ism. Tel Aviv: United Kibutz Press (in Hebrew).

DOIT. 2003. TDP Annual Budget, 1993–2003. Taipei: Ministry of Economic Affairs, Department of Industrial Technology.

Dosi, G. 1982. Technological Paradigms and Technological Trajectories: A Suggested Interpretation of the Determinants and Direction of Technical Change. *Research Policy,* 11, 147–163.

Dror, Y. 2002. Intel Develops in Israel a Cellular Laptop. *Ha'aretz* (in Hebrew). February 6.

Dunning, J. H. 1994. Multinational Enterprises and the Globalization of Innovatory Capacity. *Research Policy,* 23, 67–88.

Durkan, J., FitzGerald, D., and Harmon, C. 1999. Education and Growth in the Irish Economy. In F. Barry (Ed.), *Understanding Ireland's Economic Growth* (pp. 119–136). London: Macmillan.

Economics, E.G.P.A. 2001. The Operational Achievements of the Israeli Technology Incubators Program. Conducted for the Technology Incubators Administration, the Office of the Chief Scientist, in the Ministry of Trade and Industry, Israel.

Edquist, C. 1997. *Systems of Innovation: Technologies, Institutions, and Organizations.* London: Pinter.

Efrati, N. 1999. *In the Beginning: 40 Years of Computing in Israel.* Tel Aviv: Meta Group Israel (in Hebrew).

EI. 2000. *2000 Report: Seed and Venture Capital Measure of the Operational Program, 1994–1999.* Dublin: Enterprise-Ireland.

EI. Various years. Annual Reports. Dublin: Enterprise Ireland.

Eisenhardt, K. M. 1989. Building Theories from Case Study Research. *Academy of Management Review,* 14, 532–550.

Ernst, D. 2005a. Complexity and Internationalisation of Innovation: Why Is Chip Design Moving to Asia? *International Journal of Innovation Management,* 9, no. 1, 47–73.

———. 2005b. Pathways to Innovation in Asia's Leading Electronics-Exporting Countries: A Framework for Exploring Drivers and Policy Implications. *International Journal of Technology Management,* special issue, "Competitive Strategies of Asian High-Tech Firms," 29, nos. 1–2, 6–20.

Evans, P. 1995. *Embedded Autonomy: States and Industrial Transformation.* Princeton: Princeton University Press.

Evans, P., and Rauch, E. J. 1999. Bureaucracy and Growth: A Cross-National Analysis of the Effects of "Weberian" State Structure on Economic Growth. *American Sociological Review,* 64, 748–765.

Evans, P., Rueschemeyer, D., and Skocpol, T. 1985. *Bringing the State Back In.* New York: Cambridge University Press.

Feenstra, R. C. 1998. Integration of Trade and Disintegration of Production in the Global Economy. *Journal of Economic Perspectives,* 12, 31–50.

Felsenstein, D. 1997. The Making of a High Technology Node: Foreign-owned Companies in Israeli High Technology. *Regional Studies,* 31, 367–380.

Fields, K. 1995. *Enterprise and the State in Korea and Taiwan.* Ithaca: Cornell University Press.

Freeman, C. 1987. *Technology Policy and Economic Performance: Lessons from Japan.* London: Pinter.

Freeman, C., and Lundvall, B.-Å. 1988. *Small Countries Facing the Technological Revolution.* London: Pinter.

FT. 2003a. Mediatek to Challenge World's No. 4 Spot in IC Design. *Financial Times Global News Wire.* November 25.

———. 2003b. Taiwanese Chip Designers Facing Lukewarm Season Earlier. *Financial Times Global News Wire.* December 9.

———. 2003c. VIA, Intel Reach Patent Suit Settlement, to Jointly Face Competitors. *Financial Times Global News Wire.* April 9.

Fuller, D. B. 2002. Globalization for Nation Building: Industrial Policy for High-Technology Products in Taiwan. MIT IPC Working Paper.

Fuller, D. B., Akinwande, A., and Sodini, C. G. 2003. Leading, Following or Cooked Goose: Successes and Failures in Taiwan's Electronics Industry. *Industry and Innovation,* 10, 179–196.

Galvin, P., and Morkel, A. 2001. The Effects of Product Modularity on Industry Structure: The Case of the World Bicycle Industry. *Industry and Innovation,* 8, 31–47.

Gassmann, O., and von Zedtwitz, M. 1999. New Concepts and Trends in International R&D Organization. *Research Policy,* 28, 231–250.

Gereffi, G. 1994. The Organization of Buyer-Driven Global Commodity Chains: How the U.S. Retailers Shape Overseas Production Network. In Gereffi and Korzeniewicz 1994 (pp. 95–122).

———. 1996. Commodity Chains and Regional Divisions of Labor in East Asia. *Journal of Asian Business,* 12, 75–112.

———. 1999. International Trade and Industrial Upgrading in the Apparel Commodity Chain. *Journal of International Economics,* 48, 37–70.

Gereffi, G., Humphrey, J., and Sturgeon, J. T. 2005. The Governance of Global Value Chains. *Review of International Political Economy,* 12, no. 1, 78–104.

Gereffi, G., and Korzeniewicz, M. 1994. *Commodity Chains and Global Capitalism.* Westport, Conn.: Praeger.

Gerschenkron, A. 1962. *Economic Backwardness in Historical Perspective: A Book of Essays.* Cambridge: Belknap Press of Harvard University Press.

Gerybadze, A., and Reger, G. 1999. Globalization of R&D: Recent Changes in Management of Innovation in Transnational Corporations. *Research Policy,* 28, 251–274.

Giuliani, E. 2002. Cluster Absorptive Capability: An Evolutionary Approach for Industrial Clusters in Developing Countries. DRUID Summer Conference. Industrial Dynamics for the New and Old Economy: Who Is Embracing Whom? Copenhagen.

Glaser, B. G., and Strauss, A. L. 1967. *The Discovery of Grounded Theory: Strategies for Qualitative Research*. Chicago: Aldine.

Gold, T. B. 1986. *State and Society in the Taiwan Miracle*. New York: Armonk.

Gourevitch, P. 2000. Globalization of Production: Insights from the Hard Drive Disk Industry. *World Development*, 28, 301–317.

Granovetter, S. M. 1973. The Strength of Weak Ties. *American Sociological Review*, 25, 483–496.

Grimes, S., and Collins, P. 2003. Building a Knowledge Economy in Ireland Through European Research Networks. *European Planning Studies*, 11, 395–413.

Grinberg, L. L. 1991. *Split Corporatism in Israel*. New York: SUNY Press.

Guillen, M. F. 2001. *The Limits of Convergence: Globalization and Organizational Change in Argentina, South Korea, and Spain*. Princeton: Princeton University Press.

Guiomard, C. 1995. *The Irish Disease and How to Cure It: Common-Sense Economics for a Competitive World*. Dublin: Oak Tree.

Hall, B. H., Jaffe, A. B., and Trajtenberg, M. 2001. The NBER Patent Citation Data File: Lessons, Insights and Methodological Tools. NBER Working Papers.

Hall, P., and Soskice, D. 2001. *Varieties of Capitalism: The Institutional Foundations of Comparative Advantage*. Oxford: Oxford University Press.

Halperin, A. 1987. The Building of the Military Power and Economic Growth. *Economic Quarterly*, 16, 990–1010 (in Hebrew).

Halperin, A., and Berman, E. 1990. Skilled Labor, Security, and Growth. In D. Brodet, M. Justman and M. Teubal (Eds.), *Industrial-Technological Policy for Israel*. Jerusalem: Jerusalem Institute for Israel Studies (in Hebrew).

Halperin, A., and Tsiddon, D. 1992. The Conversion of the Israeli Defense Industry: The Labor Market. The Israeli International Institute for Applied Economic Policy Review. Tel Aviv.

Hardiman, N. 2000. Social Partnership, Wage Bargaining, and Growth. In B. Nolan, P. J. O'Connell, and C. T. Whelan (Eds.), *From Bust to Boom* (pp. 286–309). Dublin: Institute of Public Administration.

———. 2002. From Conflict to Co-ordination: Economic Governance and Political Innovation in Ireland. *West European Politics*, 25, 1–24.

Haughton, J. 2000. The Historical Background. In J. W. O'Hagan (Ed.), *The Economy of Ireland: Policy and Performance of a European Region* (pp. 2–46). Dublin: Gill and Macmillan.

HEA. 2006. The PRTLI: Program Overview. Dublin: Higher Education Authority.

Heclo, H. 1977. *A Government of Strangers: Executive Politics in Washington*. Washington: Brookings Institution.

Henderson, J., Dicken, P., Hess, M., Coe, N., and Yeung, W.-C. H. 2002. Global Production Networks and the Analysis of Economic Development. *Review of International Political Economy*, 9, 436–464.

Herrigel, G., and Wittke, V. 2004. Varieties of Vertical Integration: The Global Trend

Toward Heterogeneous Supply Relations and the Reproduction of Difference in the U.S. and German Manufacturing. In G. Morgan, R. Whitley, and E. Moan (Eds.), *Changing Capitalism* (pp. 312–351). Oxford: Oxford University Press.

Hille, K. 2003. Intel Deal Puts SiS Under Cloud. *Financial Times.* April 9.

Hong, S. G. 1997. *The Political Economy of Industrial Policy in East Asia: The Semiconductor Industry in Taiwan and South Korea.* Cambridge: Edward Elgar.

Hsu, C.-W., and Chiang, H.-C. 2001. The Government Strategy for the Upgrading of Industrial Technology in Taiwan. *Technovation,* 21, 123–132.

Hung, F. 2002. Taiwan's Chipset Sales Plunge. *Financial Times Information.* July 10.

Hung, S.-C. 2000. Institutions and System of Innovation: An Empirical Analysis of Taiwan's Personal Computer Competitiveness. *Technology in Society,* 22, 175–187.

Hwang, Y. D. 1991. *A Rise of a New World Economic Power: Postwar Taiwan.* New York: Greenwood.

IAEI. 2006. *Israel Electronics Industries Profile.* Tel Aviv: Israel Association of Electronic and Software Industries.

IASH. 2003. Israel Software Industry Statistical Information: IASH. Tel Aviv: Israel Association of Software Houses.

IC Insights. 2004. *The McLean Report.* Scottsdale, Ariz.: IC Insights.

IDA. 2000. *Ireland: Vital Statistics.* Dublin: IDA—Ireland.

———. 2006. *Industrial Statistics.* Dublin: IDA—Ireland.

III. Various years. *Zixun GongYe Nianjian* (The Yearbook of Information Industry). Taipei: Institute for Information Industry, Market Intelligence Center.

ISA. 2003. *Irish Software Industry Outlook, 2003.* Dublin: Irish Software Association.

———. 2004. *Irish Software Industry Outlook, 2004.* Dublin: Irish Software Association.

IT. 2003a. Intel Opens €12m Innovation Center. *Irish Times.* June 28.

———. 2003b. Policies of Tech Sector Urgent—IBEC. *Irish Times.* January 23.

ITRI. 2003. *Bandaoti Gongye Nianjian* (The Yearbook of Semiconductor Industry). Hsinchu: ITRI—ITIS.

———. 2005. *Bandaoti Gongye Nianjian* (The Yearbook of Semiconductor Industry). Hsinchu: ITRI—ITIS.

———. Various years. *Industrial Statistics.* Hsinchu: Industrial Technology Research Institute, Industrial Economic and Knowledge Center.

IVA. 1997–2003. *Year Books: A Survey of the Israeli Venture Capital and Private Equity Industry.* Tel Aviv: Israeli Venture Capital Association.

JIM. 1987. *Export-led Growth Strategy for Israel.* Jerusalem: Jerusalem Institute of Management and the Telesis Group.

Johnson, C. A. 1982. *MITI and the Japanese Miracle: The Growth of Industrial Policy, 1925–1975.* Stanford: Stanford University Press.

———. 1995. *Japan, Who Governs? The Rise of the Developmental State.* New York: Norton.

Justman, M., and Teubal, M. 1995. Technological Infrastructure Policy (TIP): Creating Capabilities and Building Markets. *Research Policy,* 24, 259–281.

Justman, M., Zuscovitch, E., and Teubal, M. 1993. *Technological Infrastructure Policy for Renewed Growth.* Jerusalem: The Jerusalem Institute for Israel Studies (in Hebrew).

Katchalski, E. 1968. *The Report of the Committee to Inquire into the Organization of Gov-*

ernmental Research and Its Management. Jerusalem: Office of the Prime Minister (in Hebrew).

Kennedy, L. 1989. *The Modern Industrialisation of Ireland, 1940–1988.* Dublin: Economic and Social History Society of Ireland.

Kenney, M., and Florida, R. L. 2004. *Locating Global Advantage: Industry Dynamics in the International Economy.* Stanford: Stanford University Press.

Kim, H.-K., Muramatsu, M., Pempel, T. J., and Yamamura, K. 1995. *The Japanese Civil Service and Economic Development: Catalysts of Change.* New York: Oxford University Press, Clarendon.

Kim, L. 1997. *Imitation to Innovation: The Dynamics of Korea's Technological Learning.* Cambridge: Harvard Business School Press.

King, G., Keohane, R. O., and Verba, S. 1994. *Designing Social Inquiry: Scientific Inference in Qualitative Research.* Princeton: Princeton University Press.

Klintworth, G. 1995. *New Taiwan, New China: Taiwan's Changing Role in the Asia-Pacific Region.* New York: St. Martin's.

Kohli, A. 1994. Where Do High Growth Political Economies Come From? The Japanese Lineage of Korea's "Developmental State." *World Development,* 22, 1269–1293.

Lester, R. K., and Piore, M. J. 2004. *Innovation: The Missing Dimension.* Cambridge: Harvard University Press.

Levav, A. 1998. *The Birth of Israel's High-Tech.* Tel Aviv: Zemora-Bitan.

Levi-Faur, D. 1998. The Developmental State: Israel, South Korea, and Taiwan Compared. *Studies in Comparative International Development,* 33, 65–93.

———. 2001. *The Visible Hand: State Directed Industrialization in Israel.* Jerusalem: Yad Ben-Zvi (in Hebrew).

Lillington, K. 2003a. IBM Sets Eye on Dublin for Research Agenda. *Irish Times.* September 12.

———. 2003b. Indigenous Software Industry "Struggling." *Irish Times.* December 11.

Lin, Y. 1987. A Study of an Emerging Industry in a LDC: A Case Study of Taiwan's IC Industry. Master's thesis, National Taiwan University (in Chinese).

Locke, R. M. 1995. *Remaking the Italian Economy.* Ithaca: Cornell University Press.

Lundvall, B.-Å. 1992. *National Systems of Innovation: Towards a Theory of Innovation and Interactive Learning.* London: Pinter.

Lundvall, B.-Å., Johnson, B., Andersen, E. S., and Dalum, B. 2002. National Systems of Production, Innovation, and Competence Building. *Research Policy,* 31, 213–231.

MacSharry, R., and White, P. 2001. *The Making of the Celtic Tiger: The Inside Story of Ireland's Boom Economy.* Dublin: Mercier.

Mardor, M. M. 1981. *RAFAEL.* Tel Aviv: Ministry of Defense of Israel Press (in Hebrew).

Martin, M., Mullis, I., Gonzalez, E., Gregory, K., Smith, T., Chrostowski, S., Garden, R., and O'Connor, K. 2000. *TIMSS 1999 International Science Report.* Chestnut Hill, Mass.: Boston College, International Study Center.

Mathews, J. A. 2002. The Origins and Dynamics of Taiwan's R&D Consortia. *Research Policy,* 31, 633–651.

Mathews, J. A., and Cho, D.-S. 2000. *Tiger Technologies: The Creation of a Semiconductor Industry in East Asia.* Cambridge: Cambridge University Press.

McKendrick, D., Doner, R. F., and Haggard, S. 2000. From Silicon Valley to Singapore: Location and Competitive Advantage in the Hard Disk Drive Industry. Stanford: Stanford University Press.

McManus, J. 2002. All Is Not Rosy in the Venture Capital Garden. *Irish Times.* September 30.

Meany, C. S. 1994. State Policy and the Development of Taiwan's Semiconductors Industry. In J. D. Aberbach, D. Dollar, and K. L. Sokoloff (Eds.), *The Role of the State in Taiwan's Development* (pp. 170–192). Armonk, N.Y.: M. E. Sharpe.

MoEA. Various years. *Economic Statistics Annual, Taiwan Area, Republic of China.* Taipei: Ministry of Economic Affairs.

M.O.P. 2000. *Report on Irish Venture Capital Industry.* Dublin: Matheson Ormsby Prentice and the Irish Venture Capital Association.

Morgan, K. 1997. The Learning Region: Institutions, Innovation, and Regional Renewal. *Regional Studies,* 31, 491–503.

MOTI. 1998. *Israel's Economic Overview.* Jerusalem: Ministry of Industry and Trade.

Mullis, I., Martin, M., Beaton, A., Gonzalez, E., Kelly, D., and Smith, T. 1997. *Mathematics Achievement in the Primary School Years: IEA's Third International Mathematics and Science Study (TIMSS).* Chestnut Hill, Mass.: Boston College, TIMSS International Study Center.

Mullis, I., Martin, M., Gonzalez, E., Gregory, K., Garden, R., O'Connor, K., Chrostowski, S., and Smith, T. 2000. *TIMSS 1999 International Mathematics Report.* Chestnut Hill, Mass.: Boston College: International Study Center.

Nelson, R. R. 1993. *National Innovation Systems: A Comparative Analysis.* New York: Oxford University Press.

NID. 2006. *Software Industry Statistics for 1991–2004.* Dublin: National Informatics Directorate.

Noble, G. W. 1998. *Collective Action in East Asia: How Ruling Parties Shape Industrial Policy.* Ithaca: Cornell University Press.

NSB. 2000. Science and Engineering Indicators, 2000. Washington, D.C.: National Science Board.

O'Brien, J. A. 1953. *The Vanishing Irish: The Enigma of the Modern World.* New York: McGraw-Hill.

OCS. 1974. *The Office of the Chief Scientist.* Jerusalem: Ministry of Commerce and Industry, Office of the Chief Scientist.

———. 1975. *Industrial Research and Development Background and Policy.* Jerusalem: Ministry of Commerce and Industry, Office of the Chief Scientist.

———. 1977. *Industrial Research and Development in Israel: Policy and Issues.* Jerusalem: Ministry of Commerce and Industry, Office of the Chief Scientist.

———. 2000. *Database of Annual Activities.* Jerusalem: Ministry of Trade and Industry, Office of the Chief Scientist (in Hebrew).

———. 2002. *Summary of 2001.* Jerusalem: Ministry of Trade and Industry, Office of the Chief Scientist (in Hebrew).

———. 2003. *Summary of Operations, 2002.* Jerusalem: Ministry of Trade and Industry, Office of the Chief Scientist (in Hebrew).

OECD. 1965. Investment in Education. Paris: Organization for Economic Co-operation and Development.

———. 1969. *Review of National Policies for Education: Ireland*. Paris: Organization for Economic Co-operation and Development.

O'Gorman, C., O'Malley, E., and Mooney, J. 1997. *Clusters in Ireland: The Irish Indigenous Software Industry*. Dublin: National Economic and Social Council.

O'Gr'ada, C. 1997. *A Rocky Road: The Irish Economy Since the 1920s*. Manchester: Manchester University Press.

O'Halloran, B. 2003. Business Happy with Extension of BES and SCS. *Irish Times*. December 4.

O'Hearn, D. 1998. *Inside the Celtic Tiger: The Irish Economy and the Asian Model*. London: Pluto.

O'Keeffe, B. 2003. Flinter Leaves Legacy of Competitiveness. *Irish Times*. July 4.

Okimoto, D. I. 1987. *Between MITI and the Market: Japanese Industrial Technology for High Technology*. Stanford: Stanford University Press.

O'Riain, S. 1997. The Birth of a Celtic Tiger? *Communications of the ACM*, 40, 11–16.

———. 1999. Remaking the Developmental State: The Irish Software Industry in the Global Economy. Ph.D. diss., University of California, Berkeley.

———. 2000. The Flexible Development State: Globalization, Information Technology, and the "Celtic Tiger." *Politics and Society*, 28, 157–193.

———. 2004. *The Politics of High Tech Growth: Developmental Network States in the Global Economy*. Cambridge: Cambridge University Press.

O'Sullivan, M. 2000a. Industrial Development: A New Beginning? In J. W. O'Hagan (Ed.), *The Economy of Ireland: Policy and Performance of a European Region* (pp. 260–282). Dublin: Gill and Macmillan.

———. 2000b. The Sustainability of Industrial Development in Ireland. *Regional Studies*, 34, 277–290.

Pack, H. 1993. *Exports and Externalities: The Source of Taiwan's Growth in Taiwan*. Philadelphia: University of Pennsylvania Press.

Park, P. H. 2000. A Reflection on the East Asian Developmental Model: Comparison of the South Korea and Taiwanese Experiences. In E. Richter (Ed.), *The East Asian Development Model: Economic Growth Institutional Failure and the Aftermath of the Crisis* (pp. 141–168). London: Macmillan.

Pearce, R. D. 1999. Decentralised R&D and Strategic Competitiveness: Globalised Approaches to Generation and Use of Technology in Multinational Enterprises (MNEs). *Research Policy*, 28, 157–178.

Pfiffner, J. P. 1992. Political Appointees and Career Executives: The Democracy-Bureaucracy Nexus. In P. W. Ingraham and D. F. Kettl (Eds.), *Agenda for Excellence: Public Service in America* (pp. 48–65). Chatham, N.J.: Chatham House.

Piore, M., Lester, R., Kofman, F., and Malek, K. 1994. The Organization of Product Development. *Industrial and Corporate Change*, 3, 405–434.

Piore, M. J., and Sabel, C. F. 1984. *The Second Industrial Divide: Possibilities for Prosperity*. New York: Basic.

PWC. 2000. Money for Growth: The European Technology Investment Report, 2000. PriceWaterhouseCoopers.

———. 2005. 2004 Annual European Private Equity Survey. PriceWaterhouseCoopers.

———. 2006. Money for Growth: The European Private Equity Report, 2005. Price WaterhouseCoopers.

Ragin, C. C. 1987. *The Comparative Method: Moving Beyond Qualitative and Quantitative Strategies.* Berkeley: University of California Press.

———. 1994. *Constructing Social Research: The Unity and Diversity of Method.* Thousand Oaks, Calif.: Pine Forge.

Reddy, P. 2000. *Globalization of Corporate R&D: Implications for Innovation Systems in Host Countries.* London: Routledge.

Rehav, U. 1998. *Armament Development Institutes and Their Economics.* 3rd ed. Haifa: State of Israel, Defense Ministry, Armaments Development Authority, Center for Military Studies (in Hebrew).

Roberts, E. B. 1999. Global Benchmarking of the Strategic Management of Technology. MIT IPC Working Paper 99-007.

Rose, R. 1981. *The Political Status of Higher Civil Servants in Britain.* Glasgow: Center for the Study of Public Policy, University of Strathcyle.

———. 1986. *A House Divided: Political Administration in Britain Today.* Glasgow: Center for the Study of Public Policy, University of Strathcyle.

Rostow, W. W. 1960. *The Stages of Economic Growth: A Non-Communist Manifesto.* Cambridge: Cambridge University Press.

Ruane, F., and Görg, H. 2001. Globalization and Fragmentation: Evidence for the Electronics Industry in Ireland. In Arndt and Kierzkowski 2001 (pp. 144–164).

Samuels, R. J. 1988. *The Business of the Japanese State: Energy Markets in Comparative and Historical Perspective.* Ithaca: Cornell University Press.

———. 1994. *Rich Nation Strong Army: National Security and the Technological Transformation of Japan.* Ithaca: Cornell University Press.

Sands, A. 2005. The Irish Software Industry. In A. Arora and A. Gambardella (Eds.), *From Underdogs to Tigers: The Rise and Growth of the Software Industry in Some Emerging Economies* (pp. 41–71). New York: Oxford University Press.

Saxenian, A., and Hsu, J.-Y. 2001. The Silicon Valley-Hsinchu Connection: Technical Communities and Industrial Upgrading. *Industrial and Corporate Change,* 10, 893–920.

Schumpeter, J. A. 1961 [1934]. *The Theory of Economic Development: An Inquiry into Profits, Capital, Credit, Interest, and the Business Cycle.* Cambridge: Harvard University Press.

SFI. 2004. Science Foundation Ireland Web Site. http://www.sfi.ie/home/index.asp.

Shalev, M. 1992. *Labour and the Political Economy in Israel.* Oxford: Oxford University Press.

Sharkansky, I. 1989. Israeli Civil Service Positions Open to Political Appointments. *International Journal of Public Administration,* 12, 731–748.

Sharon, E., and Naamen, Y. 1961. *Electronic Computers in Taxes and Administrative Services: A Report of a European Survey.* Jerusalem: State of Israel, Chamber of the State's Revenues.

Shefer, D., and Frenkel, A. 2002. An Evaluation of the Israeli Technological Incubator

Program and Its Projects. The Samuel Neaman Institute for Advanced Studies in Science and Technology, IFISE Report.

Smith, A. 1937. *The Wealth of Nations.* New York: Modern Library.

Smyth, J. 2004a. Fiscal Incentive Schemes Delayed by EU Review. *Irish Times.* July 8.

———. 2004b. IBM Invests €22 million in Dublin Software Laboratory. *Irish Times.* May 12.

SO. 1958a. *Economic Development.* Dublin: Stationary Office.

———. 1958b. *Programme for Economic Expansion.* Dublin: Stationery Office.

Sterne, J. 2004. *Adventures in Code: The Story of the Irish Software Industry.* Dublin: Liffey.

Stigler, G. J. 1971. The Theory of Economic Regulation. *Bell Journal of Economics and Management Science,* 3–21.

Sturgeon, T. J. 2000. Turnkey Production Networks: The Organizational Delinking of Production from Innovation. In U. Jürgens (Ed.), *New Product Development and Production Networks* (pp. 67–84). New York: Springer.

———. 2001. How Do We Define Value Chains and Production Networks? *Institute of Development Studies Bulletin,* 32.

———. 2002. Modular Production Networks: A New American Model of Industrial Organization. *Industrial and Corporate Change,* 11, 451–496.

———. 2003. What Really Goes on in Silicon Valley? Spatial Clustering and Dispersal in Modular Production Networks. *Journal of Economic Geography,* 3, 199–225.

Sturgeon, T. J., and Lester, R. 2004. The New Global Supply-Base: New Challenges for Local Suppliers in East Asia. In S. Yusuf, A. Altaf, and K. Nabeshima (Eds.), *Global Production Networking and Technological Change in East Asia* (pp. 35–88). Oxford: Oxford University Press.

Sweeny, P. 1999. *The Celtic Tiger: Ireland's Continuing Economic Miracle.* Dublin: Oak Tree.

TAF. 2002. *Calendar Year Patent Statistics.* Washington, D.C.: U.S. Patent and Trademark Office, Information Products Division, Technology Assessment and Forecast Branch. Taylor, C. 2003. Tech Lobby Calls for Introduction of R&D Tax Credit in Next Budget. *Irish Times.* November 1.

Teubal, M. 1983. Neutrality in Science Policy: The Case of Sophisticated Industrial Technology in Israel. *Minerva,* 21, 172–197.

———. 1993. The Innovation System of Israel: Description, Performance, and Outstanding Issues. In Nelson 1993 (pp. 476–502).

———. 1996. R&D and Technology Policy in NICs as Learning Processes. *World Development,* 24, 449–460.

———. 1997. A Catalytic and Evolutionary Approach to Horizontal Technology Policies (HTPs). *Research Policy,* 25, 1161–1188.

———. 2002. What Is the Systems Perspective to Innovation and Technology Policy (ITP) and How Can We Apply It to Developing and Newly Industrialized Economies? *Journal of Evolutionary Economics,* 12, 233–257.

Teubal, M., Avnimelech, G., and Gayego, A. 2002. Company Growth, Acquisitions and Access to Complementary Assets in Israel's Data Security Sector. *European Planning Studies,* 10, 933–953.

Teubal, M., Foray, D., Justman, M., and Zuscovitch, E. 1996. Technological Infrastructure Policy: An International Perspective. Boston: Kluwer Academic.

Teubal, M., Naftali, A., and Trajtenberg, M. 1976. Performance in Innovation in the Israeli Electronics Industry: A Case Study of Biomedical Electronics Instrumentation. *Research Policy*, 5, 354–379.

Teubal, M., and Spiller, P. T. 1977. Analysis of R&D Failure. *Research Policy*, 6, 254–275.

Teubal, M., Yinnon, T., and Zuscovitch, E. 1991. Networks and Market Creation. *Research Policy*, 20, 381–392.

Trajtenberg, M. 2001. Innovation in Israel, 1968–1997: A Comparative Analysis Using Patent Data. *Research Policy*, 30, 363–389.

———. 2005. R&D Policy in Israel: An Overview and Reassessment. NBER Working Paper Series.

Tsuk, N. 2004. Community, State, and Utopia: National Policy and Local Prosperity in the English Garden City and the Israeli Kibbutz. Ph.D. diss., University of Cambridge.

Van Evera, S. 1997. *Guide to Methods for Students of Political Science*. Ithaca: Cornell University Press.

Vekstein, D. 1999. Defense Conversion, Technology Policy, and R&D Networks in the Innovation System of Israel. *Technovation*, 19, 615–629.

Vernon, R. 1966. International Investment and International Trade in the Product Cycle. *Quarterly Journal of Economics*, 80, 190–207.

Wade, R. 1990. Governing the Market: Economic Theory and the Role of the Government in the East Asian Industrialization. Princeton: Princeton University Press.

Walsh, B. 1999. The Persistence of High Unemployment in a Small Open Labor Market: The Irish Case. In F. Barry (Ed.), *Understanding Ireland's Economic Growth* (pp. 193–226). London: Macmillan.

Wang, W.-C. V. 1995. Developing the Information Industry in Taiwan: Entrepreneurial State, Guerrilla Capitalists, and Accommodative Technologists. *Pacific Affairs*, 68, 551–576.

WB. 1993. *The East Asian Miracle: Economic Growth and Public Policy*. Oxford: Oxford University Press.

Weber, M. 1952. The Essential of Bureaucratic Organization. In R. K. Merton (Ed.), *Reader in Bureaucracy* (pp. 19–27). New York: Free Press.

———. 1958. *Essays in Sociology*. New York: Oxford University Press.

———. 1999. *Essays in Economic Sociology*. Ed. Richard Swedberg. Princeton: Princeton University Press.

Weiss, L. 1998. *The Myth of the Powerless State*. Ithaca: Cornell University Press.

White, T. 2001. *Investing in People: Higher Education in Ireland from 1960 to 2000*. Dublin: Institute of Public Administration.

Woo-Cumings, M. 1991. *Race to the Swift: State and Finance in Korean Industrialization*. New York: Columbia University Press.

———. 1999. *The Developmental State*. Ithaca: Cornell University Press.

Wu, Y. 2001. In Search of an Explanation of SME-Led Growth: State Survival, Bureaucratic Politics, and Private Enterprise in the Making of the Taiwanese Economy, 1950–1985. Ph.D. diss., Leiden University.

————. 2005. *A Political Explanation of Economic Growth: State Survival, Bureaucratic Politics, and Private Enterprise in the Making of Taiwan Economy, 1950–1985*. Cambridge: Harvard University Press.

Yaakov, I. 1974. Industrial Research and Development and University Research in Israel. A report prepared by Ithak Yaakov, Chief Scientist, Ministry of Trade and Industry, and submitted to the President of the State of Israel.

Yahalomi, L. 1991. Promoting International Cooperation as a Strategy for Economic Development: A Case Analysis of Israeli and U.S. High-Technology Partnerships (United States). Ph.D. diss., University of Pennsylvania.

Yeats, A. J. 2001. Just How Big Is Global Production Sharing? In Arndt and Kierzkowski 2001 (pp. 108–143).

Yin, R. K. 1994. *Case Study Research: Design and Methods*. Thousand Oaks, Calif.: Sage.

Zysman, J. 1983. *Governments, Markets, and Growth: Financial Systems and the Politics of Industrial Change*. Ithaca: Cornell University Press.

Index